AF322724

DAVID ROCKLIN

{ THE ELECTRIC LOVE SONG *of* FLEISCHL BERGER }

THANE & PROSE

NEW YORK • LONDON

2024

Acknowledgements

I am deeply grateful to Neal Thane Boulton and Pauline Aguilera of Thane & Prose, and publicist extraordinaire Alyssia Gonzalez, for believing in this book. Thank you for making a home and a place for it, and for your tireless creativity in sending it out to the world.

A lifelong, heartfelt thank you to Susan Taylor Chehak, friend and mentor, whose belief in me and in the power of writing sustains me across the years. No one could ask for a better teacher.

To Gloria Luxenberg, who told a little boy he'd be a writer one day. Thank you for seeing in me what I wasn't ready to see in myself.

My thanks and admiration to Natalia Ioset, whose beautiful photographs of Stralsund fueled my imaginings of the first home Fleischl Berger ever knew. I'm grateful you shared what you saw with a writer across the world.

I'm fortunate to be surrounded by cherished friends and a deeply supportive literary community. I'm honored to be among you. For your unwavering belief in me and what it was about this novel that made me need to write it, I'm grateful to Aruni Wijesinghe, Bruce Ferber, Toni Ann Johnson, Kate Maruyama, Aimee Liu, Sandra Hunter, and so many more: thanks for being there.

To learn about the world these characters moved through required research into everything from electroencephalograms to silent films to sleight of hand magic. I gratefully acknowledge the starting point: a scholarly article that took me down a rabbit hole far deeper and richer than I could have imagined: "The Mind Reader: the Forgotten Life of Hans Berger, Discoverer of the EEG" by Robert Kaplan.

To my best friend, my love, my wife Nina, and my two strong, inspiring badass daughters Ariel and Kavanna – this, like everything I pour my whole heart into, is for you. Thank you for our life. I love you.

To those we listen for.

"Come from forever, and you will go everywhere."

Arthur Rimbaud

CONTENTS

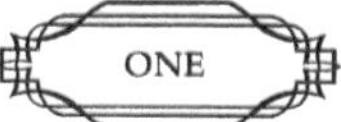

CHAPTER One
The Angel of Stralsund

The first time Fleischl Berger almost died was at the moment of his birth on the twenty-first day of May 1878. He was waiting there in the wet, as babies do, while his prawn limbs drifted aimlessly against the oddities sharing the dark with him. Then came a blast of light, buzzings like wasps, a startling drop and an icy immersion, and he only had time for a single breath and a beat of his untried heart before everything stilled. There was a great fanning flare of blue above him, and a shape within it moving as he was supposed to move, and he couldn't reach it.

He didn't know this wasn't the normal way. He didn't know that electricity, still unfamiliar to the residents of a seaside German village called Stralsund, wasn't supposed to course through the shallows of the Baltic to fill his drowning heart. He didn't know anything at all except *breathe*, which he couldn't, and *get out*. Which he couldn't.

★★★

How Fleischl came to be born just offshore from Stralsund, a foot beneath the surface of the sea, owed to his father Jurgen's aspiration to sail around the world selling flax and his mother's aspiration to leave a perfectly cozy bathtub.

At seventeen, Jurgen Berger met Astrid Elte, a Dutch Jew who produced some of the finest linen he'd ever come across. He saw her at market, where her bolts of cloth stood out for the vibrancy of their colors and the delicacy of their weaves. Hanging amid the dizzying variety of her wares was a coil of flaxen rope she'd made from the same graceful little plants with the drooping cerulean flowers he'd spent his entire childhood weeding in the fields outside Neuses. All the laborers, farmers, blacksmiths and tanners swooned over that rope. It was beautiful in a way that left working men speechless.

"They could use these on ships," Jurgen told her. It was the first time he attempted to make conversation with her over something other than price.

"They could use for at hangings too," she said.

And, with that, they had each revealed, amid the pfennigs and the flax, a glimpse into their secret selves: the dreamer and the pragmatist Jew.

In a month he convinced her to teach him rope weaving. He came to her cottage and saw how she touched the odd, hammered piece of tin affixed to the frame of her door. "Mezuzah," she told him, over and over, until the joke of his mispronunciation, which always struck him as wildly entertaining, grew stale. By then he'd been with her to Sabbath services at a neighbor's home. He found Jewish prayers interminable and full of clacking sounds. The melodies evoked a sense of melancholy he didn't grasp. But he attended services; for her, because it made her happy; and for himself, because it was an intimacy with her. There was sexual intimacy, too—after services. But attending with her gave him an insight into the secret dreamer she harbored within herself, a mystery that turned her wet, blue eyes to the sky in belief of something neither of them could see.

He, who had only ever placed faith in what he could see and touch, placed his faith in her, and in that way they began to weave themselves into one another.

Over the course of two years, he taught her how to hitch horses to a cart, how to pack the cart for uncertain weather, and how to pronounce German words correctly. Astrid taught him how comb flax, bleach cloth, and observe Passover. "Pesach," she pronounced in a throaty gargle that made him laugh. She showed him how to construct the Seder plate, how to drip a drop of wine for each plague, how to ask four (not five, not ten) questions. Above all, she showed Jurgen the empty chair.

"For Elijah," she said. "But he never comes."

"It seems a waste," Jurgen remarked. "Like spilling perfectly good wine. Wine costs."

"It costs nothing," she said, "to say *shalom* to the ones not here."

Each taught the other to do what they themselves did, though no one said the words, *in case*. It was no different than *shalom*, Jurgen learned. Words spoken or held back could mean something, or many things, or nothing at all.

By the spring of 1878 they were quite pregnant, Astrid with Fleischl and Jurgen with his dreams of a ship, the world and soaring flax sales. Neither of them could wait much longer.

"I know where our future is," Jurgen told her, his eyes dewy with thoughts of the sea. A week later they sat atop a rickety flax cart, with all their possessions packed beneath oilskin, at the rear of a line of merchant wagons waiting to pass under a stone arch into a tunnel that emerged in a harsh circle of sunlight at the far end. Slimy algae and lichen dangled from the rock ceiling. The tunnel air carried fish rot, salt and tar, and the tang of unwashed men. Everything wept water. Mussels clung to the bottom of the walls, having been swept in on high tide and stranded. The ground beneath them sucked at the curve of the wheels. It was a soup of mud, broken rock and sea water. The languages of many countries echoed from the walls and intermixed. Even Jurgen's own speech, his German and the bits of Yiddish he murmured to his beloved Astrid, lost shape and became something other.

"Show me this future of yours," she said. "And some food to help this baby live. Some fleischl."

He laughed to himself that she had "butchered" the word for meat. "Fleisches," he said.

"Quickly," she said, holding her swollen belly.

They found a Pension alongside a curved estuary of the Baltic, down a little ways from Stralsund's docks. It was a bit expensive for poor travelers, but comfortable, with a small room that had space for a bed, some chairs, and not much else. There was also a bathing room with a shallow, pocked tinsmith's tub.

He drew her a bath and said he would go in search of meat and a doctor. He imagined searching along the docks and the masted ships, under a creamy necklace of cloud, the scent of seawater and the entire, wonderful, unlikely world around him. The docks, the harbor, Rugen Island far across the Baltic narrows, the flood of sky and sunlight, blue and kindled. The edge of the world.

"*Gevalt!*" Astrid clung furiously to the zinc sides of the tub until her contractions eased. Tears fell from her blue eyes.

He kissed her and promised to return soon. "Don't go under," he told her, and left.

★★★

The heat of the bath lulled her into a most peaceful unconscious state, in which her belly wasn't about to rip open and her back wasn't on fire. She awoke reluctantly as the water cooled and the light waned. There was a constant low commotion outside the pension walls, punctuated by the grunts of men and a dull thud of tools brought against… something. Wood, she guessed. Overlaid upon the sound of all this industry was the soft, welcome patter of rain on the roof. She listened gratefully. The sound called her away from the strange city, back to her youth on the land, when rain meant the seedlings she'd planted would sweeten in the ground.

Dressing was difficult, but she managed a heavy skirt and layers of sweaters. The baby had shifted, and she could balance more easily on her feet.

She carefully descended the stairs to the street. The sun hung behind pale curtains of grey cloud. The commotion rose again and she turned toward its source. The sea.

At Stralsund's docks she found a group of strong men using an array of winches and pulleys to raise a thick wooden pole while others sat atop poles already embedded in the ground, hammering hooks and tying off black ropes. The poles rose into the swollen sky every hundred feet or so where the ocean met the land. A nicely dressed gentleman beneath a parasol shouted instructions to the sitters to take good care with live wires as he paced from the pole, counting loudly while a companion jotted in a ledger. Behind them was the sea, grey and descending to dark, and atop it the ships, and for a moment she understood her husband's yearning. The Baltic was magnificent. She considered his stubborn narrow-mindedness when it came to belief. Who could look upon this endless path to all the world and not see a hand behind it?

The labor pains doubled her over and she could spare no more thought. Wave upon wave radiated from her belly outward, blurring her vision. She stumbled into the cold shallows. Water lapped at her swollen ankles. Ships groaned in the rising tide. Men screamed at her. One of them cried for her to watch out.

There was an awful cracking sound. Something hit the rain-riddled water near her, folding the waves onto themselves. She turned as best she could to see the fallen pole and the man pinned beneath it, struggling for breath under just a foot or so of sea. She reached feebly, but there was little she could do. The contractions had her.

The men were screaming at her to get up, to move, to not touch. She closed her hand around something as a jet of blood spurted from between her legs. The black rope felt rubbery in her palm. Then it felt scalding, and then like wasps clustered and buzzing beneath her skin. Then it was all over her and behind her eyes. A most magnificent bluish light swallowed her. The baby fell from between her legs into the startled sea. Her baby's tiny hands reached for her from the shallows, where it floated at the end of her cord. Each drop of rain that hit the surface of the sea made a tiny ring, and her baby reached for those too. It all took a moment, and then mother and baby stilled.

★★★

Before he did anything else, Jurgen went to the first church he could find and asked for a rabbi.

"For my wife," he said. "I'm not a Jew. She is, obviously. We're having a baby. I don't know what the baby will be. Do you?"

The bemused pastor told him that Stralsund had all kinds, Jews and yet to be determined babies included, but it lacked a proper synagogue. There was a rabbi of sorts, he told Jurgen, who held services in his apartment just off the piazza. "He can do a bris," the pastor said, "if it's a boy."

Jurgen thanked him and left with the rabbi's address and the questions he would pose. What is a bris? Why might a son of mine need one? Why do you have a mezuzah for sale? Astrid would be warmed by his initiative. He saw himself returning to their Pension, kissing the newly acquired mezuzah which he would correctly pronounce, and he'd tell her there was a rabbi and therefore the promise of a bris.

He found a sausage shoppe across the piazza from their pension. There he bought thick, crunchy bread, some succulent fatty loin, and crumbled cheese spiced with dill. He returned through gray drizzle, along the southern curve, past a string of small shoppes, before pausing at a window lined with delicate clocks and music boxes. They were wonders of flywheel mechanics. Just the thing to gift Astrid and the baby. They would wake to a melody that would become the baby's first lullaby. One day in the distant future, their child would be a trembling elder, and that tune would ring through the halls of his memory.

He and Astrid would be gone by then, he thought. What a strange notion to consider at this moment, the very first of their baby's life. The store window reflected men hastily streaming from the piazza. Their exodus began at the far end, from the stalls near the alley that faced the Baltic.

"What's happening?" he asked one.

"They say a miracle." Jurgen couldn't place the man's accent.

"An angel."

Jurgen followed him across the piazza into a tunnel. A glow came from the end by the sea. Blue, throbbing. A low hum vibrated the stones of the tunnel walls.

Men screamed, "Cut power!"

Above the crowd gathering at the water's edge, a pole slowly winched up into view, cradled in chains. Black wires dangled from it. The frayed ends shot sparks.

He saw the great light in the shallows of the Baltic. There was someone inside it. It was lovely, but for the acrid stench in the air. The figure spun slowly within the glow and he thought of the music box in the shop window, with a dancer on a pin. She'd looked just like this.

The figure turned in the light to reveal its profile. He saw the distended belly. He saw a pendulum hanging from between its legs, down below the bulbous blue glow into the water.

He shoved his way through the crowd when the figure toppled out of the light to land face down on the cable. Two men tackled him before he could reach her.

The hum finally disappeared into the air. The blue glow extinguished. It was night. It was so bright a moment ago, Jurgen thought, and how could anyone know night had come.

"That's my wife," he said.

The men let go of him. He waded into the shallow water to Astrid. Taking her by her shoulders, he turned her over and to his horror, found that the electric heat had joined the right side of her face to the cable in an awful weld. He gazed into her eyes but she wasn't there. Her right eye had drained of all its warm sky blue and gone the color of pale cloud. He looked for her in there, but she wasn't anywhere that he could see.

One last spark flared beneath him. It was in the cord, still nestled between her legs. The other end was still attached to the shape below the water. The blue light burst silently within the cord, just below the surface, then dissipated to nothing.

"For God's sake," a woman cried. "Pick the baby up out of the water!"

Jurgen couldn't bring himself to do it. Astrid lay in his arms, reeking of fire. The skin peeled from her neck and face and petaled the surface of the sea. He couldn't let go of her, not even to scoop up his hopeless child.

"Let him through, he's a ship's doctor!"

A man waded into the sea clutching a knife. Jurgen was dimly aware of the man holding the knife over Astrid's cord.

"Nothing to be done for her," said the doctor.

The doctor took the baby's body back to shore. Jurgen saw another light flare, a reddish coal against the evening sky. Then hands fell upon him, tugging at him. Different men told him to come away. They said they would bring her too.

A ring of people formed on the beach, around his baby. The doctor no longer held a knife, but a deep-bowled pipe. He drew great breaths from it, then bent down to the little body lying in the cold sand.

Leaning against the other men, Jurgen walked to the circle. He fell to his knees. The doctor blew smoke into the nose and mouth of his baby. The baby seemed less a baby than a tiny, motionless sea creature washed up on the tide, or a bit of trash thrown over the rail of an anchored ship. The doctor's clouds entered the baby and never came back out.

"Displaces the water, y'see," a man said.

Astrid lay under a rain-soaked cloth with the tide lapping at her form.

The doctor bent over. He put his ear to the baby's chest. A sputter, then warm water dribbled from the baby's mouth, followed by hacking coughs like the snapping of bird bones. Little hands reached up to the purpling sky, imploring. The chubby arms fanned like wings. The doctor put the baby into Jurgen's arms.

"Come hold your son," he said.

It was too dark to see who he favored.

"One day," the doctor said to him, "you'll tell your boy that something happened to him. Something impossible."

★★★

At the top of the hill stood an imposing stone building that cast its shadow over a modest graveyard. In its sea-facing corner the great building cast its longest shadow over the exposed, overgrown heather and the outstretched limbs of Elms. The headstones had worn over time against the incessant salt breeze. There, the parish and its pastor were kind enough to bury Astrid.

Stralsund's lone rabbi had been apologetic. "I have only my apartment," he told Jurgen. "Certainly I have no graveyard." But he attended, to see where she lay, there among the many Christs and crosses.

Astrid's faith had meant so much to her in life, but Jurgen considered it pointless to care about such a thing now. Everywhere were carved exhortations to God, but what did those mean to the dead. The living, he thought, shouldn't waste their breath if it didn't stop the planting of one more marker in the ground.

The pastor traced a cross over his son's forehead as workers cut a hole in the ground.

"Isn't the boy a Jew?" asked the rabbi. He was young, pale, and bearded in the mossy, unkempt way of young men.

"By his mother," Jurgen said. "She was Jewish. I'm not. I'm not anything."

"We're all something," said the rabbi.

"All sorts here," said the pastor. "Christ teaches us that today should be a blessing as much as a loss."

What would Jews say about it, Jurgen wondered as he read the inscription chiseled into the marker. Astrid Berger, 1849–1873. Devoted wife and mother.

"May I offer a blessing over your son?" the rabbi asked.

"There's a blessing for motherless boys?" Jurgen asked.

"And widowers."

The rabbi intoned a melody Jurgen had heard before, at Astrid's synagogue, back when home was somewhere she knew. Not here, he thought, by a sea she'd never seen, yet still found a way to die in. It was a slow, mournful tune, and he turned his son away from it lest it make a memory in his tiny body.

He walked away from the bowing rabbi and the gravediggers as they slapped the loose earth flat with the backs of their spades. The pastor walked with him to the cemetery's edge and offered assurances that the next time he visited Stralsund, he would see the city differently. There would be grass over his wife's grave and flowers in bloom. His son would be old enough to understand that his mother was real, that she existed for a time, and there was a place where she could be found. This would come as a relief, the pastor said, and his eyes were full of faith.

I didn't bring her here for a visit, Jurgen told him. I brought her here for our life.

Stepping back through the heather, he walked down the path to the docks as a bright panic nested in his gut. His son hadn't eaten in the two days since he'd dropped from her.

Turning from the sea, he walked to the piazza and found the sausage shop open.

The butcher, a gregarious, kind oak of a man named Gert, mixed a bit of blood and raw beef into some milk. "For strength," he said.

"I don't know what to do next," Jurgen said.

"After he eats? Sleep, I would say."

"After my wife."

It sunk in over a quiet moment. "Oh. Oh, my friend, I saw. We all did. The angel."

"She wasn't an angel. She was just dying."

Gert went to his storeroom and came back with cured meats, a cloth-covered jar of milk and some blankets.

"I can't pay you," Jurgen said.

"Nor would I take it from you. Not until you tell me you know where your money will come from. You're a good man. I know these things."

"I sell flax, is all. Though I hoped for more. I brought my wife here because I thought I saw our future. Now, I suppose I'm holding all the future I'll ever see."

"If there's a future to be had, you need to see the burghemeister. Come, clean yourself up and look presentable. You've a man to meet."

"You've been more than kind to me," said Jurgen, guilt-stricken.

"I'm a Christian," said Gert.

"As am I, I guess, though he's a Jew. From her. I should really just stop saying that. I don't know if it's meant to pass along to him or not. Someone told me that."

"All sorts here."

"So I've heard."

After closing up shop, Gert led them to the wooden plank pathway along the sea to the guildhaus and the village burghemeister, a bloated cask of a man nearly bursting through his fine suit and vest. When Jurgen entered, baby in his arms, the burghemeister was gazing fondly at an ax hanging on the wall behind his desk.

"I don't accept babies as payment. Cash only." The burghemeister laughed heartily.

"I'm the husband of the angel of Stralsund," Jurgen said.

"I was there on the docks when it happened," the burghemeister said. "I promise you, Stralsund will never forget that day."

Jurgen took a bracing breath. "My dream coming here was to buy a ship, sail to other places and make my fortune. Look at me, herr burghemeister. How far away I am from what I hoped to be. I'm pitiable."

"Every man in Stralsund is far from something, my boy." He tapped his ledger with a fat finger. "Countless ships over countless years from countless places. The world comes here. What do you do?"

"I sell flax."

"Flax. Let me think. No, I don't know that I've seen flax much in the market. You can carve a space for yourself. That future is within sight."

"But I want to have a ship."

"Did you know that a man doesn't have to wait that long? That he can buy a share of a ship for a lesser price? A man can see the world that way. Here, have a map on the house. Let your imagination wander."

The burghemeister handed Jurgen an accordion of paper marked *Trade Routes To The Greater Samoan Archipelago.* Closing his ledger, he ushered Jurgen and Gert outside. "Have you seen such glory in all your years?" He waved his hand over the port and its forest of masts. "Come now, tell me you doubt you can do this, my boy, and for the price of a few years' hard work in the piazza. Of which I take but a small percentage."

"That he does," Gert said bemusedly.

Jurgen became aware of his son, cradled in his suddenly aching arms. It was as if the child had just then returned from the beyond.

"You had your child here," the burghemeister said. "You buried your wife here, may she rest. You're a part of the city's lore now. Before long we'll be standing together on the deck of a ship you own. Partly."

Jurgen considered the cold lights of the burghemeister's eyes, the way he sounded out of breath, the way the ships swayed in the Baltic breeze. He wasn't sure if he believed the burghemeister's words. He only knew he needed to.

"And then one day," the burghemeister said, "your son will take over. Tell me, what's your heir's name?"

"Oh."

He tried to think of what Astrid would have wanted. He saw her in the tub and encased in light, hungry, waiting for some meat. He thought of the myriad ways she fought with the German language, and how much he wanted her there.

"Fleischl," he said. "Fleischl Berger."

"Jurgen and Fleischl. Jurgen and Son. J&S Shipping, Ltd. An outstanding lineage. Your future is within reach, my boy. Naming it always brings it closer, don't you think? This will make a fine home for little Fleischl. Stralsund is a city that welcomes all kinds. Though we've one location I'd suggest not visiting. Surely you've seen the building on the hill? Quite a sight, but it's an asylum. Not the raving lunatic kind. They're docile creatures. No place for a child, though."

Jurgen turned his newly christened son toward the water. He couldn't help what he thought. *May you never understand what you took from me.*

The burghemeister and Gert chatted merrily as they strolled the docks back to the guild haus. They passed a shipyard filled with bins of hammers and fat kegs of nails glimmering in the sun. Atop sawhorses the size of houses, the skeleton of a ship rested. Skinned as a whale carcass, its ribs curved and its bottom punched out, he couldn't tell if it was being built or torn to pieces for scrap.

"Whaler," the burghemeister said. "Only whalers come back that battered."

"Happens all the time," said Gert. "I prefer dry land."

Fleischl cooed. His brown eyes, thick-lidded and slightly almond like Astrid's, glinted gold in the sunlight.

"Make your son a promise," the burghemeister said. "What you begin in the piazza, you end in the water. The sea shall deliver your futures."

Fleischl put his hand out to the bright flare of light on the Baltic's surface. He seemed so perfectly content that Jurgen decided to do his very best to love him and protect him from the horror of his origin. He'd buried his wife near his son's birthplace, and now they lived here. It was that simple. Everything felt ordinary, even the small storm in his heart when he gazed at the spot where Astrid should be, and at his ordinary Fleischl, who was born a foot beneath the Baltic, who would almost die again, and then again, who would grow up to be a holder of breath and then He Who Listens. His Fleischl would, in the end, be something more than ordinary. He would be impossible.

CHAPTER Two
Elijah's Chair

Fleischl's childhood attraction to puzzles came naturally.
He lived in the company of his father, a puzzle of many pieces, and
in a state of curiosity about his mother, a puzzle of blanks and spaces.

As a young boy, he accompanied his father each day to the
piazza, where he learned the family trade at their flax stall just outside Gert's sausage shoppe. People would stop by, and to Fleischl it
seemed their only interest lay in touching what his father had made,
the variously sized ropes above all. Men admired the ropes' dura-
bility, women the precision of Jurgen's braid work. You must have a
daughter whose hair benefits from your amazing skills, the women
would say, and his father would smile. Your wife must have shown
you how, they would say, and his father would slip into a silence for
the remainder of the day.

Among the people who made a point of stopping by regularly,
there was a young man his father called rabbi. The young man would
try to coax his father to pronounce it differently—"rebbe"—and
then he would tell Fleischl how much he'd grown from the time
they'd first met. Fleischl had no memory of a first time. The rebbe

was a regular who never bought anything. He just visited, offered comments on his rapid and dramatic growth, and attempted to guide his father's pronunciation, which seemed to annoy his father, or at least lead him back into silence.

"Maybe he shouldn't come anymore," Fleischl said once.

"He's a customer," his father said. "Work on your puzzle."

Their customers, the ones who watched him grow over the years, knew not to engage him when he was deep into the assembly of a new puzzle. To Fleischl, his puzzles were a kind of covenant with the world. Things became clear once all the disjointed pieces found their places, and pieces always found their places if he just kept at it. Even the blue pieces, which for reasons he couldn't grasp remained chaotic and unmoored until the very end.

The commotion of the piazza, the many tongues of buyers and sellers, his father's steady stream of instructions—fetch more seed from our bins, bring the cart, take the cart back—nothing could break Fleischl's concentration except the curious girl working each day in the sausage shoppe. She seemed in all respects to be his opposite. She was frantic where he was still, distracted where he was focused. She tolerated being barked at by Gert almost constantly, while Fleischl avoided provoking his father for any reason. She was forever per- forming, be it with a shawl around her head like a wizened crone or wielding a sharp blade as a scabbard. Always she seemed to be dancing. Dancing in small circles, dancing between customers awaiting their meat, dancing while tossing the sawdust used for sopping gore into the air like globed snow. She danced in place on those occasions when their eyes met and he suddenly, embarrassingly, gave thought to his appearance. He was serious-looking rather than handsome, or win- some, or even passably cute, with a face somewhere on the geometric spectrum between a triangle and a diamond. He had a broad forehead, high cheekbones and a narrow, amiable smile above a pointed chin. He generally saved his smiles for his poppa—not even the funniest customers earned one—and it was as if the shopgirl knew. She crossed her eyes and danced like a manic monkey whenever she caught him looking, and the feeling it gave him to be seen by her was in itself a puzzle.

If days were for the piazza, nights were for Stralsund's docks, where he learned the vocabulary of the wharf. The tall, spindly branches rising from deck to sky were masts. The lengths of chain from the hull down through the surface of the sea led to the anchor. The part of Stralsund where skeletal remains of old ships were pillaged and reused to build new ships was the shipyard.

The shipyard, especially at night, was his poppa's favorite place in Stralsund. Over the years they visited, they witnessed vessels rise from nothing and go to sea, carrying parts of the old ships with them. One night in 1886, when Fleischl turned eight, they bid farewell to the *Elegy,* a beast with sails and steam mechanisms.

"I know this much," his poppa said as the ship's lights extinguished at the horizon line. "A ship like the *Elegy* leads men to a better life. No man should stay in the place he's from."

"I'm from here," Fleischl said.

At home, he asked for a bath. He wanted the poppa back who stood in wonder before the assembling *Elegy,* not the one who watched it leave. The poppa beside the tub, astride a carpenter's bench, had a far-away look.

"What's it like on a ship?" he asked. He hoped to find his father where he was and maybe bring him back.

"I don't know," his father said. "I can only imagine."

"What happens if you fall off? Do you swim home?"

"Nothing good happens. Nothing a boy should know."

Jurgen touched the surface of the bathwater, sending little rings over to Fleischl. "You try to live as long as you can, until one of your fellows throws you a rope and pulls you out. But sometimes the sea has its way. If you can't get out, you go under."

"Then what?"

Then someone blows smoke into your lungs, Jurgen thought, and *pushes out the sea and hands you over and says here, you can't have both of them back, only this one.*

"Then nothing. Get out soon. You look like a prawn."

He left his son and stood at the window, just to see something else. When he returned, Fleischl lay beneath the surface of the bathwater.

"Get out!" He grabbed Fleischl and yanked him up from the water. "What were you doing?"

"Holding my breath," Fleischl said, terrified. "So you don't have to save me if I fall. Watch, poppa. Don't be scared."

He slipped back under. He saw his poppa's smeared and shimmering face. The distance between them suddenly felt far, so he raised his finger to the underside of the surface. Breaking it, he felt his fingertip tingle against the cool air. He held it just at the meridian between water and world, and waited for his poppa to touch him back. He knew the night, with its fears and its old ships, was a piece of the puzzle that was his father. A middle piece, with no way to know where it fit.

For years, on nights that ended with a bath, he slipped under, held his breath and waited for the touch of his poppa's finger to signal the time to get out. He became very good at holding his breath.

★★★

Each April, on the first Sunday after the first full moon after the equinox, Stralsund hosted a carnival that Fleischl was forbidden to attend. There were "improprieties," said his poppa, and "upsets." On their April post-equinox walks, Fleischl would glimpse lights, clowns, and a parade of some sort.

It was on the occasion of the 1892 carnival that he acquired a new puzzle piece.

"Improper," his father said as they passed the sea tunnel on their way home. The tunnel was ablaze with light from the festivities. "Upsetting. Also, not for us."

"It's not?" Fleischl asked.

"We're Jewish."

"We are?"

"I'm not," Jurgen said tiredly. "Your mother was. You? Be what you want. You don't have Easter. You have Passover. But when we're among others, you're not a Jew. No one likes Jews, not even Jews. Remember that."

"Does Passover have a party like the Easter carnival?"

"No. Just dinner and plagues."

"Could we do a Passover dinner?"

"I don't know how."

"Did momma ever show you?"

"I don't remember. Go find a puzzle to do."

I think I already have, Fleischl thought.

The next day, Fleischl surprised the young rabbi by saying more than, "hello," and, "thank you, yes, I suppose I have grown," when they saw each other at the flax stall. He pronounced *rebbe* correctly, asked for the man's proper name.

"Please call me Rebbe Bernhard," he replied. And while his father was occupied with another customer, he asked Rebbe Bernhard to teach him about Passover.

"First," Rebbe Bernhard told him, "we call it *pesach*."

Over the course of a few days, Rebbe Bernhard stopped by the flax stall to surreptitiously instruct Fleischl on the mysteries of *pesach*. On the first day, he told Fleischl the story. On the second day, he smuggled a Haggadah, whispered the four questions until Fleischl could at least hum the melody. On the third day, the last, as his lingering visits had caught Jurgen's sharp eye, Rebbe Bernhard produced a crude but effective drawing of a seder plate, with each symbolic foodstuff cordoned off in a kind of anatomical map.

"What are you two always whispering about?" Jurgen asked Fleischl on the third day.

"It's a surprise," Fleischl said. And on the evening of the third day, he and his poppa sat at a seder table. On the plates before them were bones Gert had provided, a pulpy mash of apple and honey, a bit of bread Fleischl had pounded flat to approximate matzo, and some grass Fleischl had plucked from the hill below the asylum.

Fleischl began a truncated story of Egypt, slaves, blood and door painting, but his father was concerned only with the anomaly alongside him. "There's a third plate."

"There's supposed to be," Fleischl said. "It's a rule."

"And an empty chair."

"For Elijah, but he's not real. He's a spirit. You leave a place for him and hope one day he comes." He got up, fetched a fourth plate and set it down next to Elijah's. Lacking one more chair, he pushed his own to the new setting.

"In case she comes," he said as his poppa left the table.

"This was a bad idea," his poppa said.

That night Fleischl fetched his own bathwater and waited beneath for his father's touch atop the surface. For a boy, his lung capacity was remarkable.

On the next Passover, in 1889, Fleischl added a fifth question to the traditional four.

"How did mama die?"

There were other words he could have said, that he'd thought about saying, but such things were impossible to say out loud. Instead, he screamed them in his head and wondered if his father heard across the expanse of the seder plates, the empty chair, the bathwater. *Did she die because of me?*

"She drowned," Jurgen said, and left.

Fleischl filled the old tin tub and went under. He heard the door to their Pension slam shut. That brought him right back out in a panic. He dried and went to the window, where he saw a lone figure crossing the empty piazza to the sea tunnel.

He found his poppa at the dock, sitting on a wooden pier. Before him was a great vessel with barnacles breathing in the night air across its hull. Its masts were crossed with cocoons of furled sails.

He sat down next to his poppa and he asked why here. *Why did you come here.*

"I like coming here." Fleischl could hear in his poppa's voice that it was true. There was a different, contented, less roiled sort of quiet about his father now. "I come here some nights when you're asleep," he said. "Maybe now that you're older, you'll take the walk with me."

"I'd like to, poppa."

They sat a while, until Fleischl couldn't hold the words any longer. "I just wanted to do something she did."

"I know you did."

Fleischl glanced around the docks for signs of anyone anywhere. They were empty, as was the piazza. Empty and dark, though through the far sea tunnel he glimpsed a tiny glow. He couldn't tell what made it, or where it came from, only that it was so small. It was an easy light to lose in the dark, and he thought about how odd a thing that was.

"You don't really ask about her," his poppa said.

"I don't know what to ask."

"Maybe tonight was a kind of question."

Fleischl thought about that.

"Let me say just this, Fleischl. She was Jewish and that mattered to her. But it doesn't matter to the world, and it shouldn't matter to you. Faith doesn't do anything. Don't look for answers in the sky."

"Where do you look for them?"

"In the earth, if I'm growing flax. In the wood and the tools, if I'm building a ship to sail on."

Is that why you come here of all places? Fleischl wanted to ask, but didn't. His poppa's quiet made itself heard, and he decided it was better to listen.

"I want better for you," his poppa said. "She did as well. That's why we came here. I don't want that to be one more thing she believed that isn't real. She believed in such things and look what good it did her. If you can't see it or touch it, Fleischl, it's a goddamn lie. It's a bedtime story for scared, lonely boys. Don't be one of them."

"Why do you come here?" Fleischl asked.

"I already told you why."

"Why do you come here to think of her, I mean. Is she here?"

His poppa considered the Baltic. Fleischl thought it strange that the sea was darker than the night sky when all it did was reflect. Or that it was so deep, and yet nothing compared to the depth of all he saw above him. Or that she was somewhere neither of them could imagine, let alone reach.

"She's up there," his poppa said, gesturing to the hill below Thalhammer and its garden of marked stones. "But that's a terrible place. Meaningless. Here, this is where she really is."

"Why here?"

His poppa said no more. For a long time, his father said no more, and that was a puzzle piece. An edge piece, to which others would soon attach.

★★★

That year, in celebration of the coming of his thirteenth birthday—well into his manhood, according to the religion he scarcely understood—Fleischl lied to his poppa. On their nightly walk past the carnival-lit piazza to the shipyard, he said he needed a coat. "I'll be there soon," he said, his mind racing ahead to the forbidden festival of Easter and the improprieties and upsets awaiting him.

What he found was music, dancing, games, tents, food and drink. There was nothing particularly improper about any of it. He thought of heading to the shipyard and insisting that his poppa accompany him, but he became distracted by an odd processional of Stralsundians behind a large papier maché puppet. A woman with a round belly danced within the frail glow of candles. The beauty of it swept him into line. Poppa would be upset, he thought.

He left the parade when it passed a tent emblazoned with blue letters. *See the astounding Phantasmascope!* Inside, he found a small crowd at a table, staring at a crude octagonal wheel with a handle turned by a man in a velvet top hat. There were images inside the wheel, connected between spools. As he turned the wheel faster, the images blurred into the fluid motions of a woman on a bench as a sliver of moon rose behind her.

"The sort of thing I dream of."

The girl next to him was fair, wiry, and brown-eyed except when the sun filled her eyes with gold leaf flecks. He realized he was staring at her and shifted his gaze to her curly chestnut hair.

"Our poppas know each other," she said, and he understood why she looked familiar. It was the girl from the sausage shoppe, now miraculously still.

"Hi," he said.

She rolled her eyes disappointedly. "You're Fleischl. I'm Greta. We know all that."

"We do?"

"Tell me where you dream of going."

"I don't want to go anywhere."

"Then why do you go to the ships all the time? I can see you from my window." She pointed to a building across the piazza. "It's the one with a candle burning in the window, in case you're ever looking. I see your poppa late some nights. He always goes to the docks by himself."

"He doesn't always," Fleischl said, aware of how unsure he sounded.

"Maybe he's the one dreaming of going somewhere. You should ask him. It's important to know these things."

He left Greta for the shipyard, but his poppa wasn't there. He found his poppa at the docks, aboard one of the largest vessels. It sat in a slip across from the burghemeister's guild, beneath telegraph lines and the slate sky. The ship's gangplank was down, so he went aboard to join his father on the sea-facing side. There he watched the Baltic churn. The waves rose up against the ship and folded back upon themselves. Lightning flashed at the horizon and thunder rolled in from the sea, from a place further off than a boy who didn't dream could imagine. He counted the moments between the flare and the sound. The heart of the storm was still far off.

"You went to the carnival," his father said.

"You went here."

He leaned over the rail. Below the surface were things he couldn't see. If he fell, no one would find him down there, trying to put a finger to the underside of a wave.

"What do you want, poppa?"

Jurgen looked at his son, pressed tight to the rail, staring at a sea he couldn't possibly understand.

"Is it really because of her? Or is this your dream? Leaving?" He saw fear in his poppa's eyes and thought, what a sad, strange boy I am.

"I don't know," Jurgen said.

"Yes, poppa, you do. Just tell me. I'll understand."

Jurgen took a moment before he spoke. "I don't make enough at the piazza to get a share of a ship. But if I took our flax to other places. Other markets."

"You should, then."

"I'd be gone, Fleischl. You'd be alone."

"I made a friend. And I'm a man. That's what momma believed."

"You astonish me sometimes," Jurgen said. "Are you sure you're ready?"

"I'm ready when you're ready. Go get money, and then get your ship."

From the rail, Fleischl saw a man standing on the dock, just staring at the sea with his hands held out before him. An odd sight, but Stralsund held all sorts. There was the man, the glow from the carnival, the great structure on the hill that was an asylum full of the certifiably insane, and a far window with a clear line of sight to where he stood, and a candle burning, and someone who'd been right about his father, and who looked for him some nights.

"I'll be fine," he told his father. And that night, he decided there would be no more puzzles. Men don't have time for such things, he thought. He was just newly a man, and had no idea yet just what a puzzle still awaited him.

CHAPTER Three
A Drowned Heart

The puzzle that was his father had come together. Maybe not completely, but enough to see it for what it was and would soon become: a man who was not a stall seller and who was not always in Stralsund. Maybe a man who was not always a father.

They were short trips at first. A night or two here, three nights there. Soon Jurgen's sales trips stretched out to last a week or longer. By 1894, when Fleischl was sixteen years old, his father would leave for Greifswald, Rostock, Bartha, Ribnitz-Damgarten—and who knew where else—for weeks or months at a time.

On the first day after his father's departure for Greifswald and beyond, Fleischl worked in the piazza through the afternoon, until shadows grew long over the cobblestones. Then he went to the Pension and sat by the window with nothing to do but stare at the church of St. Nicholas, the Artusloft, the docks and the sea, and let his thoughts drift into the unknowable stretch of time before him, during which he would be a man alone.

At dusk, all the lights were extinguished but one. A candle in a window on the far side of the sea tunnel beyond the marketplace. A figure came into its glow, waved, then disappeared. Soon Greta emerged from the tunnel with the flickering candle held up to her face. She stared plainly at his dark window.

He opened it. "If you ever see a candle in my window," she called to him, "it means come out."

"Come out for what?"

"Dinner, tonight. My poppa told yours we'd make sure you ate and got to the piazza without getting lost."

"It's right there."

"But the candle might mean, 'Let's run away and see the world.' And you won't know until you come out."

Everyone wants to leave, he thought. They must know things I don't.

That evening, he shared supper with Greta and her family in their high-gabled, cramped apartment. It smelled of liver and onions frying in fat, courtesy of Greta's mother, a short, round woman with a plain face and an implacable disposition. She slid a slick flap of bloody meat onto his plate, then took her seat and murmured a prayer before producing a jar of fig preserves from the pouch of her apron. She opened it, placed it next to her plate, and silently bade her family eat. Gert stuffed his mouth until it was a greasy smear. He talked a steady stream of complaint through the impossible wad of food wedged behind his teeth. Noisy customers. Dull blades. Sellers delivering slaughtered animals late. Demanding customers. Penniless customers.

While he prattled on, Greta's mother slowly grew red. Fleischl thought she might yell for silence, or at least peace. Instead, she stuck a stubby finger into the preserve jar and pulled out a gelatinous fig sheathed in seeds. This she popped into her mouth up to the last joint. She smiled like a plump baby and resumed slicing her liver.

Greta saw him home despite his mild protest. "We're the same age. I don't need a minder. I'm a man." He neglected to mention the newly acquired religious basis for that argument. In truth, he didn't mind some company, even in the person of a mercurial girl with a penchant for candles and, as he learned between the tunnel and the sea, mimicry.

"Are you tired?" she asked.

"A little."

"Wake up, then. And be happy, Fleischl Berger. I'm going to show you something I love."

They walked through the sea tunnel to the entrance of his pension. She surprised him by walking past him, bounding up the steps to the front door and waiting impatiently for him to trudge up. "Hurry, old man."

He unlocked the door and she went inside as if she lived there. Immediately, she set to injecting his blessedly quiet home with chaos. She pulled out the small table where he and his father ate their meals in silence and had once failed miserably at a Seder. After a moment's indecision, she took the table from its place in the right rear of the room and situated it in the middle. She rearranged chairs, found a length of linen and a bit of flax coil that had yet to be braided, and before his stunned eyes she fashioned what appeared to be the scenery for a play.

"What does this remind you of?" she asked.

He didn't want to tell her that it reminded him mostly of his father's absence, as she wouldn't dare move things around if he wasn't gone. Or maybe she would; maybe he was the timid one that wouldn't dare upend things.

"Watch." Soon there was a curtain of his father's finely made sheets stretched along the flax twine. Behind it, Greta waited at the table.

"Pull the curtain back," she said.

The tableau behind his father's sheet was a bit disappointing, though he didn't tell her so. There was an empty table and some chairs, and he was already acquainted with all of it. Greta was seated. He supposed that was new.

"Who is this?" she asked while he watched her body go into some sort of action he didn't quite understand. She puffed her cheeks, slouched her torso into a hunch, and fixed her eyes on the middle distance. "Stand still but hands everywhere," she said. "Don't look at anyone. They don't see you anyway. Breathe like it's hard. Tight mouth, no cross words. Fingers are spider legs."

"What are you doing?" he asked, alarmed.

"Bringing her in. Think of the phantasmascope."

Her hands swam through the dank air in a kind of dance. Her mouth twisted into a dramatic smile.

"I don't understand," he said.

Her fingers skittered across the surface of the table. It was all so quiet, the way she extended a finger, pointed it down, then lowered it into something that wasn't there.

"Oh. It's your mother." Bringing someone in seemed no simple matter.

She sat back. "That's tiring."

"So what was wrong when you did that just now?'

"I don't really know. I think she does that thing with her finger because that's the only good thing she has. She doesn't see us as good things."

"How do you know? She's your mother. She must love you."

That's what the ones who stay do, he thought.

"She never says anything about herself," Greta said. "So I bring her in. Maybe I'll hear a bit of her that way."

"Is this what you do in the shop?"

"So you do see me."

"You're right there where I am."

"Walk me home."

On their way into the sea tunnel, Greta told him that she liked to make her face look different when she pretended to be other people. She changed her hair, contorted her body and used butcher's tape to pull her eyes back. Once, she shaved her eyebrows down to thin threads. Once, she daubed some beef blood around her lips. "It tasted like metal," she said.

She did the same sort of thing to her surroundings when it

came time to conjure. "My poppa lets me build little places in the back of the shop sometimes, when things are slow. I can make it look like it does when you look into the phantasmascope. Like it's all in a little circle."

"Like what's in a circle?"

"Life. Everything you can imagine is so small, you can hold it. Isn't that a lovely idea?"

He thought about the woman on the bench, under a paper moon, and then he thought about stepping away from the eyepiece and around him was the carnival, ringed with people and the places they lived, worked, and died in, and the village of Stralsund around that, and the sea around everything. All of it held all of them. He was just an ordinary boy among millions.

"I can see why that would be a lovely idea," he said.

"I knew you'd understand."

They continued their walk through the piazza to her apartment. "After church tomorrow," she said, "we can take a stroll around the docks."

"I've never been to church."

"Never?"

"I'm Jewish. Maybe that's why?"

"How should I know? Unless you want me to bring you in. Then I'd figure it out."

"No. I don't want you to." The thought made him anxious. What she did felt like a taking.

"I don't know about going to the docks," he said.

"There are ships leaving. People saying goodbye. I like watching."

"I don't want to watch people saying goodbye."

"No one wants to. But that's the future, isn't it? Come, see what it looks like. Once you can picture it, it isn't scary. You can live with it."

"I don't understand why you say these things. You don't know me."

"This is how I get to know you."

"So you are bringing me in."

"My poppa told me that your poppa brought you to our shop on your very first day. Did you know?"

"No. What else did he say?"

"Nothing. What's your poppa told you?"

"That my mother drowned."

"Oh. I just knew she'd died. I'm sorry."

"He also told me to get out of the bath because I looked like a prawn."

"You and he must not talk very much."

He made it home and watched from his window until her candle snuffed out. Then he went to bed thinking of how little he knew. Sometime in the night, when sleep eluded him, he rose and went outside to see the stars—but not the Baltic. There was a note on the ground beneath a rock. The paper was spattered with dried candle wax.

Try to understand what it might have been for her, in a feathery hand, and *what it might be one day for you. Don't leave it to others to conjure your life for you or you might wind up just an ordinary dull and unimaginative boy, dreaming of no particular thing. See you at the docks. G*

★★★

He went to the docks the next day in search of her, but instead found a crowd gathered at the Baltic's edge to ogle a ship listing alarmingly in the harbor as four lighters labored to tow it into an open slip. The sight of it returned him to nights as a young boy, when his father read him stories at bath time, of men on the high seas battling mythic beasts and meeting terrible fates in the spinning vortex of a whirlpool or the beak-like maw of a monstrous squid. "A whaler," his father would say when asked what kind of ship. It was always a whaler. "Only whalers come back that damaged. Happens all the time."

"Do whales do all that?" he would ask.

"Sometimes the lutefisks help." And his father would tell him to get out because he was pruny as a prawn.

He was so taken with the ship that he almost ran into a frail old man with frazzled long hair and an unkempt nest of whiskers. The old man held his hands in a peculiar way, as if something filled them. It was the ship that held his attention. He didn't seem to notice Fleischl, or anyone else.

Fleischl wondered if the man was praying. It was Sunday, after all, and the sea was church to some. He left the old man and made his way down the dock to where the burghemeister stood atop a crate before a restless group of seafarers. Behind them, small rowers approached the battered whaler and tied themselves to netting that dangled from the hull. The whaler had come as far as it was able, from the looks of things. The rowboats bobbed against it as men climbed from them, up the netting and onto its deck, passing the ship's crew on their way down. Once full, the rowers pulled away from the listing ship and made for shore.

The burghemeister watched the ship as well, even as sailors filed past him. The ledger he held was open. On the crate next to his finely polished boot was a small, glass jar of ink. Each passing man dipped his thumb into it, then pressed it into a page of the open ledger. The burghemeister handed over a pen, with which each man wrote next to their thumbprint. There was a grim set to their mouths as their eyes darted to the sea.

So intent was Fleischl on all of it, the ship and the odd ritual overseen by the burghemeister, that he didn't notice the old man was now standing silently alongside him.

"Oh, hello," he said to the old man. "My name is Fleischl. I'm sixteen."

The old man kept his eyes on the ship. His hands turned palms up and turned slightly toward each other. Then his legs gave way and he toppled to the ground.

Fleischl took gentle hold of the old man's arms and helped

him back to his feet. He brushed the salty sand from the man's tattered breeches. The old man bent down to the ground. His fingers closed. Then he stood up straight again, hands outstretched, and walked away from the port along the sea path until he reached the guild and the burghemeister's office. There, he stood at the open door, hands out.

"Are you alright now?" Fleischl asked as he caught up.

Nothing. He may as well have been a ghost.

The burghemeister approached him at the office door. "You shouldn't be near a man like this. Your father wouldn't like it." He turned to the man. "And you!" he shouted at him. "You've no business here."

"Who is he?"

"He lives at Thalhammer asylum."

"But he's out here."

"Which is unacceptable. I'll be sure to speak to the doctor in charge."

"I've seen him before. One night from an anchored ship with poppa."

"Come away from him."

"He's out here a lot, it seems. He thinks he's holding something. What?"

"I'm certain that I don't care."

"He wasn't born this way." It wasn't like Fleischl to be disrespectful. He wasn't sure if he was being so, or if saying something to the burghemeister might cause consequences for his father. But the old man piqued his curiosity somehow. One day, his life went away and all he had was what he thought he held. Fleischl wanted to know how such a thing happened.

What he also wanted to know: whether this waited for all men. They find one thing to dream of, and lose everything else.

Greta approached from the sea tunnel.

"What are we doing today?" she asked.

Three men walked along the dock path. They wore white smocks, a cheap and heavy cotton blend. The old man turned to walk away, but they were on him too swiftly. They spun him in the direction of the asylum, forcing his arms apart. He tried to bend down but the men brought him up roughly.

"Wait!" Fleischl put his hands on the ground, then stood and held them out. "This belongs to you," he said. "You dropped it."

The old man stared at Fleischl's hands, then his eyes, and for a moment Fleischl wasn't a ghost.

The old man put his own hands out to receive the empty air Fleischl passed to him. He walked away with the men under his own power as the burghemeister trailed behind, threatening jobs and promising consequences. Once, the old man turned to regard Fleischl before resuming what looked like an ordinary walk along Stralsund's shoreline. Soon he was as small as Fleischl's fingernail. By then he was turning in to Stralsund's cemetery, onto the dirt path up to Thalhammer.

"Who was that?" Greta asked.

"I don't know."

"What were you doing?"

"I don't know that either."

"He seemed interested in this place." She stepped past him, into the burghemeister's office. "Let's see why."

He followed her inside with a sense of fatherly disapproval and the expectation that the burghemeister would bellow about consequences. There was nothing immediately evident in the room, unless the old man craved axes. Assorted legal documents, attestations, dusty volumes marked by year, receipts scrawled in a hasty hand, and maps. Maps upon maps.

One caught his eye, owing to its place on the wall. "That's the piazza," Greta said. It was the piazza, with the docks and the Baltic marked in squiggly lines and dashes. There was a small legend in the lower, left-hand corner, under the word Telegraph.

He followed the map lines from one end of the dock westward, to the hill, up a switchback trail, and on to Thalhammer.

He pointed to an odd symbol. "What's that?"

Greta leaned over the map. "Wings, it looks like. Oh, I know what that is. The angel story."

"The angel story?"

"I heard a little about it once and asked poppa, but he didn't say much. No one seems to. Something about a woman who died, and a light. I think one of those telegraph poles fell on her. They have a thing for her at Easter."

"The parade," he said. "The blue light in her belly."

"That one."

"The wings," he said, "aren't near a pole."

"I guess."

"We should go."

They put back everything Greta had taken out to examine and left, closing the office door behind them. It wasn't far to the alleyway and back to her apartment. After a supper of sausages and potatoes, he sat on the floor of her room and watched her practice bringing in the burghemeister. It was chilly outside and Greta's mother had placed oven-warmed bricks in a small stack near the headboard of her bed. Greta reveled in the radiant warmth, but he found the room stifling. It was all he could do to sit still and listen to her act out sailors inking their thumbs. When she shuffled her feet in silent invocation of the old man at the dock, her motion generated a snappish blue spark. Its aura hovered a moment in the dark above his crossed legs before extinguishing itself.

"That was a big one," Greta said softly. "Pretty."

The glow was no bigger than his pinky nail. It fanned open, then faded away.

"Fleischl? Are you crying?"

The first drip fell onto his bare thigh. It wasn't that he couldn't answer.

"I'm going to wake Momma." She sounded nervous.

After a few minutes, she returned to the bedroom with her mother in tow. She clambered into her bed while her mother quietly enveloped Fleischl in beefy arms that smelled of brine and figs.

Soon, he thought, I'll see Greta do this to bring her in.

"I miss home," he said, because he wasn't sure what he felt and had nothing else to say that might explain the hole where surely something ought to be.

"Mmm hmmm." Greta's mother didn't exactly speak. It was more a sound of the body. A low rumble. After a while, she retrieved coats for the both of them. "Come," she said.

Whenever he looked back on that time in his life, he couldn't recall hearing Greta's mother say another word.

★★★

The burghemeister's bier haus at midnight was a smoky cacaphony. Drunken men, mostly sailors, crowded every table. Down to the last of their coins, unable or unwilling to go home.

Greta's mother led them through the confusion to a hexagonal table where Gert sat with the burghemeister. He appeared well on his way to a stupor.

"Can't sleep?" he slurred. And then, to everyone's delight he howled, "Get them a stein!"

Greta took the burghemeister's hat from his head, placed it atop her own, then doffed it to him. "A stein!" she belted. "Get these kinder some cake!"

The men burst out laughing. Gert rolled his eyes. "Is that me?" the burghemeister asked, genuine puzzlement in his voice. "I think that's me I hear! Wondrous! Yes, get them cake!" He laughed himself into a coughing fit. "I thought I recognized you. The fleisches man's daughter." He clapped Gert on the back. "And you." He turned his attention to Fleischl. "What do you have to say?"

"A pole fell on the angel of Stralsund," Fleischl said, "but the wings aren't drawn on a pole."

The haus and its proprietor fell silent.

"Wings?" the burghemeister asked. "What pole? What are you talking about?"

"The map in your office," Greta said.

"How did you…"

"The wings are on the water," Fleischl said. "She died in the water."

The burghemeister sat down. "Oh, my boy. I know who you are now. Has no one ever told you?"

Fleischl hadn't meant to say anything, exactly. He certainly hadn't meant to know anything. He'd meant only to endure Greta's showing off, and maybe have cake as long as they were bringing some out, and hopefully grow sleepy and not see any more static sparks, which confused him as something unnameable that nevertheless belonged to him. But some part of him had acted without his conscious intention. It took a piece and placed it against another, and there it was.

A perfect fit for a man too old for such things.

"Mein kinder," the burghemeister said. "It wasn't a pole. One fell near her, but not on her. It never touched her. It wasn't exactly the water either. It was the telegraph wires."

"So it's her. That's my mother on the map."

"Maybe the boy doesn't need to hear this," Gert said. "Had his father wanted it for him, he would have said it all."

Fleischl glanced around the room. Everyone stared at him. There were only two women, three if he counted Greta. Her mother and a maid bringing drink and food to the tables. Sausages, he noted. He wondered if Gert sold his sausage here, to the burghemeister. Yes, of course he did. He sold them to the burghemeister and the burghemeister sold them at a profit here at the haus. Triple the price, Fleischl figured. It made sense once he saw Gert's face. How timidly he spoke.

"I'm not a boy," Fleischl said. "And my father's never told me anything."

The burghemeister took Fleischl's hands in his own. They were soft hands, unmarked by labor. "My boy, your mother's story is a story to be told. Gather round, you seafaring men. All you lot know about is what the sea takes. Listen now to what she gave back."

Fleischl listened. The others, Gert and Greta, listened.

"The telegraph wires, *kinder*, they fell into the sea. Just a foot or so of water. You were born at that moment, when the power to send words across Germany went through your mother and she couldn't hold you any longer. You were born drowned. But you were too strong for even the sea. You came back. Do you hear? Freya, a candle for the cake!"

The maid brought out a hastily baked cake smeared with frosting and studded with clumped sugar. Embedded in the center was a tall candle more appropriate to a dinner table than a small cake.

The burghemeister lit it. "They say a man has two birthdays, herr Berger. The day he falls from the womb, and the day he can look himself in the eye and not look away. Happy birthday, to the son of the angel of Stralsund!"

The room erupted in cheers. They didn't know his name and most were drunk, so they sang good wishes to the angel. After he blew out the candle and Freya took it away for slicing, the burghemeister brought him to the window. "There." He pointed to a telegraph pole standing near the shoreline. Its pinnacle seemed to scrape the underbelly of the blister-bluish night sky. "That one. It's likely not exactly the same pole, mind you. But that's where it was."

The cake returned. Freya brought plates and clean forks. Everyone gathered at the burghemeister's table for their slice.

Fleischl stayed at the window. Greta came to his side. He could see her reflection shimmering in the haus light, dreamy and glowing.

"I think I see you differently," she said. "I may even have to act you now, Son of the Angel."

"She wasn't an angel," Fleischl said. "Just a dying woman, no better or worse than any. Maybe just… easier to see in the dark."

"Did your poppa tell you that?" Greta asked.

"No. That's me."

"I like getting to know you better than I thought I would."

She smiled. He saw her in the window. Across the cloud that

was her reflected face, a smile and the far sea, each folded into the other.

She laughed quietly and couldn't stop. He began laughing as well. She touched his hand, generating a little spark that prickled his skin. He thought he saw a brief light no bigger than a star, though it could have been anything. It might not have been a spark at all, because neither of them said a word and neither of them jumped.

"Do you want to go see the pole?" she said.

"Maybe. Not now."

He waited for his desire to speak itself out loud. It took a bit. The world grew lighter outside.

"I want to see her," he said.

★★★

Astrid Berger, 1849-1873. Devoted wife and mother

"It's a nice inscription," Greta said. "I mean, I suppose."

Dawn broke over the hill. Ribbons of color deepened across the windows of Thalhammer. The sunrise was wrapping its arms around all the crazy people, Fleischl thought, before deciding that clearly he was in a mood, and that all the bits churning inside him were what passed for depth in unimaginative boys.

It would be fully light soon. He wondered why Greta's parents hadn't come looking for them. He supposed it had something to do with the bierhaus, and with him. Sons of dead mothers occupied a certain station, maybe. Especially those whose birthplace was enshrined on a map of steps.

"I mean, it doesn't say much," Greta said. "It would be nice if it said more."

"It's enough. For all I knew her."

"Do you remember anything of her? Of course you don't. You were just moments born."

"There are things." The words felt like the first stirring of a headache. "Not memories, as you said. I can't have those. But things, that maybe were a part of her. Or maybe I dream of her. I must have seen her, for at least an instant. Maybe such things stay in there somewhere. I don't know."

"Like what things?"

He couldn't quite find words for the bits he could conjure. A light. A drop of water. Somehow, those felt the same. A kind of fanning out.

"I can't remember," he said, finally. "Blue, maybe?"

"Maybe when your poppa comes home, you can ask him about her."

"I don't know if I can."

The world took shape as daylight fell across Stralsund and the sea. There was a ship near the horizon line. The line was such an odd, maddening thing. He could see it from where they sat, in a cemetery in the shadow of the asylum. But on board the ship, those men couldn't see any line. They saw a different one, that they would never reach. One always further off. That's what Poppa said.

"You want to know what you want to know," Greta said. "You don't want to just ask him random questions. 'What was she like?' 'She was like a lot of things.' See what I mean?"

"I don't know what I want to know. He had time with her. I didn't."

Something moved past a window of the asylum. He thought it was a reflection, so he looked around for a bird or a cloud.

"Is it really true that there's an asylum in there?" he asked.

"Yep. Scary, isn't it?"

"What do lunatics do?"

"Yell. Talk to people who aren't there. I'm not sure. Ask your new friend."

He saw the shape again in Thalhammer's window. It was a person, thin and vague.

"You'll stay with us tonight. Maybe all the nights until he's home, and after he leaves again."

"Is that ok?"

"I wouldn't have it any other way."

"Me too."

"I'm sorry your mother died."

"I'm sorry having me meant my poppa can't have her."

She put her arms around him. He felt the good weight of her against him. He felt the sun falling upon his skin, and the dew drying on his trousers. He heard a ship's bell, and far-off birds, and Greta's soft breath. From the high hill he beheld the half-timber warehouses on Gersten Street up to the Wickhauser dining hall where men from everywhere gathered to eat and drink. The sea spread its fingers through Stralsund to the countryside and in doing so, lost its salt and became the river Tallonsee. The sea took enough. In the angel of Stralsund fable, it took his mother. In the failure of his father to say a word about it to his own son, it took one of the threads that bound them.

He cast his eyes one last time toward the window. The figure raised its arms out before it. The arms spread, the hands opened as if holding something. Now the light was high and the window clear, and he saw that the old, bearded man from the docks held nothing at all.

CHAPTER Four
Sea Tunnel

In the year of his seventeenth birthday, he woke each morning in the early hours, brought his flax cart to the piazza marketplace
and worked, then dined and stayed with Greta and her family.
He and Greta spent more and more time in each other's company.
Gert would occasionally remark on their inseparability, but mostly
just watched the two of them as they chided each other at the
supper table.

He still walked at dusk along the docks and brought Greta
with so he could hear her create the people they saw in the piazza
(the grandiose burghemeister remained his favorite), and through her
he saw more of the world than he would otherwise have noticed.
He liked how the world was when it came through her, and so he
wanted her to come to the sea. Especially there, because that's where
the old lunatic could be found.

"He had to serve on a ship," he said one spring evening while
she rummaged through her clothes for something warm. "Or else
why the fascination with every boat that sails into port? Why can he
only see the ships and nothing else?"

She pulled a sweater over her head. He watched the weave of

the wool slide down her body. It stirred him. He turned away from
her as the heat rose in his cheeks.

"You see me," she said, "if you choose to."

He told her what little he knew as they walked through the
piazza to the sea tunnel. The old man almost always came on those
days that ships sailed into Stralsund's port. The ships drawing the
lunatic's interest were primarily German. He thought, or wished, he
held something.

"I pretend to pick it up," he said, "so maybe he thinks I can
see it too. I think I know what it might be. He's always standing near
where the burghemeister stands."

"I understand why this matters so much to you. You want to
know what can happen to a man because of ships and the sea."

I know a little of what the sea does, he thought.

"Keep trying," Greta said, "and maybe you'll piece it together."

On those occasions when he encountered the lunatic without Greta, he tried to communicate with him. He never really
expected a reply, and didn't know what he would do if he actually
received one. He talked about the weather, about flax, about how
the weather affected flax. Sometimes, he talked about his life. That
he didn't actually care about flax. That he knew something his father
didn't want him to. That he feared he wasn't the son his
father deserved.

The lunatic remained inscrutable until one cold Sunday
afternoon in November, 1895, when the *Schnitzel* sailed into
Stralsund.

He and Greta came upon the ship while on a walk after
church. Men were lining up before the burghemeister, waiting to
press their thumbs into his list.

They peered at the paper in his hands.

Be It Known:
The undersigned affirms and warrants that his death at sea is an act of

merciful God's will, and shall hold _______ harmless. All risk at sea is assumed by the undersigned.

In the blank space, the word *Schatze* had been written in a paler color than the words around it.

"That's the ship name," a young man said. He stood next to Greta, his eyes on the list. "But everyone calls it the Schnitzel."

"Why the Schnitzel?" Greta asked him.

The name cut close to her family's trade, Fleischl supposed.

"Just look at her!" the young man said. "Barnacles all over her hull. She looks breaded, doesn't she?"

"She does," Fleischl agreed. "Are you going to be on it?"

"I am."

Behind the hopeful sailor, Fleischl saw other men waiting with their families. Some of the women wept. Those children who were in tow shifted restlessly or broke away to chase gulls, or stared in open want of the harpoons lying in a pile by the ship's gangplank.

"So it's a whaler," Fleischl said. He spied the lunatic trudging toward the *Schnitzel,* hands out. "This is its first voyage."

"It is," the burghemeister said as the sailor stepped up to make his mark. "How did you know?"

Fleischl thought of the feeling of his prawny hand in his father's, listening to old tales. "It doesn't look damaged. Yet."

"He's seeing you," whispered Greta.

The lunatic came to Fleischl's side, hands out as usual. Fleischl wasn't used to seeing anything in the old man's eyes but sky and sea, but today there was fear, glistening like drops of sunshower.

"Don't worry," he told the old man. "I'm not going."

The lunatic walked away, back to the hill and Thalhammer. There was a light on in Thalhammer's window, facing the sea. If he waited long enough, a figure would appear.

"It's a master list," he said.

"That's what his hands are doing?" Greta asked.

"I'm nearly positive. He's holding it open for men to leave their marks. Maybe he's holding it for someone who sailed off and never came back."

"He was holding it open for you."

"I know."

"One day it really will be you," she said, "leaving your mark. It will be your father and he'll take you with him. That's the future he wants for you."

"My father dreams of it. He loves it, not me."

"What in the world do you love, Fleischl Berger? That's what matters, not what anyone else loves."

That night, he lay on her floor and thought about what she'd said. He thought about the city and above it, the expanding network of telegraph wires. He thought of the sea, their walks, candles in windows and the view from his mother's grave. He thought about deciphering the blathering of a lunatic and deciphering the silence of his father. All the odd-fitting pieces of his life. Now Greta had told him that one piece was missing. What in the world did he love.

They snuck out late to the burghemeister's office for three straight days, where they went through all the rolls of all the whalers that ever left Stralsund. Men had been lining the boardwalk for a hundred years to leave their names and the whorls of their thumbprints. Putting together a list of their own, they formed a plan to contact the surviving captains and mates of those ships with loss of life. Perhaps one of them would know the lunatic.

"A telegram would be faster," Greta suggested on the night he posted his first letter. He thought about it, and about the telegraph office where the burghemeister would cheerfully take his money and tap out his words. He thought about his words traveling up the poles.

He assumed that's how it happened, having no understanding of electricity or telegraphs beyond their ability to generate despair. Into the wires and out to the far world his message would fly. He thought about the sounds the wires would make as they carried his words out.

The hum and crackle.

"I can't," he told her.

Before spring came, he'd heard from all save the first mate of the Freund. The ship had left Stralsund's port on May 5, 1844 with a crew of 93, bound for the migration lanes off Spitzburgen's arctic waters. It returned in roughly two equal pieces, tugged by salvage ships, on June 2, 1846. There were 81 survivors.

They wrote to and received a reply from a cooper who gave an account of the last night before all went wrong. The first mate's name was Anton Lautin. He came back. Aboard was his brother, Johannes, who didn't. The brothers held fast to a seafaring tradition of their own making. When one went in the whaleboat, the other remained on deck until the boat was spotted bobbing safely on the waves. Anton held no love for the harpooning life. Johannes loved his brother and the harpoon, and little else.

"What do I do now?" Fleischl asked Greta.

"Go tell him what his name is," she said, "and who he's been waiting for."

"I need your help."

"What can I do?"

"Bring him in for me, and then for him."

★★★

They knocked at Thalhammer's door and asked to see the person in charge. One of the white-tunic men brought them to a small sitting room and told them to wait. "What's all that?" he asked, eyeing Fleischl's armful of linen and rope, and Greta's bag of makeup and clothing.

"Tools of our trade," Greta said sweetly.

Soon a well-groomed young man came and introduced himself as Dr. Laszlo Rapholtz, the asylum director. He was an oddly proportioned figure, with a short, square torso and long legs, as if God had been interrupted mid-construction. He wore simple black breeches, a hunting shirt of deep mauve, a white cravat, spatterdashes, and unpolished black boots.

The doctor shook Fleischl's hand, then bowed to Greta in a courtly, old-fashioned way. "Who are you here to see?" he asked.

"Anton Lautin," Fleischl said.

"I don't recognize that name. Is he on staff?"

"He's an inmate here."

"We prefer 'patient'."

"He's the one allowed to visit the docks. The older gentleman."

"You know his proper name? Are you a relation?"

"You didn't know who he is?" Fleischl asked. "What do you call him?"

"How could you have found out his name? I've spent countless hours trying to reach him."

Fleischl explained his process. Rapholtz made notes. "Deductive reasoning." he sighed. "So simple. And the mysterious item he thinks he holds?"

"The master roll from his ship, the *Freund*. What have you called him all this time?"

"Minah. Or nothing. The patient in room eighteen. Come, I'll show you to him."

They followed Rapholtz through the asylum's many corridors. Every several feet or so, there was a door with a number and a hook from which clipped papers dangled. Many of the doors were open. Inside, the beds were neatly made with crisp, faded white sheets. Chamber pots were tucked beneath their metal frames. Everything was arranged identically in room after room.

"They have no windows," Greta said.

"And they have those." Fleischl pointed to a bed in one of the rooms with unbuckled leather straps dangling to the floor. "May I ask how you tried to reach Anton?"

"Those are for patients who get unruly," Rapholtz said. "Our number eighteen certainly isn't one of those. He's quite docile. He doesn't even sleep in his room. He sleeps in here."

The room they found themselves in was octagonal and tiered.

The first and second floors were ringed by a metal walkway that hugged gently curved walls lined with shelves of haphazardly placed books. The crowded shelves encircled the room entirely, but for an immense window.

"That must offer a view of the sea," Fleischl said.

"And the cemetery," Rapholtz added.

"How does he get out?" Greta asked.

"I'll show you something no one here knows about. Well, number eight—I mean, Anton does, and I. And now I'll show you." Rapholtz went to a section of bookshelf a few feet past a large couch draped in sheets. He took hold of a handle hidden between two thick tomes. The bookshelf split, then opened out to a doorway. Beyond it lay a tunnel built of oblong rock, like the cobblestones of an ancient street.

"No one seems to know why it's even here, or why it was never filled in," Rapholtz said. "It leads all the way out to the bottom of the hill, can you believe it? This is how he leaves and returns, unless our staff goes to get him. Please don't tell anyone. I just have always felt it a lovely little secret thing buried in a room of knowledge. It had a purpose, no doubt, and one day I trust I'll learn why it's here."

"If I may ask," Fleischl said, "why is Mr. Lautin able to leave? Are others allowed to? Not through the tunnel, I mean, but at all?"

"No. My work with the others has been much more successful."

"I should think success is measured by how many men *do* leave," Fleischl said.

"And that is what an unschooled man would say. Let me impress upon you the value of informing yourself before you speak."

Fleischl wondered if the doctor spoke to his patients in a similar tone. But the doctor wasn't entirely holding his attention now. He'd noticed the sheet draped over the couch. It was moving. "Isn't the goal to repair these men?" he asked as a hand slipped out from under the cover to brush against the library floor. "Let them join life again. Oh, and there seems to be someone under there."

"Well, of course there is. That's Mr. Lautin, who you came to see. It's near his sabbatical."

"Sabbatical?"

"To the sea, of course. I'm very curious as to how he'll receive you, so to speak, here in his room. But to answer your question, one might think the way you do, were one never matriculated through the alienistic curriculum. The goal is to build their confident sense of self, so they may see themselves as perfectly adequate. We give them what they need to build a new life here. Not to force themselves upon an old life that no longer wants them."

"With restraints," Fleischl said. "And doors that lock."

"There's no cruelty here, young man."

"Do you talk to him?"

"To what purpose? Number eighteen, you have visitors. Isn't that a wonderful thing?"

He whispered to Fleischl, "I'm mindful of his real name, thanks to you. But we must bring him along gradually. Like everyone here, he's broken. We know so little about the wheels that turn the mind. Let me make this clear to you: in the end, all men of psychiatry do is tend their wounds. We can't heal anything. That, I believe, is likely impossible. I don't know how, and I don't know anyone who does. But try to talk to him if you must. Of course I tried it and it was pointless, as you'll soon see. Now, please explain the sheets."

"We didn't know if we'd be allowed to bring wood and hammers," Fleischl said. He tried to smile as disarmingly as Greta had.

While he strung the linen along his father's expertly woven rope, he admired Greta's zeal for rearranging other people's furniture. She did it unapologetically. He wondered if he would ever be as bold as she, worrier that he was. Puzzlemker that he was, he fretted over the notion of moving the chairs and desk back to their original places.

The doctor seemed amused by it all, though he recognized in the knit of Rapholtz' brow the familiar grumpiness he sometimes detected in his father. It made him want to apologize and promise that all would be put right.

When at last everything was ready, and Rapholtz was seated with a notepad in his lap, Greta signaled him to pull the curtain back. Anton remained at the library window as the sheet receded. He seemed oblivious to the change of scenery emerging behind him. Fleischl went to his window. "I brought some things that belong to you, Mr. Lautin. I brought your name, and your brother's, Johannes." Lautin turned away from the window. He tilted his head slightly, a dog hearing a distant whistle.

Greta stood behind the desk. To everyone else in the room, it may have appeared as if she'd just stood up from composing a letter. But by the placement of her hands along the top of the chair, the slight sway of her body, the manner in which she'd pulled her hair under a cap, the coal-drawn beard she'd rubbed onto her cheeks and chin, and by her eyes, the frantic scanning of some middle distance, Fleischl hoped Anton saw what she was bringing in. A man at sea, waiting at a ship's rail like any other day that the whaleboats went out. That man didn't know it wasn't just any other day. It was that day.

"I've corresponded with your cooper aboard the *Freund*," Fleischl said. "He told me you were the very best first mate a man could ask for."

"He's not even listening," Rapholtz said.

"He is," Greta said. "You just don't recognize it. You have so many men to watch. Fleischl only has him."

"It couldn't have been easy ordering to sea the very whaleboat your brother was in," Fleischl said. "But your shipmate told us what happened. Listen, Anton."

Greta moved to the center of the library. She stared at nothing that anyone could see and after a moment, began to speak in the voice she'd practiced. A hoarse, deep growl, versed in all things whaling. "When the first whale in months breeched that twenty second day of June, 1846, you didn't want to go. Johannes did. He always wanted to go. He dreamt of the harpoon and the kill and you didn't think anything would happen. He'd gone and come back so many times before. But a dying whale with so many harpoons in him can take the hunters down with him. They don't come back. Only their memory returns to port."

"Anton," Fleischl said, "and Johannes. There you are, watching for him. Do you remember? Say it to me, Anton. Johannes."

It took almost an hour of repeating the names, but as the sun dipped toward the horizon, he thought he felt something in Anton let go. He couldn't explain it, not when he tried later that night with Greta, or even to himself. It was nothing he could explain. Anton's eyes found him and held. It felt real and it didn't last a moment before a ship's bell sounded from somewhere on the Baltic, and Anton was gone into himself again.

"Quite the moment," Rapholtz said when Anton was back on his couch, the blanket up and over his head. "But a moment was all. There will never be a cure for such men from simple talking, my boy. But I'll allow, to see a man's past returned to him along with his name. You, sir, show promise, though you've some naivete appropriate to your age and station. And you, young lady. Quite a performance!"

He turned back to Fleischl.

"Have you thought about your future, sir? You could be here, studying the mind of man. Think on it. But today is, I fear, a valuable lesson in perspective. All your effort reached me, and perhaps him, but now it's gone as if it never was."

Tell me," Greta said, "might one apprentice here to learn the science?"

"Perhaps," said Rapholtz. "No one's ever asked."

"Fleischl's quite good at puzzles. There would seem no bigger puzzle that putting order to your library, if not one day your patients."

"Interesting. I'm willing if you are, Fleischl. We could write a paper together on this. I shall think of a name."

"But the piazza," Fleischl said that night on the floor of her room, after trying and failing to describe what it was he felt and how quickly it left Anton's eyes. *Something happened to him* was as close as he could come. "The flax stall."

He knew Greta heard everything he did not say. A ship. Our walks. My life until now.

"Do you know why I really love pretending to be someone else, or making up those silly little sets?"

"Because you're good at it?"

"I am good at it. But that's not why."

She sat on the floor next to him, close enough for their shoulders to touch. She leaned into him and it was as if she was back on the deck of the *Freund,* steadying herself against a gale. For a moment he let himself believe he was strong enough to hold her up.

"Do you ever wish someone somewhere would look at you so closely that they memorized you?" she asked. "Then they could call you up from the past one day when they're old and you are, too, or you're gone." She looked away. "Everything we think we remember is a little bit true and a little bit of a lie, isn't it."

He called up his father from his not-so-distant past. At the docks, telling him his mother was out there somewhere. She couldn't be seen, could only be believed, but he swore that she was there, and then he said how it was folly and weakness to believe in what couldn't be proved. The soil, the wood, the sea, but also not the sea when it came to those who were gone. He thought of the empty chair, which was wood, and he wanted to get up and leave like his father. The world was too big. But where the soft rim of his shoulder touched Greta's, the world was small enough to hold.

The candlelight caught a fleck of gold in the brown pool of her right eye.

She smiled as if she'd heard everything he was thinking. Such things were impossible. They weren't soil or wood.

"I do this because maybe I'll find out what in the world I love," Greta told him. "I'll make a moment someone will remember perfectly. A little memorized piece of my life that will always be right, no matter what. It will matter that much to someone."

"It matters to me," he said.

"I'm glad." When she spoke, he could feel her breath on his skin. "Maybe what we did today will be the thing in the world you love."

"Maybe it will."

"Try it," she said. "And if it turns out not to be, try something else until you find it. Nothing is forever, until it is."

★★★

He was working in the piazza the following morning, bartering with the usuals, when a voice called out. "How much for the wool?"

"Wool is for beggars…"

His poppa peeked out from behind the customers. Pulling him into a hearty hug, his poppa said, "you make me so proud. Come, let's have supper. I've some news to share with the man I see before me."

They crossed the piazza to a vendor of fine baked breads and bought loaves of black rye.

"You look taller."

"Maybe," Fleischl said. "I don't know."

"And you were alright without me?"

"I was fine. Keep going until you have enough for your ship. You don't have to stay."

"That's a part of what I wanted to tell you. I've made what's needed. It's time."

At the tunnel's end, Fleischl paused to consider the dividing line where the sun fell and the ships leaned into the Baltic's shallows. "I came here a few times," he said.

"I was hoping you'd learn to love it."

"What's the rest of your news?"

"We now own one-fifth of the *Elegy*. In a week we'll be aboard."

"We," Fleischl said, because he knew.

"I want you to come with. *J&S*, remember?"

★★★

After a quiet dinner and an airing out of the Pension, Fleischl lay in his own bed until he couldn't hold it in any longer. He found his father asleep in a chair.

"Tell me again how she died."

His father roused with the familiar annoyance in his eyes, but Fleischl saw it quickly peel away. It was no different than Anton. A kind of letting go, a moment of recognition, then lost. Back to the place where secret hearts lived.

"In the water," was all his father said.

CHAPTER Five
We Are All Electric

"How long, poppa?"

It had been six days of excited, one-sided chatter about the future and walks to see the *Elegy*. His poppa brought gifts for Gert and cheerily commented that Greta was a lovely young maiden who would make "someone" a good wife one day, followed closely by "no surprises for your poppas, you two!"

At the burghemeister's bier haus, he raised his stein and called loudly for a toast to a safe voyage. When they were alone at night, he set out the Elegy's trade route and all the stops he planned to make.

His father's eyes were alive with promise on the cusp of their departure.

He shared his itinerary with Fleischl. He'd sketched a detailed map of land and sea with Xs at all the stops. He'd drawn a diagram of the ship itself, or as much of it as he knew, which seemed considerable to Fleischl. Corridors, cabins, a roundhouse, a galley, the holds and all they'd contain. It looked like the hull held a city.

He told Fleischl of his grand plan to sell flax to the army across Germany and elsewhere. "They need bandages. Wads for cannons.

I don't even know what they might use it for! We start here, and then there, and at harvest we'll be back in Germany, at Kiel's camp, selling the last in time to gather more."

"How long?" Fleischl asked, but the tavern was too loud, Gert's table too joyous, his poppa's eyes too bright, and he too quiet. As always.

On the morning of the *Elegy's* departure, they stood with Greta and Gert at the dock, among a group of men gathered at the feet of the burghemeister's soapbox. They had each packed a full bag of clothing and, for Fleischl, some paper for writing, a puzzle, and a comb for his unruly hair.

Ahead of them was the young harpooner he and Greta had met on the day the *Schnitzel* sailed off for parts and whales unknown. His mark made, his weapon slung cavalierly, he turned and nodded in Fleischl's direction. "Looks like good work," he said, gesturing to the rope Jurgen carried.

"I made it," said Jurgen. "I can make you one if you want."

The boy went up the gangplank.

"Must be meeting a whaler somewhere," Jurgen murmured as they stepped up to the burghemeister's roll. *Dowid* was the boy's name, scrawled childishly next to a fat thumbprint.

"How long," Fleischl asked again, because Greta came alongside him, her eyes full of fear and impatience. *Say something*, she mouthed.

"About a year," Jurgen replied, "give or take. It's a long way to Zanzibar, but the sights we'll see along the way! It's winter now. We'll be back in time for next harvest at Kiel, as I said."

"Zanzibar," Fleischl repeated. Greta squeezed his hand. "Home in 1896. Maybe."

"Hopefully, for the holiday. It's worth it. I must admit, I feel nervous. I feel like a boy again. Don't you?"

"I am a boy," he said, to his own surprise. What sort of man tries to keep up with boys, he thought as he surveyed the others at the docks.

"You don't have to go," Greta whispered. He let go of her hand and went to be next to his father.

"Such a proud day," the burghemeister said, gesturing for the Berger men to step forward.

Jurgen pressed his thumb into the roll and left his mark. He turned to Fleischl and took his son's face in his weathered, trembling hands. "Our future must be a bit fearsome for you, and yet here you are. We'll be together and I'm glad. I think we need this, you and I. Don't you agree?"

"J&S," Fleischl said.

"Limited." His father clasped his hand. "It's just us and the future we build."

A moment longer and Jurgen stood on the *Elegy's* deck, suitcase in hand, waiting for his son at the rail.

The afternoon glare robbed Fleischl's eyes of clarity and rendered his father's face a shadow. His father could have been looking at Stralsund. He could have been any other traveler. The port was empty save the men angling for work. Whalers and trade ships had already departed or were still some months from their return. A few men passed on their way to the piazza to get an early start on commerce. Locked into their lives, they paid no mind to the man alone on deck, yearning for a different sky far from everything.

The burghemeister held the inked cotton out for Fleischl. Jurgen leaned over the rail.

"It's not just us," Fleischl told him. "Don't forget the empty chair."

"It's almost time," Jurgen said. "Come up."

"You think it's because of me she died."

Jurgen put his case down. He didn't look surprised. "That's not true. I've never said that."

Fleischl left the burghemeister holding the roll, and Greta, and went to the edge of the dock below where his father stood aboard ship. He gazed up at the light and the cast silhouette of his father over him.

"I know the angel story. I know it happened because I was born."

"It's not your fault. It will never be your fault."

"You see her every time you look at me. It's been there and I didn't know what it was. I can't go with you, poppa. The sea is yours. My part is here. The shallows. This is as far as I go."

His father regarded him for what felt like hours. He heard the burghemeister quietly close the roll. He would have been the last. Dowid came to the rail next to his father. He glanced disinterestedly at Fleischl, then to the high parts of Stralsund.

He saw his father smile. For all the years to come, he'd never be sure what that smile carried, at the golden hour when light met water and made of the world a great looming.

"Take good care of him," Jurgen called from the rail. He pointed to Greta.

"I will," she called back. "I promise."

"Poppa I'm sorry."

Jurgen picked up his bag. "It's only a year," he called to Fleischl. "Next time."

"Yes, poppa. Next time."

On the docks, the men not selected dispersed like the frigid low clouds, toward the piazza, the haus, the guild. Soon the burghemeister left. He reappeared in the guild window, seated at his desk before the ceremonial axe.

Fleischl remained for as long as his father was visible on deck while the work of a ship carried on around him. Men hauled provisions of animals living and dead, crates of drink and salthorse, and Fleischl thought, that's what he'll live on for a year. This is who he'll see each day instead of me, for a year.

Greta took his hand again. It was so cold he barely felt her skin. She told him they weren't going for a walk that night. There was nothing to see. Instead, they would stay warm by the fire, and she would tell him a story he might want to hear.

"Poppa!" The *Elegy* broke free of the port. "It's too cold.

Go below. When you come home, I'll be right here!"

His poppa waved a last time before stepping away from the rail. He and Greta walked away. Down the path, he saw Anton staring at the sea from the library window.

They entered the tunnel. Green moss wafted above them on currents of tangy air. There was a rusty metal door ahead, and light behind it that dazzled the wet walls.

They emerged in the circular library. Rapholtz sat at a desk, jotting in a bound black leather notebook. Anton took up his place on the couch.

The doctor looked up at the sound of their entry into the library. "Excellent. I wasn't sure you'd be able to locate the tunnel entrance. It's quite overgrown."

"We remembered," Greta said.

"I've just said goodbye to my father," Fleischl added. "A year at sea."

"Difficult for any good son."

Anton came to Fleischl with open hands. Fleischl put out his thumb. "There'll be no whales," he said, and rolled it across empty air.

"No Johannes," Anton mumbled.

"I'll start tomorrow," Fleischl told Rapholtz.

That night, for the first time, he lay in Greta's arms. He listened to her story and felt sleep coming like a tide. He was glad she told it in her own voice. It was his favorite.

"There is a man who stands at the foot of a great journey. He will begin his life again and the sea can't stop him. Nor can it stop the son. It's a kind of quiet, the leaving, and the son has known many quiets all his young life. He came to the world in the oddest, brightest quiet of all, and had no need to spend any more time listening for it. The son isn't alone. He will never be alone."

★★★

In the first two months of his father's absence, Fleischl became a familiar sight for Thalhammer's patients and staff. He visited with

Anton each day at the library window, where he repeated Anton's name and that of his brother. Sometimes he would invoke some of Greta's words (not well) and talk of the sea, and his father came to mind along a wave of guilt at how they'd parted. He and Rapholtz drafted a paper, *On Hearing and Listening: External Stimulus As Treatment For Dementia.* At Fleischl's suggestion, Rapholtz added to the title before submitting it to periodicals. *Treatment For Dementia and Loss Of The Self.*

Between visits with addled men—Fleischl became most familiar with Geralt, who suffered mild to moderate seizures when in the presence of the color green, and a hysterical contracture patient known only as "Knot"—Fleischl composed and discarded letter after letter to his father. He didn't know what to say. Each draft circled the same sentence like a ship reeling along the ledge of a whirlpool. *Why didn't you tell me what really happened to her, and then to us?*

He imposed order upon the library's chaos, and among the treatises and unfinished thesis papers by one Rapholtz, L., he occasionally found things that interested him. There was a scholarly article by a rising figure in psychiatric circles extolling the "talking cure." He took that to study in order to perhaps be nimbler in his debates with Rapholtz. There were issues of a periodical called *Revive*, with photos and daguerreotypes of asylums and descriptions of clinical practices and experiments from around the world. He took those for Greta, who loved photos. Even grim ones.

To his surprise, he found a Bible among Rapholtz' old papers. One day in the deep February freeze, Fleischl asked how a man of science could also find room for belief.

"I never said I believed in God," Rapholtz told him. "I like the rituals. They bring me comfort."

"It's like the tunnel," Greta said when Fleischl told her. "It's just there, and maybe one day he'll figure out why."

Over the weeks and months, Fleischl unlocked Thalhammer's locked doors and introduced the concept that learning about addled men might lead to a memory, and from there, to what they loved. To Rapholtz' oft-expressed belief that Anton's brief awakening had vanished (if it had ever happened at all), Fleischl brought Greta's optimism.

"Let me at least try," he told Rapholtz. "Nothing is forever until it is."

Still, Thalhammer's men remained in stubbornly full thrall to the phantasmascopes in their heads.

"Imagine how exhausting that must be," he said to Greta on one of their evening walks. "To maintain that. To see only what they can handle, and nothing of the wider world. What causes that?"

"I suppose seeing the wider world that did whatever it did to them is too much," Greta said.

"I'm trying to understand them. Rapholtz isn't. But they deserve at least that."

"Fleischl, what's wrong?"

He wanted to say, "nothing." It was reflexive, and he supposed he learned it from his father. Saying nothing meant nothing was wrong and he could return to being quiet and listening to Greta's voices.

"I hear you," she told him, "even when you're quiet."

"I know." His silences resembled his father's, back when his father hadn't the money for a ship. A failing sort of quiet.

"What's to come for us?" he asked Greta.

"I didn't know you thought of such things."

"I'm starting to."

"This is what I believe. The answer is different for each of us. There's us, Germany. I listen to poppa and the men at the tavern while you stare into space. There's trouble in the north. Bismarck insulted France or some such. We could be at war, or not. You and I don't know of such things because we only think of what's coming for us. For me, I long to be on a stage somewhere else in the world. I want to be seen by everyone in all the grandest places. I want to be so much more than I am now. I want to make people cry and laugh and forget. Did you know there's a theater in Pankow called the Wintergarten, with

pictures that move across a screen? There's a world doing what I want
to do. It's coming. In some places, it's here. I want that to come for me.

Then there's you. Your poppa will come home. It's a long time
yet, but across a life it's no time at all. When he does, he'll want to put
you on a ship and off you'll go, selling flax in Madagascar and Tipperary.
You won't want to. You don't want the future coming for you."
She pointed to Thalhammer. "You want what's in there."

"Why do I want that?"

"Maybe lunatics remind you of someone. If you could only
hear what they hear in their heads, you'd get them back from where
they go when they become lost. It's a building of empty chairs,
Fleischl."

"You think you're smart. Tell me what to do."

"About what?"

"I don't want to break my poppa's heart."

"Ah. That."

They went to a bench near the spot where the *Elegy* had been
anchored two months earlier. The bench was relatively new, with a
shiny plaque dedicated to the memory of a son lost to the sea.
"I'm sure your mother didn't want to break his heart," she said, "but
she did. You didn't want to make him raise you without a wife, but you
did. I don't want to break anyone's heart by leaving here one day, but I
might. We do these things and some of what's around us breaks.
It's what happens. If it matters enough to stop us, we were the most
breakable things of all."

He felt a bit giddy, and a bit sick. The bench faced the sea,
where his father sailed with his son's words alongside him.

"I wonder if there are asylums in Pankow," he said.

Greta kissed him. It was warm and lingering. "Here's what
I think," she said. "You work at the asylum. Learn from that doctor.
Learn all you can. When your poppa returns in the winter, you'll both
make peace with your mother. He'll see the life you're building, just
like he's building one. He'll understand. A man chooses what to make

his life from. That's what you're doing now. That's what all this is."
She kissed him again.

"You should eat with us," she said, "but sleep at your home.
Now that we're courting, it isn't right that we share a room. Come
over when you see the candle."

She took his hand and placed it inside her blouse, over her
breast. His palm was cold as the sea, but she didn't flinch. "Tonight,
wait for the signal telling you it's time to come out. Bring me some
Revives. I want to see photographs from other places."

"I'll go get a few," he promised, as her heartbeat came through
her rising breast, into his hand like words into his ear.

★★★

Getting back into the asylum was simple enough. He knew the
tunnel's entry point by heart, overgrowth be damned. It was quiet inside.
All the patient doors were closed. Whatever visited those men at night—
lost fathers, lost brothers, the dread color green—only they knew.

On the Theory That Some Minds Must Never Be Alone. He made a
note of that possible thesis, for the future.

In the library, he took a stack of Revives and quietly crept back
out so as not to wake Anton. There was a photograph of an apartment
in the April 1894 edition. Outside its window, swollen clouds wove
together above the basilica of a church. In the hazy foreground there
was a table and an odd cylinder atop it, with joints and wires sprouting.
One of the wires trailed over the table, along the floor, up the wall and
out the window, into the storm like a kite string.

We are all electric.

He sat down on the dock bench to reread the first sentence,
and then the paragraphs below it.

We are all electric.

*Are you familiar with the experiments of Galvani? I commend you,
read his De Viribus Electricitatis in Moto Musculari, 1791. He posited that the
muscles can be made to respond to electrical stimulus. This is due to the currents*

of energy that course like estuaries through all living matter. A battery and a dead frog is all one needs. You will see dead flesh twitch and contract as if not dead. For energy does not die. It hides and it thinks it is silent. Think of what man could do, what he could heal, what godly thoughts he could construct, if the polarity of the body could be harnessed!

I shall await your reply to this theory here in these pages, for I don't wish to be in direct contact with crackpots.

A.B.

Before leaving the bench, Fleischl leafed through every subsequent issue of Revive to see whether A.B. had received any response. Nothing. No words of encouragement, no batteries, no dead frogs.

He thought about the article all the way home. There, he opened the windows to let the chill night air freshen the moldy Pension. He went downstairs to the courtyard and built a fire, then warmed bucket after bucket of well water until he'd filled the old tin tub. Beneath the pension window, he slipped under the surface and held his breath until clouds of color burst behind his eyelids. The water cooled to his body's temperature. He felt adrift with no one there to tell him *get out.*

Afterward, he looked out at Stralsund. The sky was stitched with telegraph wires that disappeared into the distance. They were silent. They only made noise when something carried along them. He went to Greta when the candle ignited, kissed her and told her what he would do.

At dawn the burghemeister came to open the guild hall. He saw a cart of flax goods alongside the building. When he went to the front door, he found Fleischl waiting.

"I think I want to send a telegram," Fleischl said.

"My dear boy." The burghemeister embraced him, for few Stralsunders made use of the contraption inside the back room of the guild hall. Of all people, the son of the Angel.

The burghemeister took Fleischl's dictation, then looked up

the nearest telegraph station to Paris, where Revive could be found. He began tapping away at the great keys. The pinwheeling of wires and gears, the mechanism by which language flew. When it was done, the burghemeister gave him a sheet with his own words on it, so he might say, yes, this is what I meant.

DEAR HERR AB STOP THEY SAY I WAS BROUGHT BACK FROM DEATH AS INFANT STOP BLUE ELECTRIC LIGHT STOP BORN WITH A DROWNED HEART AND NOW I WRITE YOU STOP FLEISCHL BERGER STOP ALSO I COWROTE A PAPER NO ONE HAS READ IT WOULD YOU STOP

Fleischl took his written words outside. It was too early to see Greta again. He would go to the piazza, set up early, eat a bit of cheese and rye, and wait.

Above him, the telegraph wires thrummed. They passed an audible quiver one to the other, down the water line.

"Thank you, momma," he said.

CHAPTER Six
J&S, Ltd.

7 June 1896

If we're to be stranded somewhere, at least it's in paradise.
We came as far as Apia before the winds turned to storms and the captain
anchored us in the horseshoe bay of a small island to wait for the weather to
pass. Could be a month, he says. This may be my last letter for a time, as it's no
longer safe to row ashore where there lives a Christian missionary who ferries
our mail to a cargo ship on the island's far side. For now, we batten down. It
appears we'll miss the bulk of trade, so today our caption decided we'll come
home again when it's safe rather than complete the journey. Such are the ways
of the sea, he says. Who am I to question.

It's nothing but boys on this ship. Hard as they play at it, most are
afraid. Sometimes so much so that they make themselves ill. We carry them to
the roundhouse for prayer and a little comfort. I read to them at night like I did
with you.

We've much to talk about, you and I, and we'll do so when I'm back.
You're a man, not a boy, and as a man I say this to you: she was not only your
mother but my wife. When it's your time to love, you'll understand. Until then,

I'll hold all there is to say until we see each other again. It will be soon, thanks to the weather.
Poppa

Fleischl returned to Thalhammer and took a seat on the couch next to Anton. A fine, late fall light bathed the shelves up and down the wall by the tunnel door. Together, he and Greta had managed to organize the library. She had a keen eye for touches of comfort and beauty. A casually strewn blanket on the couch, some small, vibrant paintings she'd bartered for at the piazza. Rapholtz had gone so far as to say that Fleischl had a future in psychiatry, given his meticulous organizational skills and his predilection for puzzles.

That wasn't the future Fleischl worried about.

"What was the date on that letter?" Greta asked when she came by. She'd managed to convince Rapholtz to spend a bit of money on an old desk. Over time, she'd decorated with odds and ends from the shipyard: a rusted sextant, a compass, a yellowed map. It gave the library a nautical theme, which seemed fitting.

"It's more than three months old," Fleischl said. "He's certainly due back soon. Then he'll make me leave when the *Elegy* goes out again. I just know it."

"Talk to him. Tell him what you're doing. For God's sake, show him the battery."

On the desk next to A.B.'s detailed instructions on how to build and use the battery, a pair of lines hung in garlands from hooks on the library's second floor balcony, where they'd been affixed to the bare wires of a bulbous fixture. A Leyden jar sat on the desk, its insides covered over with cemented foil. Its lid was punctured in the center, through which Fleischl had strung an antenna-like terminal per A.B.'s surprisingly elegant hand drawings. A delicate chain connected the terminal to the wires atop the desk, ready to be plunged into the flayed quadriceps of a newly deceased orange-bellied frog he'd clipped to a piece of sanded driftwood. That was Greta's touch, "to give it more of a habitat milieu."

"Show him what?" Fleischl asked morosely. "That his son knows how to make a dead frog jump?" He touched the battery wires to the frog's legs, sending them into a macabre dance that fluttered the small stack of letters between he and A.B. The most recent lay on top. *The heart makes a sound,* A.B. wrote, *and by it we can find and mend it as best as is possible in this age. Something mended your drowned heart, my friend. How do we hear that? Oh, and please do send your paper. I lack good reading.*

Greta took his face in her hands. He'd grown fond of their strength. They were rough and calloused. They forever smelled of the unique chemical exchange between meat and salt. There was so much within her. A poetic heart and the unknowable ability to capture the essence of others. It gave him hope that there might be something more to him as well. Some spark that broke free of his odd birth and lived on in him. If he found it, he might show it to his father.

She gave his face not a kiss, but a gentle, insistent twist until he was pointed at Anton on the couch. "That's not a jumping frog corpse you see. That's a man who's been given back his name."

That evening they dined at the burghemeister's bier haus, on sausage and the newest addition to the menu, thanks to Fleischl's constant tinkering with the battery.

"You've made Parisians of us all with these frog legs," the burghemeister said as he stood over their table. "Bony. Reminiscent of roast chicken. But I must say, delicious."

"Not just a doctor of the mind and a seller of flax," said Gert. "A purveyor of exotic meats." Gert took a frog leg from the plate and examined it with the keen eye of a jeweler. "So much," he said, "for so quiet a young man."

"Still waters and all that," said the burghemeister. He placed a stein in front of Fleischl. "A toast to your father's imminent return."

"One for me," said Greta.

"A lady doesn't engage in bier haus toasts," said the burghemeister.

"A lady doesn't tear meat from bone," said Greta, "and yet…"

"I know many a young lady who works in the kitchen," the burghemeister chastised.

"Indeed," said Greta. "And I promise you, they all drink."

The burghemeister laughed heartily. "With your father's permission, for I know when I've lost an argument."

"By all means," Gert said. "I gave up all hope of a frilly thing in lace years ago."

They raised their steins and toasted Jurgen Berger's name.

"I have no son," said Gert, when the toast was over and they had taken their drinks. "But I can tell you, nothing makes a man prouder than a son following in his wake. Everything we do, we do for you. So that your path away from home is clear."

Fleischl felt Greta's gaze.

"Your futures," Gert said. There was wetness in his eyes. Fleischl's stomach churned warmly. Greta's lips came to his ear. "Don't," she whispered. "Hold on to what you want to be, Fleischl Berger.

I'm going to tell you what I see in you. I've been thinking of how best to show you. I just need a bit more time, and the battery and all the wires you have."

★★★

Fleischl waited. He waited at the guild for A.B.'s letters. He waited at the port for the *Elegy*. He waited and waited. And on the 29th day of October 1896, he came home from the piazza to find a note under his door. *Your presence is required in the library tonight, but not until you see the signal. Do not come before!*

He waited at his window until he saw the flame in hers, and then he went to Thalhammer. It was just past ten when Rapholtz ushered him into the dark library and sat him down on the couch.

His eyes adjusted. Shapes familiar and odd emerged from the gloom. The table next to him was clear of objects. There was a long series of sheets sewn together and stretched taut across the length of the library. They blocked off most of the room's sea-facing curvature.

He heard the short, sharp turn of a gear, and saw the contours of three batteries. The coiled vines of the wires spilled over the edge of the desk to disappear in the murky room.

He heard a soft click just before a faint light grew behind the sheet. For an instant, he saw the silhouette; it could only be Greta. He heard the sound of small pieces moving. Then the light faded, taking her silhouette with it.

"The son isn't alone. He will never be alone. He doesn't know what he can do. But he can do things."

Soft blue light rose in the room, glowing from two points, one at each end of the sheet. Another shone near the middle. The sheet began to ripple in the azure glimmer. It was strong in some places, faint and evaporating in others.

"Oh," Fleischl whispered. The sea.

Her silhouette reappeared behind the sheet, alongside the middle light. She held up shapes. They didn't look like anything, just odd, incongruent forms at the end of sticks. Then she brought them closer to each other.

"I didn't know my story," she said in an old, roughened voice. The pieces came together as pieces of a puzzle to form a man's head. She held it above her and looked up at it.

"I have a name again." God, she sounded exactly like Anton.

The shape of Greta turned profile. Her belly was swollen. Around her, the blue sea light eddied. Her shadowy form began walking toward the far end of the library.

More clicks. A light ignited behind her—a sudden, violent flare. Another burst, closer to her this time. She continued. Her gait was heavy and awkward. Her hands cupped her belly. She trailed lights and walked as if she didn't notice. The other end was blue and beckoning.

He stood. He hadn't meant to.

She was nearly there when a final light ignited above her head. It fell to her feet and then there flashed more lights than he could count, one over the next. It was beautiful and quiet, and his heart hurt like nothing he'd ever felt.

Her arms fanned wide, then descended down, but the sweeping shapes remained at her shoulders. Wings.

The room went dark. Fleischl felt for the couch behind him. All that was visible behind the sheets was a small, weak, blue light near the floor.

A last click. Her shape appeared back at the end nearest him, where her walk had begun. Just her, her outline, her spread wings. Her voice rose. "He can do this," she said, "because he was born not with a drowned heart, but a heart full of light."

She peered out from behind the sheet. "It's nice to see you at last, Fleischl Berger."

She came to him, sat down and held him. The wings she wore were a clever contrivance. Balsa and feathers and a glue that carried the musty scent of old books. And yet he cried. She kissed the salt from his cheek and he reached for her breast. He needed to know its weight and permanence. Somewhere distant he heard Rapholtz, who must have operated the lights, get up and leave. He spared a precious moment to thank him silently, just as Greta opened her mouth to him. Rapholtz might have helped her set the lights up and create two more batteries, and in so short a time. The lights had been beautiful. The ones that took Greta's silent version of his mother and the sea, and the last one. The weakest, smallest blue glimmer that he understood to be himself, on his very first day.

When her breathing grew deep and even, the way he'd heard it when they were children, he rose as quietly as he could and rested her head against the worn leather of Anton's couch. He needed to write while he could still hear it.

Poppa -

When you come back, let us talk to each other. You're my father and we're together in this world. She's not between us. She never should have been.

She's with us, listening for the moment we understand that. We're J&S. Let us be that, if not aboard a ship, then in life.

I'll try to understand you if you'll do the same. I know how hard it was to lose her and to raise a son alone. Perhaps you can understand the son you raised. He's waiting for you. Let's each talk, and then let's each listen.

Fleischl

He put it in the morning's mail to be posted, then returned to the library and lay back down next to Greta and slept. Somewhere, a small blue light glowed, and a drop fell to the surface of a great sea, and then another. The light swelled until it was a perfect circle and inside it was a shape with its arms reaching out. From a far place he heard a voice. He thought he ought to know who it belonged to, but something wasn't right about it.

She's not the angel, it said.

He woke to a warm sensation on his bare chest. For a moment he thought he was immersed in bathwater. A pale shaft of dawn light stretched across his skin from the library window where Anton kept watch over the docks.

Thankfully, he and Greta were covered. He moved her arm off of him. Every muscle in his back objected when he stood.

The library door opened. Rapholtz peered in. "You're awake. Thank goodness. I didn't want to wake you this early, but there are some things."

Fleischl nodded groggily. "Was that you, operating the batteries?" he asked.

"I'd like to think I'm a bit more than that, Fleischl," Rapholtz said as Greta sat up and yawned loudly. "Remarkable talent, she is. Quite the actress. Young lady, your father was both gratified and displeased to learn that you were here through the night. And herr Berger…"

Fleischl pulled a shirt over his head. "Am I in trouble?" he asked.

"There are reports of a ship approaching," Rapholtz said quietly. "It will be in port soon. The *Elegy*."

"That's my poppa. I should go." He turned to Greta. "Shouldn't I go?"

"I'll be there," she said. "Just let me wash up a bit. Maybe see my family and let them yell at me."

Fleischl went to shake Rapholtz' hand. "There are things to say to my father, you see. But after, I will be back. I want to be back."

"And I will be here waiting for you. Take care now."

After Fleischl left, Greta pulled on her shoes. She splashed water on her face and cast a dejected eye at the mess that was the library. "I'll just straighten up a bit before I go," she said. "It won't take long."

"You shouldn't do anything but go to the dock," Rapholtz said. "Go now. Don't let him be there alone."

"He's just nervous."

"I'm told something happened," Rapholtz said.

Anton pressed his hand to the window. His head bowed until it rested against the glass. Then he turned and walked past Greta and Rapholtz as they stared at the empty hands he held out. He was careful not to drop anything.

★★★

"Precious few bodies."

The last of the lighters drifted against the dock truncheons. Three men heaved a shrouded corpse from one of the boats to the wood planking of the port. Others took it and lay it next to its white-sheeted brethren.

Fleischl counted fourteen in all.

He stood next to Greta and Anton, watching the lighters and dinghies row out and back, ferrying the dead and the maimed.

The burghemeister waved him over. He took Greta's hand and picked his way through the knot of onlookers at the slip.

"That's everyone," the burghemeister said.

"My father."

"He's not here, *kinder.*"

"You've seen beneath the sheets? You've been aboard ship?
I didn't see you looking at anything. How can you know?"

"Fleischl."

"Don't speak of things you don't know!"

He tore his hand free of Greta's and went to the furthest part
of the pier. "Poppa!" he screamed at the ship. "Jurgen Berger!"
"A storm," the burghemeister told Greta as they watched Fleischl pace
furiously, waiting for the lighters to touch shore. When they did, he
knelt and searched each bandaged face.

"Ships anchored to each other like links in a chain," the burghemeister said. "Parlay between crews. When the gale took down the
one closest to the sea outlet, they were still tethered. One took the
next down, and the next and the next."

"Which one was he on?" Greta asked.

"Middle one, I heard. The *Elegy* went down, and one went on
top of her. He's under the other ships."

"God." Still, she had to look, if only to spare Fleischl doing it.
It didn't take long. There were so few men. Bloated, sea-salted faces,
blue from drowning, and no lights to bring them back.

She approached Fleischl and put her hand on his shoulder.

"There are rumors," the burghemeister said. "Some made it to
shore, perhaps. That one there did, but he's the only one they found.
Myself, I just can't imagine anyone living in a storm sea. Only a strong
young man, maybe, and even then. The rest are surely lost."

They watched the lighter draw near. In it was the rower and a
man cradling a trembling shape under a blanket. The blanket twitched,
then again. The survivor, that miraculously reached shore.

Fleischl's guts knotted themselves as the lighter's blanketed
passenger emerged from cover, saw where he was—atop the sea—and
tried to get up and out. The blanket fell the rest of the way off.

"Dowid," said Fleischl. "The boy with the harpoon. He spoke

to my father the day they left. He might know."

Dowid climbed unsteadily out of the lighter, toward the out-stretched hands of men on the pier. They led him to the docks. He cradled a thickly braided coil of rope.

"Goes mad if anyone takes it from him," the lighter pilot said to Fleischl.

"What happened?" said Fleischl. "Did you see any others swimming with you? On land? Was my father with you?"

Dowid didn't respond. He didn't meet Fleischl's eyes. His grip on the rope tightened.

Fleischl grabbed for it. Muck fell from the rope. J&S, it read, stitched delicately in thread of some color that had been washed almost to vanishing by the salt.

"He made this for you," Fleischl said. "Jurgen. Jurgen. Did you see him at Apia?"

There were things that could be done, he thought. Ship's rolls and reports from the port of call at Apia on what had transpired, survivors to interview, natives to locate for accounts of addled, wandering white men who spoke not a word, or who screamed a strange sounding name. Fleischl. All of it might yield scraps of information with which to piece together a chronicle of events, and he might find his father in there. Because he wasn't here. His father might be on Apia somewhere, far from home. Or he lay beneath all of it. Even farther. He seized Dowid by the neck. "Where is my father? The man who read to the boys in the roundhouse? What's wrong with you?"

Greta's arms closed around him as the men guiding Dowid pulled the two of them apart. One of them men was a large, oil-skinned Kanaka. "S'matter with him is, he's seen too much of what the sea does, boy." He took fresh hold of Dowid's arm to lead him away. Dowid went rigid. He rearranged his embrace of the rope so that he could hold one end up.

"What's this mean?" Fleischl asked him.

Dowid walked away. He was back under the surface of the sea.

"What was he doing?" Fleischl asked the Kanaka.

"Wasn't there, boy. But I know the sea enough. That one's one in a thousand to get out. The rest are done and gone, sorry to say. Make your peace with it or live in torment. Most of us who've seen, we do both."

Soon, Dowid was a small smudge at the far end of the docks.

"Rapholtz," Greta said behind him. "He might be able to help. Or you. Then, maybe he'll tell us."

In the night, there had been a moment. Late in the sort of darkness he recalled from childhood, a grainy, cloudy darkness that made objects across his tiny bedroom appear to be moving. He was inside her, moving, and her face was clenched. For a moment he thought he'd hurt her. His mind filled like a sinkhole with all manner of terrible possibilities. She bleeds. She hates me. She's had better. She's broken. He looked closely at her as his member withered and fell out. But she was fine. She asked if anything was wrong, and kissed him, and the brackish thoughts left him to settle among the bits and pieces of her story, there in the library.

He left her crying at the dock, his thoughts reeling from her kiss to fake wings and burnt lights to the broken ship and his poppa reading to strange boys. Soon he was in the piazza. Soon he was home but didn't stay. Soon he was at his mother's grave, and then the docks again, empty of all life. He sat on the memorial bench and thought of no particular thing. He was cold and numb and waiting to be found.

★★★

There was so much to do.

He met with the burghemeister to settle his father's account. The smallish debt was more than satisfied by the proceeds due Berger, J. from an admiralty and marine casualty policy of insurance taken out by the majority owner of the *Elegy*. Fleischl even had a modest sum left over.

"Enough for a share of your own ship," the burghemeister said. "Your poppa would be proud." Owing to his sad state, the burghemeister didn't charge Fleischl for the gravesite next to his mother's. No grave needed digging given the lack of a body to bury, which also kept the cost down.

He chose a simple headstone that matched his mother's. It made no explicit mention of the sea, though the underscore to his father's carved name was a slightly curling wave.

He spent his days at the piazza, selling flax. People bought from him in far greater quantities than usual. They bought things they needed and things they didn't. They came to speak highly of his father regardless of how well they knew the man. He was good. You look so much like him. You were the most important thing to him. Make him proud. From now on I shall buy all my flax from you.

Rebbe Bernhard came by one grey morning. He brought two prayer books with him and offered Fleischl one. "You can just repeat the words," the rebbe said.

"They won't change anything."

Fleischl returned to his work as the rebbe stepped away, began to bow and sing, and generally attract the attention of a small group of curious passersby. It was a melancholy melody the rebbe chanted. The words felt pitted and somehow breakable. He turned away from all of it, lest it find a way into him. The words weren't anything he could see. Not like flax.

He saw Greta each day, through the window of the sausage shoppe. Occasionally their eyes met. In those moments, he wanted nothing more than to go inside and take her into his arms. But doing that would invite the moment after, and he didn't know what that was.

He saw her at night, at her window. On the first night she lit her candle. He turned his lamp out and slept in an empty tub.

On the third night he came home to a letter in her unmistakeable hand. *Dowid is at the asylum. Rapholtz is there. You are there too. It's where you belong and that hasn't changed. Nor my heart. Don't get lost too.*

The day before the funeral, Greta came out of the shoppe.

She waited outside the door, watching him as he sold his wares. After a while, Rapholtz joined her. He carried a bundle, carefully wrapped and tied with twine.

"We miss you in our halls," Rapholtz said. "I hope you return to us soon. I shan't write any more papers alone."

"What's that?" Fleischl asked, and they teared up at the sound of his voice.

"They recovered some things," Rapholtz said. "From the ship. It belongs to you. The burghemeister said it's ivory. Carved. He called it pearly."

"Parlay," Fleischl said.

"Yes, that."

"It has your name on it," Greta said quietly. "It's not clear what it is. We suppose he had it carved for you."

Fleischl untied the twine and uncovered the bottom half. It fit easily in his palm, but was a heavy piece nonetheless. He pulled the wrapping all the way off.

"It's difficult to know," Rapholtz said apologetically. "Its shape. It doesn't resemble anything. I thought the human heart, but no, now that I see it."

"Fleischl?" Greta asked, because he was crying. "Fleischl, please say something to me."

"It's a puzzle piece."

It erupted from him. It came from everywhere. It followed him as he ran to the only place left for him in Stralsund.

He lingered in the shipyard, among the bones of the old vessels and within sight of the first transported pieces of the *Elegy*. At dusk he went to the dock and the bench and stared at the sea as it slowly lit with the first stars. At least one of the ships anchored out in Stralsund's sound was due to depart the following day. He didn't know which, or where in the world it might go, or for how long. He didn't know how close it might come, if at all, to the places on his father's map. He didn't know anything at all about what the ship might do, or what he might do.

From the bench he saw the sea tunnel and through it the easily lost candlelight. It was like the dimmest, furthest star. He saw the contours of Thalhammer and the cemetery. Over the time he sat, they lost their shape as the twilight deepened around them. His father's service would be conducted up there, near noon the following day. But he'd learned. His father wasn't there. He'd never be there. The sea had him. Maybe it spat him onto Apia land devoid of memory, or else, why the quiet? Why no word to anyone who could tell his son?

Maybe it didn't. Maybe the sea kept his father for itself. Either way, he knew in his heart that his father's last thoughts were—had to be—*why isn't my son with me.*

All he had were pieces. A bit of parlayed ivory. A map of all the places his father had hoped to reach. A drawing of the *Elegy's* insides. Everything else felt bigger than any one man could hold. Greta and all his love. Rapholtz, Thalhammer and a hoped-for future. The piazza and his father's every unfolding day. The days were meant to keep going. No one had told him otherwise.

"I don't know what to do now," he said. He waited for an answer. Everything was silent. Everything but the Baltic.

Candles don't make sounds, he thought. Not from this far away.

★★★

I fear that I may not be nearly enough to ably serve as your assistant and co-author. I am humbled that you thought me equal to the task. Perhaps one day I'll be of use.

He signed his name, folded the letter, and slid it into its envelope. He'd kept it brief. A succinct recitation of the ways frog legs flickered at various charges. A request that the proper apologies be made to A.B., should he ever write back. And the last bit. He didn't know what else to say.

His skin prickled in the cool night air. The bathwater lapped gently as he got out to dress. Retrieving a coat of his father's, he closed the door of the pension and left for the tunnel entrance to Thalhammer.

In a while, his hand was on Anton's shoulder, gently jostling him awake. Anton sat up on the couch. His eyes blinked away sleep. After placing the puzzle piece on the table, he held out his hands. Anton stood. He hesitated, then did the same.

He placed two envelopes into Anton's upturned palms and asked him to see them through.

"I'm afraid," he said.

★★★

At the noon hour, a small group gathered around Jurgen Berger's gravesite. A priest stood sentry, bible in hand. Rebbe Bernhard lingered nearby. Every few moments they smiled comfortingly at the gathered, cleared their throats and returned to their respective texts. Gert, Greta and her mother stood on one side of the headstone. They exchanged uneasy looks with Rapholtz. The burghemeister consulted his pocket watch.

"Did something happen to him?" the burghemeister asked.

"This is all very upsetting," Gert said. "He's alone in the world now."

Greta winced.

"Let's give him a few more minutes," Rapholtz suggested.

"Gotte," the burghemeister said. "What is that lunatic doing out? This really is unacceptable, Dr. Rapholtz."

Anton walked over the soft mounds to the assembly. He placed the first envelope in Rapholtz' hands. He gave the second envelope to Greta.

She opened it and found her letter to Fleischl with a line struck through what she'd written. Across the top, in Fleischl's hand, "I sell flax."

She cast her eyes across the cemetery grounds, and when they found the distant docks, she began to weep.

"There's a ship leaving," she said to the burghemeister. He turned to the docks. They all did.

★★★

By the time they arrived at the slip, the *Jura* was out at sea. Greta took the master roll from atop the burghemeister's soapbox, where the Jura's captain had left it. Her eyes were bleary with tears, and she couldn't read it. Gert took it from her and ran his finger down the list.

"I don't see…"

He fell silent. Greta's sobs rose into the air. In time, she breathed, wiped her eyes on the sleeve of her dress, and took the master roll back to find the very last name, next to a thumbprint.

J&S Ltd.

CHAPTER Seven

Kiel By the Baltic

For seventy days he crossed the sea atop five hundred tons
of iron and wood at five knots. He paced the deck of the *Jora* alongside his fellow passengers, some of whom bore the marks of good
breeding. They'd embarked from Hamburg and were intolerant of the
food, the salt air, the ribald ship's crew, and the small, stuffy nature of
their quarters. They were equally intolerant of men such as Fleischl,
who didn't wish for company and wished even less for small talk,
German or not.

When he wasn't alone at the ship's rail, monitoring the
ceaseless sea, Fleischl could be found in the dining hall among the
emigrant class. There were some twenty Teutons bound for Samoa
as he was. Most of them labored for one subdivision or another
of the same Goddefroy syndicate that owned the *Jora*. In the ship's
belly he made the acquaintance of tailors, masons, vinedressers,
a farming bailiff, a whitesmith, cutters, steelworkers, and all their
wives and children.

Among their number was a butcher named Albert who, like
him, traveled alone. Fleischl couldn't look him in the eye. The man's

hands bore a familiar landscape of callouses and old scars. He supposed Albert thought him rude or haughty, and not simply a quiet young man sick with regret for leaving behind those few who still cared for him, and sick with fear for what lay ahead.

He never became accustomed to the seasickness or the soul-crushing monotony that was life aboard a ship. Those states of mind, he found, were broken only by terror-filled nights contemplating a lonely death on the black bottom. One day, should Dowid's catatonia ever abate for even an instant, he would make a point of asking whether his father had been afraid like that.

Of course, that would mean his return to Stralsund and Thalhammer, and he wasn't able to think about that yet.

He started and stopped letters to Greta. *I'm sorry. I'm afraid. There's a chance I'll find him. There's a chance this is all for nothing. I should have gone with him. I should have stayed with you.*

Tell me you understand.

Not a single one did he ever finish and sign. By the day that the watch of the *Jora* spotted the first signs of land, the trash bin in his cramped cabin was at last empty of all the balled sheets of paper he'd generated to her. Every last one of his futile attempts to explain himself, declare love, or beg forgiveness were fed by a kindly coal heaver into the *Jora's* monstrous furnace.

"One day more," the heaver told him while he stoked the furnace fire with his ramblings, "and we're in the Bay."

That night Fleischl lay awake and tried to conjure all the sights and sounds of gale winds, thunder and pounding waves. But the ship was so still, and the sea so gentle. He couldn't hear anything, no matter how closely he listened. Nothing but footfalls on the deck high above, a quiet tidal murmuring through the walls, the occasional cry of someone down one of the countless corridors. Everyone lay with their thoughts of where they'd left and what waited, he supposed.

He took out his father's diagram of the *Elegy* and wandered its rooms down to the roundhouse. He'd traced the ship so many times on the voyage. It always ended where his father said he read to scared boys. He curled up with the drawing and waited for the light to lift. This is what I am, he thought. A son looking for his missing father. And if he's not missing, if he's simply dead as all fathers one day are, then I'm no longer anyone's son. I don't know what I am.

At dawn they came to the islands of Savalis and Tutuila, and made for Upolu. As they entered the crescent harbor all the bells aboard the *Jora* sounded at once, in tribute to the fallen. The crew paused their labors and came to the ship's rails bearing garlands of dry flowers, coins, flasks of rum, and stone-weighted letters. The other passengers who'd risen that early wandered the deck, watching the ceremony without comprehension.

He'd been on deck half the night in a ceremony of his own making, watching the wide net of stars fade into the morning light.

As native lighters, slim and brown as cigars, floated toward them from shore, the *Jora's* captain explained to the passengers that all Apia-bound vessels sounded their bells and cast keepsakes into the bay, down to those who'd been lost in the storm. He spoke of how lucky all of them were not to have been there when the *Elegy*, the *Nipsic*, the *Eber* and the *Vandalia* met the violence of the typhoon.

The *Jora* crew dropped their offerings. The Samoans lit torches in the bay, then dipped them into the water to snuff them out. Other passengers asked how many in all had gone down. Everyone looked over the rails at the surface of the sea, while the captain told them estimating all the loss was hard to do. Nothing exact about such business, he said.

"Imagine being there," one of the passengers remarked.

Imagine not being there, Fleischl thought.

Some of the crew gathered together after leaving their gifts to the deep. They prayed in clusters. Passengers came to the outer edges of them and bowed their heads. Fleischl listened but didn't hear the *Kaddish.* There wasn't anyone else like him on board. At least no one that would say.

The lighters were there to ferry ashore those who'd come for work or visits with emigrant relatives, or crewmen in need of refreshment and distraction. He waited at the rail for his turn. He had a bag, some money, his father's papers, and nothing to give to the bay.

When his turn came, he climbed into a thin canoe. The water turned them toward the far beach. There was no tonnage beneath him now. The sea, gentle beneath an iridescently blue sky, felt almost magnetic against the wooden lighter. The waves curled up to the wood like obedient pups looking for sleep, and the lighter pushed back as it cut a course to the beachhead. On shore the sea came and the land sent it away. The sea never stopped, and he wondered how a man who read to boys could do anything but be taken. It was all so impossible and for nothing. His carriage along the surface of the same sea was as futile and stupid a gesture as any man had ever made.

He saw huts of thatch and corrugated iron as they neared shore. The sad little shacks were dispersed every hundred yards or so, along a line of lush screwpine and snakewood. Here and there he spotted shutters and eaves and took them for signs that Europeans or Americans lived in them. Men who didn't want to live where they were from anymore, or who'd forgotten altogether.

He made a plan to knock on those doors first.

Disembarking into the gently lapping shallows, he walked onto the sand at the end of a long line of men he didn't recognize from the voyage, along with a small group of women and children. Where they'd been during the voyage, he couldn't say. The *Jora* was never so evidently a city unto itself than when viewed from the land. It only stood to reason that its hull contained multitudes. He might have heard some of them walking the corridors or their voices carrying through the walls. The closer they'd sailed to Apia, the odder it was, the notion of voices just floating away like that. It was one of many trivial things that he found himself fearing as they neared the end of the voyage.

You may be here, he thought as he glanced around the beach at the shacks. How like little iron-roofed chapels they were. Or you may be there, and he turned to the sea.

Between the shacks were small shrines made from local wood, lacquered with varnish and covered with sheets of glass that had gone cloudy from sea salt. The largest one was as tall as he. According to its legend, it had been a gift of the American consulate. It bore names in two columns beneath the name of the ship they'd served on and went down with. The *Vandalia*. Above that was the date of the storm.

He read the men's names until one bayman blurred into the next yeoman or afterguard. Some were marked *deceased*. Others simply *lost*.

He walked among the shrines while the others went off to their destinations. There were memorials of various sizes, including ones for the native Samoans who'd died trying to help.

He found the one erected in memory of lost Germans. Near the bottom was his father.

Berger, Jurgen - lost

"Is there someone you know?"

The man next to him was Samoan. He spoke passable German. "Also English, French and a little Mandarin." He was kind enough to let Fleischl cry a while.

"Lost means no one knows," the man said. "But what else could it be? Bodies washed ashore like they do from time to time, and we try to return to them their names, but most are strangers when we scatter ashes. Some we gave to them," he said, pointing to the German consulate seal at the top of the shrine. "If we knew they were German."

"Have you seen any survivors on the island?" Fleischl asked. "Maybe a man who doesn't remember things?"

"No one like that."

"Where can I go to find out if he was buried, or scattered?"

Saying the words felt like the first moments he'd spent beneath the surface of the old tin tub, waiting for his poppa's blurry figure to come touch his finger.

"Hamburg house of Josef," the man said, as if it was an

incantation of some kind. Seeing the confusion on Fleischl's face, the man offered to take him where he needed to go.

Fleischl thanked him. He wanted to pay, though he didn't know in what. He didn't know much of anything, it seemed. He was a dull, unimaginative boy, after all.

"Where did you scatter the ashes?" he asked as they turned toward the tree line and began to walk.

"In the bay."

Fleischl followed the man through the stand of trees to the village's lone road. It began at a store in the village's west end that was owned by a rich German trader named Greusmuhl. From there it wound dizzyingly eastward all the way to the consulate, where his Samoan friend told him he would make the acquaintance of Theodore Weber, Imperial Consul, and H.G. Unshelm, representative of the Hamburg house of Joseph Cesar Goddefroy. Along their walk, the Samoan pointed out the name and purpose of each odd amalgam of wood and the omnipresent corrugated iron. There was a courthouse, the Hotel ZurStadt, a pharmacy, a doctor's home, a seamen's church, and a bakehouse. There were trading posts for coconut, cocoa, and coffee. There were grand homes for the wealthy outsiders, homes with verandas, balusters and venetian blinds.

As he wound down along the street, he felt a growing dread at the whole venture. Nothing he might find would satisfy. A dead father, a missing father, or a demented father. What did any of it matter? What would any of it tell him about what to do next? He'd run away like the boy he always suspected he was. Now he was too far gone to simply go back, no matter what he discovered.

He grew increasingly quiet. By the time they reached the German consulate, his Samoan friend seemed ready to leave him.

He sat down gratefully in a high-backed rattan chair on the consulate veranda. From there he waved goodbye to his newfound friend, who he didn't expect to see again. The consulate staff brought him a cool drink, and in an hour he was sitting in another rattan chair, in a spacious office, listening to the Imperial Consul's practiced recitation of condolences and statistics on the composition of the island's foreign population ("twenty seven Germans in all," the Consul said, "and I'm acquainted with each and every one of them") and assuring Fleischl that, had there been even a hint of a wandering, wayward Stralsundian among them, he would certainly know about it.

"And so, the bay," Fleischl said.

"I'm afraid so, young man. Is there anything I can do?"

"You've been gracious to see me. May I trouble you for some paper and a pen?"

"Of course."

"There's a post office of some kind here? I believe a missionary brought letters to and from the *Elegy*."

He received directions. It was a short walk to the post office. At the front desk, he finally completed a letter to Greta.

You were right. He's not here. Are you?

He handed it over to the postmaster, a stocky, hirsute Bavarian, and asked if somewhere on the shelves there might be a letter that came from the *Elegy* but was never delivered.

"No," the postmaster said after checking. "But perhaps the other way."

He left the front desk again and returned with the letter that Fleischl had sent to his father. "The ship was gone by the time this arrived," the postmaster told him.

"I'll take it to him," Fleischl said.

He found a small room for the night at the ZurStadt. In bed, he listened to the far murmur of the bay, that came to him through the screwpine like a heartbeat. In the morning, already coated with a sheen of oily sweat, he dressed and returned to where he'd begun. The rail of the Jora.

Atop the polished wood he lay his father's map, the *Elegy* diagram, and his own letter. Next to him, the first mate checked passenger names and welcomed them aboard. Those few times he bothered to look away from the water, Fleischl didn't recognize anyone. New faces, leaving for somewhere else.

Soon all were on board and the crew raised anchor. The first mate and the captain stood down a ways from him with papers of their own, and sextants out. Something about degrees from the equator and the path to circumvent storms. It was near the time of year again.

The first mate wandered over after the captain left. He watched Fleischl select one of the papers, struck a match and set it alight. When the flame consumed all but a corner of his letter to his father, he let go. The letter caught in the wind, crumpled mid-air and flew in separate directions, down to the waves with a last little light before extinguishing.

"Where are you headed?" the mate asked. "Home again?"

Fleischl shuffled the remaining pages. *Elegy* below, map on top.

"Where this takes me," he said.

★★★

28 October 1897
Kiel

 DON'T WRITE ANYMORE STOP GRETA NO LONGER IN STRALSUND IS FAR AWAY FROM US BECAUSE OF YOU STOP EVERYONE LOSES LOVE STOP YOUR'E NO EXCEPTION STOP YOU LOST YOUR FATHER TO THE SEA AND HER TO YOUR SELFISHNESS STOP LEAVE US IN PEACE STOP GERT STOP

Fleischl tore the telegram to pieces and climbed back onto his flax cart. It was new, with shining brass screwheads and a polished beech bench. The horse was new as well. He'd bartered for both in Prague in exchange for oil and three coils of rope. The rope brought Dowid to mind, and with him his father, and then Greta and balsa wings and the terrible, malignant regret that first descended on him in Stralsund's bay and held him across ten thousand miles at ten knots, into a northern wind to Apia and beyond.

He'd lost count of the number of letters he'd sent to Stralsund in hopes they would reach her, only to be met with silence each time. Until Gert's reply. She was gone to her future. Her family hated him. Finding his way back was unthinkable. The past was no longer where he'd left it.

From Alexandria he made his way by train to Marrakesh, then on to Cairo, following his father's map of army encampments. He reached the places his father never saw, and at each stop he felt his father watching from the rail of every ship.

In Paris he sold flax at an open market near the Tuileries and took an evening to attend a play at the Theatre de l'Odeon. A farce of missed connections and outlandish misunderstandings. He only laughed later, in the barn of a new flax client far outside the city lights, as he thought of how she would have done each voice. Waiting for sleep to take him, he wondered if she slept under the same dome of stars, or whether she'd gone so far that it was a different day where she was. With luck, she was on a stage somewhere, creating angels and devils, drunken louts and, perhaps, cowardly boys who left broken girls in their wakes. Their wakes would be water.

In Villefranche, at a cafe by the shore, he puzzled the waiters and a small coterie of French soldiers on holiday with his requests. "A litre of wine, s'il vous plait, a small green salad, and a bone from the kitchen." From those he made his seder plate and as the soldiers watched, he dragged over a chair from a nearby table and bade all the missing to come find him.

The winter season brought him at last to Handwehrzebirk and the 37th Regiment Base at Kiel, on the shores of the Baltic. Poppa's last stop, where the land and water met in a way that seemed familiar. The sentry at the gate directed him to stay on the prominent path until he arrived at the canteen. He passed between two barracks to an open field littered with dozens of structures lined up next to one another like bread loaves set out to cool. Peering through the window of one, he saw wires dangling from the ceiling in low and unsafe coils. They almost touched the tops of the metal bunks. The walls were gray and bare of ornamentation. So much did it remind him of Thalhammer that he goaded his horse to pick up its weary pace.

Columns of men filed past the barracks and out onto the wide, muddy field. They set to grappling until they were filthy as pigs. They fought for handholds, the better to throw each other over their shoulders. The canteen building stood at the far side of the field, against a looming bluff hollowed out by the Baltic. At the foot of a two-hundred meter tower of rock, at the edge of the dark, churning water, men could purchase cigarettes and candy, get their mail and stand at the shoreline and dream of ships coming to carry them home. Behind them, make-believe battles raged that one day might turn bloody and real. Above them, a dense forest bearded the edge of the cliff. Moss blanketed the stone wall, all the way down to the boulder-strewn beach.

He stood in the canteen doorway, studying the cliffs and the sea and imagined her by the same sea, just a different end of it. A theatrical clearing of a throat broke his reverie. A young soldier stood by his cart, petting his horse and watching the field. "Upside down," the soldier said.

"Beg pardon?"

"Those fighting drills. They lift you up and quite abruptly turn you upside down. Then they throw you to the mud. It's most unpleasant."

"It looks unpleasant."

"I'll be there before long." The young man was bespectacled, blonde and pale. His face was partially obscured by the oddly large cap he wore. He clung to Fleischl's horse as if it could save him.

"You haven't done those yet?" Fleischl asked.

"Not yet. It must be a ghastly feeling, being tossed around like that. You can't stop it."

"I suppose they're teaching you fellows how to stop it."

Logic seemed called for. "So the enemy can't do it to you unless you allowed him to. Which, why would you, I suppose."

"You may be right. Maybe you can try it while you're here."

"Oh no. Not after hearing you describe it. I don't think I'm capable."

"I'm Pieter."

"Fleischl Berger."

"Yes. The flax salesman. I've been directed to bring you to your appointments so you don't wander about camp. Secret things around here, you see."

"I can imagine."

For the next two hours, Fleischl followed Pieter to a succession of officers in the medical unit, requisitions, the mess and canteen. By the waning of the afternoon light, he was out of everything flax.

"I'm told you have extra things," Pieter said. "For the officers."

"I do. And some things for soldiers such as yourself. But only a few."

"That's good. Because there's only a few fellows I like."

Pieter brought him first to the officers' quarters, where Fleischl proceeded to distribute cognac and cigars he'd bartered for aboard the *Jura*. After, Pieter brought him to the mess hall and introduced him to his friends.

"This is Fleischl Berger," Pieter said, handing over a tin of hackfleisch auf toastbrot. "He has something for us. Just us."

After dinner, such as it was, Fleischl waited at their barracks until the last calisthenics were done, the flag lowered and folded, and the order given for lights-out. Bribing the officers proved worthwhile; he received permission to stay a while.

One of the soldiers was a gentle brute named Anders. Anders lit a series of oil lamps set low, "so as not to draw looky-loos. Lots of busybodies in camp. Now, let's have it!"

Smiling at the oversize child before him, Fleischl handed out several *cartes des visite* of nude and semi-nude women. Passing a flask of schnapps, the men ogled and giggled.

"I've seen hairier," Anders said sagely.

"But enough about your mother," said Josef, a thin, adenoidal youth.

The schnapps worked its way through each of them. Fleischl felt woozy and warm. The banter was oddly comforting. He hadn't grown up around others his age—except Greta. It occurred to him that he had no friends at all.

He glanced out the barracks window. The cottony treetops high above, on the plateau, could only be seen by the dent they made in the vastation of stars.

"You should stay," Pieter told him. "It's late."

"I am a bit weary," he said. "I'll stay as long as no one minds. Am I even allowed?"

"You brought them contraband. I can't imagine they'd send you away. You'll be glad you stayed. Not just for my company, I assure you. It's going to be quite dramatic. A demonstration of power tomorrow, indeed!"

He listened to Pieter laugh softly, and he thought about the things he ought to do. He ought to tend to his horse, who remained unwatched and hungry in a stall. He ought to at least ask permission of someone besides a lonely soldier, rather than simply materialize the following morning. He ought to get up and find a latrine. Instead, he lay down on a bunk. It felt like being at sea again. The room spun lazily and seemed to generate a steady hum between his temples. He thought of Greta and his father. It was strange, and not completely unwelcome, to listen to the breeze rise outside the walls of the barracks and be reminded of the wind's thistling passage between the stones of Stralsund's graveyard.

It wasn't precisely sleep that found him. More a feverish sort of semi-consciousness during which Greta appeared at his side and spoke to him in an uncanny rendition of his father. She told him he was prawny. When she leaned over to kiss him, her lips were black with master roll ink.

★★★

The soldiers woke before dawn and assembled in formation at the shoreline. True to Pieter's prediction, Fleischl was allowed to stay. No one asked him to leave, anyway. The requisitions officer did impress upon him the need for utmost secrecy.

The movement of men was fascinating to behold. A large contingent he estimated at six or seven barracks' worth spread out across the sandy shoreline, interspersing themselves among the boulders near the Baltic. The men were on horseback and in trenches facing the bluff wall. Several units lined the edge of the cliff above. They looked out onto the sea like sentries of old.

An officer provided him with a horse and told him to situate himself at the water's edge, near a cove below the cliff. It was the perfect vantage point from which to see the men threading through the trees to the very edge of the bluff. A thin line of train track cut into the bluff's ascent at alternating angles. The engineering of such a thing was stunning to consider.

His horse remained indifferent as the shallow Baltic lapped against his legs, swirling about his ankles. The sun climbed past the vanishing point of the sea to lay a golden ribbon across the water.

Pieter trotted over, looking ill atop his own horse as it bounced along. "See it out there?"

Fleischl squinted. Past the glare, he made out the contours of a ship. "I see it."

"That's the target. It's been towed here for today. Just an old husk brought here from some backwater."

"Target?"

"Keep your eye on the cliff. You'll see soon enough."

The chilly air would give over to rain. He wanted to be well on his way by then. He wanted to keep to his schedule, which already was off by a day, thanks to a night's drinking. He wanted to put the sea behind him again.

Out on the water, the ship came to a halt.

"Where did the ship come from," he asked again. A sudden

cacophony rose from the tree line high above, nearly drowning out his question. But Pieter heard him.

"Shipyard," Pieter shouted. "No one aboard so it doesn't matter."

"What shipyard?" shouted Fleischl.

But Pieter had turned to stare at a train as it rolled to a slow stop high above, having wound its way from somewhere in camp to get all the way up there. Then a great tilting crane, a magnificent bird of metal and wire, appeared alongside the train car and bobbed down. After a short time, it hauled a massive, black cylinder up into the air.

"Cannon," Pieter shouted at him. "It's going to shoot at the ship."

"What shipyard?" Fleischl screamed.

The cannon hung from the crane's tether like a spider dangling from its silk. It descended delicately onto a frame. The air rang with the voices of men and the crackling of wood under strain. Sunlight glinted from the cannon's black metallic skin as a team of soldiers swung the weapon to point at the sea.

Anders brought over a spyglass. He handed it to Fleischl first and gestured to the bluff, where soldiers stuffed the barrel full of flax, then breech-loaded a ball as big as a man, itself as black as the cannon.

He trained the spyglass on the sea. Anders shouted at him to look at the bluff so he wouldn't miss anything. He made a great flapping fuss of his arms to conjure explosions and fire, but Fleischl was still focused on the approaching ship. It was old and hulking, a beast of another age. It belched a puff of coal smoke, just enough to cause it to turn so its starboard side faced the shore.

"Sand," Pieter shouted. "It's about to fire."

"What did you say?"

"Stral-SAND," then the world split apart.

An unholy sound opened from nothing. Fleischl kept the glass on the ship, waiting for it to blossom wood and boilers in a fiery flower. Everything around him descended into mayhem. Men were screaming. Pieter was in his ear, "it's coming down!" loud enough to deafen him but he screamed back, "it's still there!"

Behind him, men's shouts were no longer words. Rocks and soldiers cascaded over the collapsing lip of the bluff, hurtling down to splatter like rain against the hard ground.

He dropped the glass and clawed for the reins to control his terrified horse. The cannon plummeted down from the failing cliff. Something—the firing of it, the weight of it—had burst its frame and the cliff with it. The first storm of rocks and boulders hammered down onto the men closest to the cliff wall, driving them into the shoreline before splintering and flying into the water, mowing down the men in their path. The cannon followed, end over end.

Fleischl yanked the reins to bring his horse around, but the animal reared up, shrieking and wide-eyed. Its legs gave out and it fell on its side. Fleischl spilled onto the ground as sky and sea traded places. He saw a bird soaring belly-up, and then his head caromed off the rocks, sending a shower of sparks across his eyes. Distantly, men cried his name. They told him to get out, but his leg felt shattered.

Twisting where he lay, he spotted the cannon. It was as long and as thick as five telegraph poles strapped together. It rolled at him, picking up speed as it careened down the slope of stones to the Baltic, closing in, pounding the earth beneath it as it went.

He tried to scramble away, but his leg was pinned beneath the horse. The deep chill of the sea washed over him. There was another sound rising in his ears, loud enough to drown everything else. A pounding like a drum.

A razored grief swelled within him as the cannon tumbled closer. He wasn't sure if he was screaming or if the swelling, deafening sound came from something else. It didn't begin or end. It had no shape and didn't belong to any moment. It drowned out everything, even the loud crack of metal on stone, the shocked, abortive whinny of his horse, and the water.

He lay down and let the Baltic have him. The blackness fanned open to engulf him. He reached, but the water got through and carried him off.

★★★

"He shat himself."

"You would too. Look how close. Cannon passed right over him."

"Horse meat for dinner, I'll say that. Wonder where its head is."

"Flattened by the cannon, looks like."

He felt as if he were struggling to swim, grasping for purchase in a sickening darkness. Was he on land, or had he been carried out to sea? At last, he felt some rock, something sticky and wet. It could be the shore. He thought that someone might have dragged him to where he was.

He got hold of a jagged hunk of metal, which scalded him. Then the blackness and the screaming began to abate, and for that he was grateful. He let himself sink, as if to the bottom of a tub, where he could hold his breath in peace.

★★★

Through a cottony sheet, he touched a thick bandage and a splint. He recognized it as his own flax product, from the way the weave felt against his fingertips. Pain radiated from his knee into his hip and lower back. His head throbbed mercilessly.

"You're an unholy sight," Anders said.

Shifting, he heard the low squeal of metal against the wall. He felt the spongy sinking of a mattress beneath him, and under that the stab of a stray spring coil. He was in a bunk. From the murmur he could hear outside, he sensed he was beneath a window,—or close to one, at least. The one he'd been in the night before?.

I should open my eyes, he thought. The light will surely hurt, but I should try.

Outside, the voices of men grunted in unison. The turning of wheels. The cries of horses echoing from stables.

"Do you remember anything?" Pieter asked. "You've been here almost three days now."

"What happened," he said.

"Some say it wasn't loaded right," Pieter said.

"That's not it," Anders said. "From what I saw, all that was supposed to be connected, was. But you know how it is. Connections can break."

"It fired but not at anything," Pieter said. "Just the sea. Then it crashed down through the frame and, well, everything else."

"It was tumbling right at you," Anders added. "A miracle, nothing less. It hit a rock or something."

"Or his horse," Josef added.

"It just turned somehow. A matter of inches."

"Feet, really," Anders said.

"Whatever the case, it was on you, Fleischl. And yet here you are. Don't be afraid."

"Or sad," Pieter said. "It does no good. The doctor's been here, and he'll be back again soon. Have hope."

"Hope of what?" Fleischl asked.

"Others weren't as fortunate as you." Anders lay one of his massive hands on Fleischl's shoulder. "Fourteen dead. Some fell. Most fell, I suppose. One stood right up against the frame when it fired. Nothing left of him."

"Some were crushed," Pieter said, "like you almost were. Flat as a Jew's skullcap."

"I saw it," Fleischl said. "All of it." He began to cry. He couldn't help himself. "I couldn't do anything."

He went to wipe his eyes and found them open. He held his hands out in front of his face. "I can't see. My eyes."

"Go get the doctor," Anders said, and someone got up and ran. One of those who remained took his hand and squeezed it.

"I'm right here."

It could have been Pieter. Maybe Anders. He didn't know who spoke to him. He didn't know what it looked like out the window he thought he might be under. It was hard just then to picture the delicate lines his father had sketched to create the *Elegy's* roundhouse. No one had told him to memorize all that you've ever seen. It can disappear from behind you as you go.

When the doctor came, he wept. All my useless eyes are good for, he thought.

The doctor had a voice like rebbe Bernhard. Quiet and a little high, though not as kind. For all he knew, the doctor was just another boy putting his time in, staring at the sea and calling for home.

"Please help me," he said.

"What's your name?"

"I can't see."

"I know. Your name?"

"Fleischl Berger."

"You're able to answer, so you're better than you were yesterday."

"I don't remember yesterday."

He heard the scratch of pen across paper. He'd never noticed how like a loom that sound was, the way the comb bound thread to thread.

"Are you a soldier?"

"No," Fleischl said.

"Did this happen in battle?"

"Did what happen? Did something blind me? Nothing hurts in my eyes. Why is this happening?"

"No one here's been in battle." Anders' voice was gruffer than the others.

"Yes, I know all that. I'm merely recording his responses to set a baseline. Can you tell me where you are, herr Berger?"

"Kiel," Fleischl said. "A bunk. I don't know."

He heard someone strike a match, and the hiss and spark of the flame. In a moment, heat rose near his cheek, then up to his eyes. But he saw nothing. A terrible fear wrapped itself around him. He would never see again. He was lost in a great black storm. He would be piti-able. He would live at Thalhammer as one of those men.

He heard more writing. It went on longer this time.

"Someone read me what he wrote," Fleischl said, and someone with a voice that wasn't gruff did.

29 October 1897
Kiel
Regiment count: indeterminate
Survivors: indeterminate
Wounded: indeterminate
Account: unknown ordinance discharge and/or weapons failure near regiment location. Disproportionate impact on one non-unit survivor and/or guest. Regiment leader brought affected to infirmary, transfer to quarters on medical discharge. Degenerative condition and suspected malingering. Semiotic method. No ocular response.

"What does that mean?" Anders asked.

"It means," Fleischl said, "that my eyes are fine. It's my mind that broke."

The doctor offered him something to help him sleep. Anders objected to the notion of bearing Fleischl off with a drug. Better to talk to good men, Anders said.

"I don't want to dream." Fleischl took what drug the doctor offered and drifted off in tears. Through a gathering breeze, he heard the doctor say that he'd return. When Anders promised him food, some schnapps and jokes that would make a barman blush, the words found him beneath a film of gauze. The last words he heard barely got through at all. "What about the other," they said, "the telegram?"

★★★

He awoke to the sound of a murmured conversation, someone nearby rummaging for something close, and the rustling of paper. "He's awake," someone said. "We should read this to him. It's been long enough."

"Give him a moment," said Anders, "for the love of God." His burly voice was familiar to Fleischl now, and as comforting as an aged caftan.

He heard the gathering of chairs. Then the men were around him, speaking in chipper, forced voices. They swapped stories of old loves and of their early naïveté at Kiel. They called out which of them wept most often for home (Pieter), which masturbated excessively (Anders, by his own proclamation), which passed stools that stank worse than rotting vegetation (their commanding officer). Then they grew quiet, and Fleischl understood that he was meant to fill that space with something sunny. Something humorous and weightless, so they would all know he was fine. He was well and content, and not terrified at being sightless, or hearing the falling men in his every thought since that day. October 29th, 1897. Burned in him for all time.

Someone else stepped in to fill the silence for him when he wouldn't. "Fleischl." It was, as far as he could tell, Josef. Quiet until now. "Something came for you the day of the incident."

"A telegram," Anders said.

"For me? From who?"

"It's not from anyone," Josef said. "Fleischl, I think it's cruel and a poor attempt at a prank. If it was my choice I'd throw it away so you never see it. I'm sorry. That's not what I meant to say."

"But it's not your choice," Anders said.

"I don't understand," Fleischl said.

"By its mark," Josef told him, "it was sent at the time every-thing happened. Which is impossible."

"What does it say? Read it to me."

The barrack door opened. By the phlegmatic, insistent throat-clearing, the good doctor had returned. Another chair pulled up. A box of matches opened. Alongside it, the opening of an envelope, the unfolding of paper.

"How are we feeling?" the doctor asked.

"Read it," Fleischl said. He reached in the direction he thought he might find the telegram. He held out his hands for it. What I must look like, he thought. Hands holding nothing. If you could only see me now, Anton.

The match struck and heat came to his eyes as his fingers brushed stiff paper.

"Are you sure?" one of them asked him.

Somewhere down a long dark tunnel there was the smallest, the frailest, and easily lost of lights.

"I see something," he said, and took hold of the telegram. "I see a little light, like a candle."

The frantic scrawling. Hands fell upon him and it seemed that a tear did, too; perhaps it was his own. His new friends told him how happy they were. The doctor called it a promising sign. Soon, with a little luck, there might be more to see.

"Anders."

"I'm here."

"Read it, won't you."

"It says 'Fleischl, did you die.'"

The men grew quiet. Fleischl folded the telegram along its creases. It had been opened and closed a number of times.

"And it doesn't say who sent it," he said.

"Small wonder they wouldn't want to be known," Anders said.

"Maybe," Josef said, "word of the accident has gone round since. But this came the very day. Maybe an hour after at the most. I don't see how it's possible."

"A poor excuse for a joke, I'd say," said the doctor.

Fleischl clutched the telegram as a sensation gathered in his eyes. It made him think of the first time he'd opened them beneath the water in the bathtub. It carried the little light with it, and he wondered if it was just a remnant. Then the doctor's match came clearer, and with it a blurred hand.

"Is the telegraph office far?" he asked.

★★★

He hobbled into the telegraph office in Kiel leaning heavily against Anders. At the counter, he presented the operator with the telegram and asked where it had originated from.

The operator stood in front of a large board with numbered needles corresponding to letters. He examined the paper through bottle-like lenses that seemed to make pools of his eyes. "Berlin," he said. "Odd message to send. Thought so as I took it down."

"I want to send one back to the same office," Fleischl said.

The operator took out a pen and some paper. "Message?"

"Who is this? Why did you say that?"

The operator turned to the contraption and began pecking out letters.

"How long until we get a reply?" Anders asked.

"Depends on whether the sending party is still where they were. Whether they can be located by the messenger. They didn't sign, but the Berlin office ought to have a record. Whether they even want to answer you, I'll just say, is an open question too. This odd message, you see. If a reply comes, where shall I find you?"

"I'll be by here daily," Fleischl said. "More than once, I imagine."

They followed the operator's recommendation of a good tavern and slept atop the cart to save money. They smoked, drank and spoke a little. Anders alluded to his life before the army. Fleischl, who hadn't asked in the first place, didn't pry.

On their third dawn in Kiel, the operator found them at the tavern. He gave Fleischl an envelope and said, "I believe this answers your question."

"He's blind, you idiot." Anders took the telegram and read it to Fleischl.

DO NO WRITE AGAIN STOP I WONT BE FOUND SO DO NOT TRY STOP YOU ARE ALIVE I DO NOT NEED TO HEAR ANYTHING ELSE STOP GRETA STOP

"Do you know this person?" Anders asked.

"I'm grateful for all you've done. You're my first friend in a long time. Go back so you don't get in trouble."

He turned to the window and looked out upon the light gathering across the sky. It was purple and pink, with a hint of burnt orange, and buried in it like submerged wrecks were odd shapes form-ing. Through the ironwork of the window frame he saw the last of the rain puddles on the street. The mountains in the distance and the sea below were bathed in a brilliant band of sunlight. Against it all, the cliffs looked so small. They'd been scalloped away. There was no longer a lip or a forest at the edge, only a jagged crescent that resembled the bottom half of a jawbone.

He supposed the shoreline looked equally brutalized. Strewn with rock, broken tree limbs, the remaining bloodstains of the dead that hadn't yet washed back into the Baltic.

"Fleischl," Anders said, astonished. "Can you see?"

"I can. Still a bit hazy, but yes."

"My friend, I'll tell the others. Where will you go now?"

"Home," he said.

★★★

He clambered down from his cart and surveyed the piazza. It was past the noon hour. The chimes of the cathedral rang into the tunnel, out to the marketplace, and back again to the wide space of the docks.

He'd felt the need to see the coast before anything else. He thought of Anders, who'd promised to visit one day but probably wouldn't. The last thing he'd said was, "This Greta wasn't at the base. She was somewhere in Berlin. Yet she said, on the very day of the calamity, that she knew something had happened to you. Such a thing isn't possible, which makes her cruel or a liar in a way I don't under-stand. I hope one day, you do."

He passed his old pension. It could be let by now, he thought. Not that he wanted to return to it.

Where is home now, he wondered, as the searing pain in his leg reached down to his toes. At least his sight had returned. Nothing else in his life felt the same.

He began walking to the shipyard end of the docks and the hill beyond, where the sun's shafts bent through the trees that ringed the cemetery. As he got close, he saw Anton in Thalhammer's library window. Then he rounded a curve in the trail and entered the overgrown mouth of the tunnel.

He didn't have to rap on the library door of the asylum. Anton was there, waiting for him.

They went to the window. It was quiet and he felt as warm as a bath. The dock was empty. No ships this day, he thought.

"Look who it is!" Rapholtz exclaimed as he entered. "You've come back to us! Are you well? Are you back to stay?"

Anton held out his arms, palms up. He smiled.

Fleischl closed his eyes. He saw paper wings, a sunset along the road back to Stralsund, the falling bodies of men. The cannon falling end over end. Greta on the couch the night he felt her skin against his. The scream that came from somewhere and passed from him and passed onward, like a ship leaving port. Like a voice along the wires. Nothing fit, and he'd always been so good at puzzles.

"Fleischl, you're crying," Rapholtz said. "You're safe, my boy."

He was crying. He only heard it, just then.

"Something happened to me," he said.

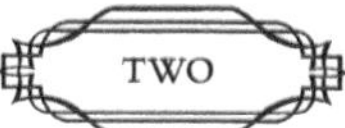

CHAPTER Eight
One Thousand Seven Hundred and Two

"There's ample precedent," Rapholtz said, "for what happened to you."

Every surface in the library was covered. The desk, the table where the batteries and their tangle of wires rested, even Anton's couch, featured a collision of strewn journals, manuals, periodicals, and papers both published and unpublished. They addressed all the conceived maladies of the mind that Fleischl had been keeping company with in the days following his return. Dysphagia, dysphonia, psychogenic non-epileptic seizures, dystonia, astasia, and his own personal affliction: hysterical blindness.

"Mental maladies in physical form," was how Rapholtz described them. "Stemming from traumas of the emotions or of the brain. Blindness, permanent change in eye color, deafness, muteness, even a malformation of limbs that were perfectly healthy until something awful takes place that the mind can't digest. There's a growing interest in it, though I find it prurient and deeply troubling, to be honest. There are even studies on how to provoke such trauma just to study its effects. Extremis, they call it. I call it repugnant. But to you. You, my boy, suffered something no man should go through. Consider yourself fortunate. You have your sight back and you're not dead. Leave it at that."

"You know me better than that, Laszlo." He leaned back in his chair and rubbed his eyes until clouds of colors burst in the room. His back was stiff and his leg ached, though appreciably less than it did during the first days after Kiel. On his journey home, every bump in the road took him straight back to the shoreline as it cracked open beneath him. At night he still heard the terrible screaming. He spent most nights wide awake and fearful that it would happen again. He would trust in the world's permanence and close his eyes, and it would find him again. A roar that seemed to come from everywhere and nowhere. A great blackness that would descend on him, and this time he wouldn't reach the surface. A man could only cheat death so many times.

"It was simply too much for your mind to hold," Rapholtz said. "So your mind tipped over. When your mind calmed, your vision returned. The chances of it ever happening again are slim, according to what we've read. You won't suffer such extreme horror twice in a lifetime. The odds of that are certainly in your favor."

Rapholtz lay down his omnipresent pen. He looked exhausted, and Fleischl flushed with guilt. Busy as he was with his patients, the man unfailingly spent time talking, calming, studying, and reassuring his young charge. For that, Fleischl was grateful, even as the question he truly wanted to ask hung unspoken in the air of the library.

He smiled at Rapholtz' haphazard scrawling across the top of the notepad. It was what Rapholtz wrote before seeing any new resident at Thalhammer and before commencing any new paper. Once, Fleischl thought the note was a kind of prayer, though not one any bible would contain. Now, in the light of what happened, Fleischl thought it less a prayer and more a map.

Make observation. Form hypothesis. Make prediction of outcome. Create and conduct experiment. Analyze results.

"Laszlo," he said. "About the other."

"It won't do you any good, my boy."

Fleischl removed the carefully folded telegram from his pocket. The things he carried with him, that he supposed he'd always carry, had grown by one. He moved the *Elegy* drawing and his father's list of places to the side. Between the old battery and stacks of periodicals, he unfolded Greta's message.

Rapholtz leaned forward and read it yet again, as he had on Fleischl's first night back. Then, Fleischl wasn't in any condition to talk about it and Rapholtz too stunned and sick with worry to find words for it. It had been days. Everything was quieter now.

"A strange, unexplainable occurrence," Rapholtz said. "The world is full of them. Just the other day I was grumbling over the gloomy weather when suddenly the clouds parted and the sun shone through." He smiled. "I'm not making light of it. I know how it must have felt, getting this after what happened, and from her, of all people. But Fleischl, it's a coincidence. A terrible one, but nothing more."

His mentor's smile held. That's how mothers and fathers are supposed to smile at their children, Fleischl thought, when they want to distract them from something terrible.

"I suppose," he said.

"It troubles you."

"It does. I can't stop thinking about it."

"Is that because you can't explain it," Rapholtz said, "or because it's her?"

"Because what happened is impossible."

"I presumed we'd talk about this sooner or later. I have some notes."

"You always have some notes."

"I'm a creature of habit above all else."

Rapholtz looked over his pad. "Let's start with elimination.

Is there any possibility that news of the accident reached her somehow?"

Fleischl turned the telegram to face Rapholtz. "Dated the very same day. Sent about an hour after, from Berlin. That's incontrovertible. The men at Kiel, the doctor, they all assured me it wasn't possible that word of the accident went across the country. It barely went out across the camp in that brief a time. An hour after it happened, they were still pulling bodies from the rubble. I wasn't even in a bunk yet. I was still on the beach where they'd dragged me from the water. No, my friend. It's not possible that Greta could have heard about what happened. And yet she sent this. That's incontrovertible too."

"It's interesting, you know."

"What is?"

"You keep referring to it as something she heard or couldn't hear about. Hearing. At the heart of this impossible thing, she didn't somehow see what happened. She heard it."

He thought about that. "Maybe that's because when I think of the moment, that's what I remember most vividly. That's what still feels overwhelming when I find myself suddenly taken with it. Not what I saw but what I heard. A horrible, deafening sound all around me."

"That she must have heard at the same time," Rapholtz said, "from across the country."

"I know."

"Alright. Another possibility to rule out. Someone pretending to be her, playing a cruel joke on you."

"I've thought of that. No one at Kiel knew of her. I scarcely spoke about myself. Certainly not about my father, and certainly not about Greta. This came from Berlin, I remind you. Where news of what happened couldn't possibly have reached at the hour it was sent."

"What does that leave us then? Coincidence, I suggest. It's not some miracle, Fleischl."

"No, it's not. Miracles aren't supposed to be as horrible as this."

"Although," Rapholtz said, "some might call it a miracle that a blinded man found his sight again."

He grew restless. He felt suffocated by the library, so he stood and went to the window alongside Dowid. Since the wreck of the *Elegy*, Dowid had found—if not quite solace, then at least place. He spent each day watching the sea alongside Anton. Theirs was a quiet vigil, broken only by Dowid's questions. There were precisely two, asked incessantly, and each day Anton answered them patiently, the way an older brother would guide one younger.

"How many steps?" Dowid would ask.

"One thousand, seven hundred and two," Anton would reply.

"Can the sea reach us here?"

"Not today." And they would fall into their usual, comfortable silence.

Fleischl felt Dowid's eyes on him. "It's just me," he said.

Dowid turned away.

"It's just hard to talk about," Fleischl said to Rapholtz. "As hard as it is to think about, talking about it is worse somehow. Saying it so it's heard, I feel so alone."

"I know, my boy. But you're safe here, and so is what happened, and whatever you need to say about it. We'll come to understand it together."

"I don't know what to do now," he said.

"About what comes next for you? I can't answer that. I can only help you understand the choices you have. I make an observation. You feel lost."

"I do."

"I'll give you a hypothetical. You can go back to selling flax, though I'm not sure you'd want to. You can stay here. Make a home. Help these men who wander aimlessly inside themselves. You have a gift for that. Create those marvelous dioramas like you did for Anton."

"That wasn't me. That was her."

They both knew it was true. Greta lay at the heart of everything.

"As for what happened at Kiel," Rapholtz continued, "may I suggest that you have two courses. Believe it or forget it."

"Sounds simple."

He gazed out the library window. Stralsund's docks were quiet and dim. Its sea tunnels were empty. The hour was early and the piazza was still ringed by a predawn mist. Soon there would be lamplight, carts rolling in from the countryside and a gathering of men at the burghemeister's pedestal to depart on one of the ships. Thumbs rolled in indigo, leaving their marks.

At least I can see these sights again, he thought.

Rapholtz joined him at the window and put a fatherly arm around his shoulders. Quite the portrait, Fleischl thought. Four men framed in glass. Two patients, their minds far away, a doctor who cared for them, and a dull, unimaginative boy straddling the line between.

"Go on a quiet walk," Rapholtz suggested. "Eat something. Read some of the letters and papers that came while you were away. Take the first small steps that might just lead you back to your life. Somewhere, you're bound to run into what it is that you're supposed to do with all that's happened."

"Believing it," Fleischl said, "or forgetting that it ever happened, right?"

"In the end, I think our entire lives fall into one of those buckets."

"I'm not one to simply believe. I'm my father's son in that way."

Rapholtz' arm grew tighter around him. It had been a long while since someone hugged him.

"I'd suggest to you," Rapholtz said, "that the son who went a year and more in search of a father who will never be found is more capable of belief than he knows."

★★★

Taking the corridor past the washing room, he departed

Thalhammer and wandered to the shipyard as the morning deepened. The men who staffed the yard didn't seem to mind the silent figure stepping between great wooden pylons to stand in what remained of broken vessels.

A play of light came through the torn places of one old ship. There were initials carved in slats that had formed a cabin wall or faced the sea as part of the bow. Perhaps once there was a seaman dangling from ropes, scrubbing away barnacles, and he took out a knife to carve proof of his own existence into the ship on which he sailed.

Greta came to mind. In light, behind a sheet, in the circular glow of a candle. Once, it felt like the only clear thing was her.

You know how it is, Anders had said. *Connections can break.*

Some of the yard men came to the foot of the ship's skeleton. They unfurled an immense oilskin and began the task of covering the cracked hull in which he stood. "I'm here," he said, surprising them.

One pointed to the horizon and said something in an unfamiliar tongue. The meaning was clear enough. Clouds gathered at the far end of the sky, and though he hadn't noticed before, the air carried an unmistakeable weight.

The first low rumbles of thunder found him as he passed the old lowhouse along the planked walkway. His father had told him once, men at sea count the moments between the quicksilver rippling the clouds and the thunder they made. Count it twice, and if you can't count as high the second time, the storm's coming your way.

He waited for the distant flash, then began counting. By the second one the wind had picked up considerably. He reached half the number of moments before the sky shuddered and he with it, at the awful sound shaking the air. It brought him to the cliffs as they crumbled. His heart began pounding.

Near the burghemeister's guild hall, he rested against the telegraph pole. He knew better than to designate it the very one, but there were parts of his childish heart he couldn't speak sensibly to.

This is the one. *Poppa knew everything about everything. Greta heard me. Did you die.*

A hum ran through the wood of the pole, startling him. There was a dim light on in the guild hall. Someone was sending a message out along the wires.

The rain fell harder over the Baltic. He crossed the planks toward the dock and the ship that was anchored there, nearest the guild hall. He didn't return to Thalhammer even as concussive blasts of thunder thrilled his heart. The frigate's gangplank was down. He went aboard and made his way to the side facing the Baltic. He didn't know the ship's name. He didn't want to.

The storm pelted him as he leaned over the ship's rail. The Baltic churned violently against the hull, sending tremors through the deck. Static filled the air. Then the black sea flared brilliantly and the thunder came at once. A bolt split the underbelly of the clouds and painted them blue. The waves ignited in time. The world was held in a great fan of light.

He felt it all through the rail and into his palms. A shimmer of numbness. Far from the ship, a buoy faded back into the blackness of the water. The lightning must have struck it, he thought.

He climbed onto the rail and sat with his legs swinging out over the waves. Rain lashed his face. His hold on the wood was tenuous. The ship felt as if it was about to tilt. It was the worst place to be, on the rail, on a storm-ravaged sea, and he didn't know what compelled him. It was just that he needed to be nearer the Baltic when the next burst of lightning came. With it would come the moment when the dark sea lit up like a scene inside a phantasmascope.

The storm swept against the hull, throwing him off the rail. He was falling. The ship was turning and he was free of it with nothing below him but that which had already taken so much away from him. His heart tore free along with the rest of him. Then hands seized him as if from the sky. They pulled him back up along the side of the ship and over the rail, and then threw him to the deck.

The mate standing over him looked to be no more than a boy. "Do you want to die so badly?"

"Who does," Fleischl said as he stumbled toward the slick gangplank. Once off, he ran for the hill. Another, further peal of thunder sounded as he made it to the library tunnel, passing through rattling stones. By the time he opened the bookcase door, startling Rapholtz at his desk, the rain had slowed and the sky had lightened. The world outside the library window emerged.

"My God, look at you," Rapholtz said. "You're soaked through."

"There's a third choice." He came in shedding drops of rain. At the window he slid to the floor, spent. Rapholtz brought him a blanket and draped it over his shoulders. Fleischl held his hand up. "Feel my pulse."

Rapholtz took hold of his wrist. "Rapid," he said. "It's practically pounding."

"I was terrified out there. Not as badly as that day at Kiel, but I felt fear all around me, and it's made me think of something."

He told Rapholtz of the ship, the storm and how close he came to falling. "You said I have two choices on how to live with what happened to me. Believe it or forget it."

"I recall."

"There's a third way, and that's what I'm going to do."

He lay his fingers against his own wrist. His hammering heartbeat slowed. The afternoon light spread as the storm left Stralsund. Before long there would be another place sinking into darkness.

"I'm going to prove it," he said.

★★★

The second thing Fleischl did was to locate and pull every last bit of writing the library contained concerning the brain. There were books on the brain operating normally and abnormally, the brain transmitting its signals in a normal manner and the brain corrupted into thinking it was deaf, dumb, blind, bent or in another place and time altogether. The brain could be, in the words of just one, "out of awareness, but not out of operation."

He set that line aside for its potential applicability to Dowid.

To that considerable pile of material he added what documents he managed to borrow from a curious and accommodating burghemeister. In the guild hall's sloppily maintained records he unearthed an article on the basic principles of the telegraph, along with schematics so yellowed with age that DaVinci might have drawn them up. Beneath them, he found the old map of steps and with the burghemeister's permission, took that as well.

The first thing he did, before ransacking Thalhammer's library and the guild, was share a light breakfast with Rapholtz in the library and, in the breaking light morning, assure his mentor that he wasn't trying to kill himself.

"I believe you," Rapholtz told him over black bread, butter and coffee. But he didn't sound wholly convinced. "How do you intend to prove this?"

"I'll follow your method. Step one: make an observation."

Rapholtz watched Fleischl turn over a sheet of paper and slide it against his cup. Step one: *electricity*.

"I was terrified at Kiel," Fleischl said. "May no one ever go through something like that. Aboard the ship the other night, I was afraid of the storm—and of almost drowning, of course. But it wasn't nearly the same. I could think. I had time. Kiel was a sudden onslaught. An overwhelming surge that swept all my senses away. It was like my mind cracked open."

He gestured to the battery on the desk across from them. "Electricity, Laszlo."

Rapholtz regarded the battery with the same kindly, skeptical expression that he wore while listening to Fleischl excitedly press his case.

"Why not?" Fleischl continued. "The heart has it. Tissue has it. We know that. Apply enough electricity and dead frogs jump, right? The brain has electricity too. We don't know how much or what kind. But we all know the sensation of something terrifying us. We *feel* it."

"Fleischl…"

"*Two*," Fleischl interrupted. He tapped his finger on the paper. "Form a hypothesis. Right there."

Rapholtz read the next line. Two: *The brain, when sufficiently stimulated, is capable of generating enough electricity to create a transmission effect, that under the right conditions (as yet unknown) can be received.*

"Under what conditions?" Rapholtz asked.

"I haven't gotten that far yet. This is all just coming to me. I may be utterly wrong. I have to consider so many things. That day, the weather. Was I rested, hungry, thirsty? I don't know, maybe the sea being so close. We're saline as well as electricity."

"No." Rapholtz slid the paper back across the table to Fleischl. "I'm asking what condition was an essential element?"

Fleischl didn't answer.

"Let me help you. You had to almost die."

"I know."

"If this happened…"

"It did happen."

"Then to prove it, ever, brings you to step four, correct? Conduct an experiment?"

"Yes," Fleischl said quietly.

"You would need to come that close again. Is that what you were doing aboard the ship?"

"No. I told you. I wouldn't, not ever."

"Step three, then. Make a prediction."

"I can't. Not yet."

"Neither can I. So I suggest we modify step three. Let me make something more akin to a diagnosis."

Daylight had by now flooded the library, but Fleischl hadn't noticed.

"A man loses his mother," Rapholtz said gently. "Then his

father. Then the woman he loves, and she's the one he believes may have somehow perceived the moment he almost loses himself. No one else. Only her."

"There is no one else."

"And that's why you need this to be true, my boy. There are no words from those we lost wandering around in the air, waiting for us to hear them when we couldn't hear in life. I wish to God there were. If you want to hear, listen while they're with you. That's all that's real, Fleischl. Treasure this odd bit of magic the world gave you at Kiel. It saved your life, returned your sight, and left you in a state of wonder. Tell stories about it to your grandchildren if you want. But don't chase it into the sea. You've lost too much already."

Fleischl stood up from the table, rubbed his aching leg and went to the bookshelves. He took down a volume he'd been eyeing. *An Anatomical Guide to the Brain's Hemispheres.* "My father once told me that belief was for scared little boys," he said as he paged through detailed line drawings of the brain's corrugations. "He said I should only put my faith in what I could see or touch. The soil, if I was to be a farmer. Wood, if a shipbuilder. The sea, if I was to be a man like him."

He returned to the table and set the book atop his paper. "What if, Laszlo? What if we really have this in us?"

"That doesn't sound like science. That's belief. I thought you didn't have much of that. What's changed?"

"I went looking for him," Fleischl said. "I listened to you. You were right. I looked for him on the soil, in the woods, and in the sea. All that's left of my father now is belief."

Rapholtz considered the man before him. After a while staring at Fleischl's rendering of the scientific method and its questions, he said, "For now, get some rest. After rounds and dinner tonight, you can tell me how I can help you in this odd journey you want to make. But be assured, if I see you come anywhere near danger, I'll do more than stop you. I'll have you committed. You and Dowid can count steps together."

"Agreed."

After Rapholtz left the library, Fleischl pulled all the books he could find and made his plans to visit the burghemeister's guild, where he would locate whatever he could on the most prominent example of transmission he knew of. What must momma and poppa think, he mused. The telegraph, still in our lives.

He picked the battery up from its tangle of wires. Nestled within the coils was a lone bulb. He attached it to the wires. The battery hummed weakly. In a moment, the tiny glass orb grew a bud of dim blue light.

It still works, Greta. Imagine that.

★★★

The telegraph is a machine of simple principle. It sends information by making, then breaking, connections.

A heartbeat across wire.

Electricity across distance.

Makes use of magnets, bars, plates, dots, dashes.

Grey cells live in a network.

The right side is where cardiac contraction begins. The electric conduction of the sub-endocardium. Atrioventricular bundle.

The dominating rhythm of the heart is heard everywhere in the body.

Papers were littered across everything in the room. The desk, the couch where Anton slept in the fetal ball he favored, and the floor. The floor led to the window, which led to Dowid, posted on his evening watch over the Baltic. He'd made an unholy mess of the library, not that Rapholtz minded. Since their discussion three days earlier, Rapholtz had been supportive, solicitous of his ideas and open in his sentiment that his young mentee was navigating perilous waters in what could turn out to be a lifetime pursuit of the impossible if Fleischl wasn't careful.

"See that?" Rapholtz asked more than once over the days. He'd point to the ivory puzzle piece on the table next to the array of batteries. "It's but a small part of the whole. It's not meant to be everything. Don't let anything be everything. Men go mad that way."

Fleischl surveyed the madness of notes, sources, opinions and unmoored suppositions he'd jotted down in diligent pursuit of scientific method numbers two through four. Form a hypothesis. Make a prediction. Conduct an experiment. Prove it. Believe it. Forget it ever happened.

He'd gotten precisely nowhere. He lacked even the roughest of maps. He didn't know where to begin or where to go next. It was simply a matter of time before Rapholtz or his own thoughts told him to let go of the thing that happened. Relegate it to a memory to be brought out only occasionally, like an old keepsake at parties. Take the necessary steps toward the rest of his life, whatever that would be.

He tried to think of that life. What he came up with was the ones who wouldn't be there with him.

Feeling maudlin and thoroughly adrift, he left the library and its chaos of papers. Dowid didn't even notice. In the washing room he filled one of the concrete troughs and lowered himself into deep hot water made milky by the asylum's old pipes. His body was weary but his thoughts refused to be still. He slipped beneath the surface to the place where the world always seemed the quietest. But it all followed him, and after holding his breath for almost three minutes—a personal best, he suspected—he came up.

He wasn't ready to face the nattering collection of ideas he'd abandoned, so he went to his cramped room and busied himself with tidying up his cot, desk, and nightstand. Rapholtz had left letters and some periodicals that had come for him during his long absence. Fleischl had yet to attack the pile. He began sorting the documents into two piles: to be read soon, and to be read sometime. It felt like progress of a monumental sort given what waited for him in the library.

Making his way through letters from the insurance syndicate, a few from his compatriots at Kiel ("no excuses for not writing us," Anders wrote in a sloppy hand. "I know you can read this"), there was one he paused at.

A.B., Berlin

It had arrived at Thalhammer almost nine months ago to the day. He tore the envelope open.

Herr Berger:

I write you partially as co-author of On Hearing and Listening (I trust it wasn't you who thought of that dreadful subtitle about loss of self). I assume the work is primarily Dr. Rapholtz' from your co-author status and the overall pedantic, practical discourse which doesn't align with the other capacity in which I write you. You are young and a bit naive in your zeal, I believe. Nonetheless, the paper was mildly interesting. It might find some usefulness after a good deal of revision.

About that other capacity: I write you principally as the author of that telegram sent to my attention, and because of this statement in particular: I was born with a drowned heart. Something to do with electricity, you say? I ask, why are you coauthoring adequate papers with such a thing as this in your life?

I invite you to continue a correspondence with me. You just might be interesting. Whether you write me in reply or not is of course not consequential. I would suggest you shouldn't just disappear, though. Not after so auspicious a debut into the world.

A.B.

He posted a reply the following morning.

Herr A.B.:

May this find you well. My deepest apologies for not replying sooner. I was traveling abroad for over a year and went further than letters could reach. I would very much treasure a correspondence with you, if I may be forgiven for the long silence.

As for my drowned heart, I can say that something happened to me in the very beginning, and it now appears that something has happened to me again. Difficult to explain, even more so to understand, and perhaps most of all to prove.

Are those not the things most worth spending your days on? came A.B.'s reply in two weeks' time. It was pinned to the most recent issue of Revive, along with a note that said, *"See p. 18"*

He turned to that page and was greeted with the glistening, exposed pink brain of a suffering rabbit and a second letter. The scalped animal, Fleischl learned upon reading the adjacent text, was alive at the moment of the photograph.

Prominent physicists posit that the brain, much like the heart, emits electric phenomena that can be artificially induced. This notion will be presented in Berlin on 20 February 1898. This may be of interest to a young co-author with unusual ideas.

He sent a telegram that afternoon.

I WISH TO ATTEND STOP MAY WE SPEAK ABOUT THIS WORK STOP INDUCEMENT IS REAL I HAVE SEEN IT STOP IT HAPPENED TO ME STOP

He sent a small barrage of telegrams at a pfennig per word. They detailed Kiel and the telegram, though not her.

A.B. replied by telegram.

THIS SOUNDS ABSURD STOP CONFERENCE IS FOR SCIENTISTS AND INVESTORS ONLY STOP FEE IS NOT INSUBSTANTIAL STOP

So Fleisch answered.

I WILL PAY STOP

"This A.B. ridicules me," he told Rapholtz after sending his last telegram. "But look at the photographs. The wiring to the brain. Transmission, Laszlo. This could help me."

"I'll go with you," Rapholtz said, "because it might do you

good to be among men of ideas. But you need to be prepared. Not everyone will consider your experience worthy of study. My guess is that few will, if any, and most will dismiss it, and you along with it."

A telegram arrived that evening from A.B.

I WILL RECEIVE YOU AND PAYMENT STOP PLEASE EXPLAIN WHAT YOU HOPE TO ACCOMPLISH STOP

In the morning, after a long night's struggle over what to say, Fleischl's telegram went out.

HOW TO BE HEARD STOP

CHAPTER Nine
A Fairy Fable In Shadow Show

After arriving in the central borough of Mitte, he and Rapholtz located a spacious pension near the Spree, in the shadow of the Berliner Dome. At a cafe near Alexanderplatz, they washed fatty chops down with strong red wine that fortified them against the bitter winds that whipped their outercoats as they walked to the university where, at the hour of six, a small contingent of lab-coated men and, to Fleischl's surprise, one woman, took their seats on an amphitheater stage alongside a shackled, paralyzed monkey.

From the wings of the stage, a mastiff of a man emerged to steady applause. He was of vague middle age and had a prominent forehead. His dark hair featured one narrow shock of silver running from front to back. He wore a finely tailored, charcoal colored suit. He appeared to be built in all respects for combat, with shoulders so broad he could sit for Rodin. He stood in stark contrast to the sorry monkey, whose wide eyes swept the room in terror as one of the lab-coated men went to a table and returned with a formidable saw.

"I bid welcome to so many eminent guests," said the man. "I consider myself fortunate to serve as Chancellor of this institution.

I am, as so many of you know, well-placed." He paused for effect. "I enjoy making the acquaintance of like-minded men. I may not be of the sciences. I came to my station through industry and wise investments. I oversee a diversified portfolio. Were any of you to review my many holdings, you would surely wonder what business I have being here. I will say this: I share with you a seeker's mind. We all want to peel back the veil, and in my case, profit from it."

"You can certainly be counted on," someone said, and the audience laughed.

"Without my money, most of you would be teaching in the hinterlands. We are hand in hand, gentlemen. And so our experiment today. I daresay it holds some promise, but I'll defer to you. For those of you who do not already know, my name is August Bliekroder."

"A.B.," Fleischl whispered to Rapholtz. "It has to be him."

"Enough from me," said August. He stepped back from the edge of the amphitheater stage to a waiting chair. "The monkey grows impatient."

At his gesture, the student wielded the saw against the pitiable creature's head, then lifted the top of its skull fur and all.

One of the lab men brought forth an immense contraption. "I give you the galvanometer, and the DuBois-Reymond electrodes."

Both the people on stage and those in the audience took copious notes. But the woman, Fleischl observed, simply sat there next to August. She seemed dour to the point of mourning. She watched the audience in a manner that he found oddly similar to that of the monkey.

"Electrodes," he whispered to Rapholtz. "We might make something with those. A way to transmit. I don't know, *something*."

"Don't ask anything," Rapholtz said.

"And once positioned," the lab-coated man continued, "there… we'll only have a brief period of activity. May I suggest that all those interested in close observation come down to the front of the hall."

Fleischl joined a line of men shuffling toward the stage below. He weaved his way through the crowd to the front, near the electrode table. "Non-polarisable electrodes," the man explained. "Made of cotton thread embedded in clay. I connect them thusly to the galvanometer to measure fluctuations. And we begin."

He strung the electrodes out toward the disturbingly calm primate. "We measure excitability at two points along the spinal cord. We place one electrode at the lower spinal node, the other at the point of cord entry to the brain, at the height of the cerebral hemisphere. Observe the galvanometer."

The thread of the instrument vibrated gently. Linen, Fleischl saw by its coiled weave, like a twist of bread dough.

"We now provoke the desired activity." He produced a small torchier, struck it and brought it close to the monkey's glazed eyes. "Do you see?" He nodded toward the galvanometer. Its string vibrated with greater frequency as the monkey's jaw slackened. A rope of luminous saliva descended from its quivering lips as the last of its life slipped away.

A murmur rose among the scientists. One asked when the paper might be ready. Another asked about production. "My lawyers are addressing the small matter of patent rights," August said.

"How can he say a light in its eyes provoked anything?" Fleischl muttered to no one in particular.

Onstage, August reached into his suit coat pocket and produced a folded sheet of paper. Behind him, the seated woman sighed.

"Gentlemen," August began. The audience quieted. "Let's talk about something altogether different, shall we?"

At his gesture, the woman rose and brought a chair. He sat down and dismissed her with a wave. She returned to her seat, her cheeks ruddy. She was older than the fellows seated around her, with a matronly form. She'd been attractive in her youth, and the minimum of age lines around her eyes and mouth betrayed an age younger than one might have initially guessed. She wasn't elderly. She seemed worn somehow. Her sour expression, Fleischl thought, might stem from the sort of menial catering that he'd just seen her perform for August.

He didn't like it much. He also didn't like the way August snapped open the paper as if he was swatting away a fly.

"We have a dreamer among us." August uncreased the paper and rested it in his lap. "Now, I like dreamers. In my life I've come to understand them, whether they're of a high sort, as are so many of you scientists and doctors, or of a considerably lower sort. I mentioned my holdings before. I have positions in places like this, and not three blocks from here, a cabaret where on any given night you can be entertained by mesmerists, hypnotists, magicians, palm readers, and even women."

He paused for the titters to quiet. "To be perfectly candid, these sorts of investments offer me a better return than you lot. My point is, I'm acquainted with dreamers of all kinds. There's room for them in the new age. But I wouldn't conduct a galvanic experiment at the Tingel-Tangel, and I won't allow charlatans and spiritualists in here with all of you. I believe I do a commendable job separating wheat from chaff, but it appears that my assistants have failed me."

He held the paper aloft for all to see. Fleischl's stomach churned at the faint yet unmistakable typeface of a telegram.

"I was born with a drowned heart," August read. "I nearly died and this was heard from hundreds of miles away. I intend to prove this impossible thing that happened to me."

"Don't," Rapholtz hissed in his ear. Onstage, August called for the dreamer, should he be in attendance, to leave *sans* refund.

He pulled away from Rapholtz and made his way through the other attendees to the lip of the stage. As August gazed down at him, he produced a tight, humorless smile. "For all the mockery you enjoy at my expense," he told August, "Let's take a good look at this idiocy you call science."

The attendees formed a tight circle around him, sensing a battle. At least, that's what Fleischl thought. In truth, they expected a rout.

"By all means," August said with a smirk of his own. "Educate us. But stay close. I wouldn't want to try hearing you from a long way off."

"Bastard."

He climbed onto the stage with no sense of what he should do. Now that he was close to the deceased (and still wired) monkey, the only thing he had to offer was *poor creature* and perhaps *it looks like a battery I built once from your instructions.*

Instead he said, "It's attached wrong." One electrode was attached atop the animal's gelatinous brain, the other along its lower spine. "The electrodes should be at different regions of the brain. What does the animal's spine have to do with anything?"

August looked to his lab-coated men for answers. One of them said, "It traces the electric current as it travels." But he sounded less than certain. Over the man's scrawny shoulder, the woman fixed Fleischl with a look that suggested she found him ignorant at best, and possibly worthy of extermination.

"Yes, yes," he said tartly. "There's electricity in the heart and then it moves around. "That's not what I was talking about. That's not what transmission is. Not by a wide margin. This placement is no better than placing your hand on top of the waves to find out what the bottom feels like. And that machine is crude. How can it detect anything? All it does is scribble some lines."

"Waves," the woman said before August caught her with a look that quieted her.

He'd ceased being a source of amusement to August, judging by the death of the great man's smile. Not that he cared. If this was the beginning and the end of his correspondence with A.B., let it all come down. "The battery is here," he said, jabbing his finger at his own temple. "And it can go farther than you imagine. Judging by all this, you don't imagine much at all."

August bellowed at him. "Get out of my university. You're not only a deeply unserious young man, you're petulant and capable only of crying like a spoiled child when challenged. Well, I stand here and I challenge you. Prove your point or leave. You've said nothing of weight or import. You've no credentials and now you attack an invention that's the product of research and industry. And you've done so on the basis of nothing but your own arrogance. You deem it a failure." An uproar rose among the crowd as the dressing-down continued. "You dismiss an experiment you don't know the first thing about. And yet you came here why? To study here? To prove your sad story, you traveled across Germany because you're that important? No, I'll not tolerate you another second. If you're looking for a venue better suited to your talents, may I suggest the nearest ratskellar."

Fleischl looked around for anyone who might offer a supportive nod or a look that said *I think you may have a point*. The lab coats glared at him. Their number had dwindled by one; the woman had left the amphitheater stage.

The audience was no better. He left the auditorium to jeers and catcalls. At the far end of the room, he found Rapholtz.

"Bliekroder is a bombastic egotist," Rapholtz said. "That's evident. But I warned you, did I not?"

"I didn't realize it would be quite that humiliating."

"And you deserved every second of it, it pains me to say. You went up there with no idea of what to say. Worse, of what you believe. You didn't debate. You threw a tantrum. You may find his tone appalling but if you had a valid point to make, so did he. Beginning with petulance."

"I don't need to hear this from you."

"Where are you going?"

"I need some air."

He left Rapholtz for the amphitheater door and the frozen Berlin night. With each step away, he considered how accurate Rapholtz and, though it disgusted him to admit, August were. It was a childish gesture to leave at the first provocation. But it would be a far worse humiliation to return. Not fond of either choice, he walked for what felt like forever toward the brightest light in the heart of the city's curtain. One of those burning little lights belonged to a threadbare cabaret, the Kabarette Bretl. It was situated in a line of brash, open door storefronts on Kurfurstenstrasse. The atonal sounds of brass instruments and coarse shouting filled the street. The other side, in contrast, was largely dark but for one small space with shuttered windows, behind which a soft glow illuminated the designs on the windowpane.

He crossed the pavement for a better look. The design was a scroll, and it was inscribed hieroglyphically.

Hebrew, he realized, as the melodic thrum of men's voices came from within.

Behind him, a group of revelers in evening finery stumbled out of the brightest, loudest establishment, the Kabarette.

It only took a moment for him to decide. Go be with your own, he thought ruefully, and made for the brashest open door on Kurfurstenstrasse.

He passed through a beaded curtain into a dark, circular room upholstered in deep reds and clogged with smoke. The tables were full and fifty or so men talked drunkenly. Some had louche, made-up women at their sides, lighting their foul cigars or bringing their coins to the barman for drinks they quaffed themselves with their bellies against the barman's rail.

On the venue's tiny stage there was a man in an absurd velveteen topcoat and matching cape. He doffed his opera hat, reached inside and withdrew what appeared to be a cooked omelet.

"It was in there the whole time," said a drunk man at a table near the stage.

"Philistines," sighed the man on stage. Fleischl took him for a magician of sorts and wondered what kind of thinking had gone into an act that culminated in a cooked omelet. He clapped before realizing he was the only one to do so.

The magician pointed at him. "You there! Your name, young sir!"

"Fleischl."

"Our next volunteer, Fleischl! Come to the stage, my boy, and partake of the wondrous."

"I just came in for a moment."

The magician produced a cane from behind his back with a

flourish, and said, "I'll keep it to a moment then."

The audience hooted at him to hurry up, and Fleischl made his way reluctantly to the stage. It was even tinier up close, with a few chairs and a table, on top of which rested, incongruously, a fireplace poker, some feather boas, another evening hat, and a plate of eggs.

Eggs, he thought, were a prominent feature at the Kabarette Bretl.

"Why me?" he asked the magician.

"Because you're not falling down drunk," he said. "And now," he cried out to the audience, "the vanishing pfennig!"

He leaned to Fleischl and said, "I need a pfennig."

Neither the trick nor the man's powers of distraction were impressive. A bit of wax on the magician's hand and a pfennig in his palm. When he closed his hand, then opened it upside down, Fleischl and those seated closest could clearly see the coin stuck to his fingers. But everyone laughed and clapped, and to Fleischl it seemed less a cabaret of the wondrous than a rundown association of Berlin's castoffs. Everyone was drunk, loud and lecherous, but they were also together in something.

Outside, the city was cold, its affluent denizens hidden away behind locked mahogany doors and hansom cab screens.

They were all hurtling toward an unknowable future, he thought. So what was the harm in being with one's own, whoever they may be?

Someone bought him a drink, then another. Over the course of a few hours, between the Magnificent Magnified Cane, the Advantageous Wager, the Prisoner Released and the Conundrum of the Three Jealous Husbands, he grew lustily drunk. He'd also become the de facto assistant somewhere along the line to a blurry succession of highly unskilled sleight and jugglery artists.

Near midnight, the Kabarette audience insisted that Fleischl gift them with a trick of his own.

"I don't know any tricks," he said.

"Everyone knows at least one," said the newest act. He was a

self-proclaimed Mesmerist and he mounted the stage carrying an armful of props. He had a large glass globe, a candle, and a complex rig of
wire and disassembled hangars.

Fleischl envisioned the candle moving, the glass globe aglow,
the declaration of spirits in their midst because spirits, having made
the journey from the far side, wanted nothing more than to visit a
seedy cabaret.

The audience cajoled him. More drinks came. He asked for a
piece of paper and the mesmerist's candle.

"That's your trick?" someone heckled. "Burn the place down?
Not that it would matter."

The sheet of paper was no bigger than an octavo. He held it
near the flame until it felt hot and crisp, then asked for the favor of
someone's armpit. A fleshy, slurring woman rose to the occasion. He
slipped the paper between her arm and her side and rubbed it vigorously until static burst minutely against his fingertips. Then he went to
the nearest wall and held the paper up. It stuck to the wainscoting as if
magnetized.

"Bravo!" cried the mesmerist. "Crude," he said to Fleischl as an
aside, "but effective."

"I trust no one here believes I'm magic," Fleischl said.

"No one needs to believe," the mesmerist said, "until we do.
That's the secret. A drink, a laugh, and if you're lucky, perhaps a moment
when one of them finds themselves wondering if something really did
happen. Something real."

"Do you ever wonder?" Fleischl asked him.

"Wonder?"

"If something really did happen."

"Have another drink," said the woman whose armpit static had
affixed the paper to the wall.

"Something happened to me," he said because he needed to,
and these people were drunk. They were no one and they laughed at
themselves and each other. If they laughed at him, he didn't think it

would hurt. It meant he belonged.

So he told them of Kiel, and of her.

The room was quiet but for the sound of the barman taking glasses off the rail. Then the mesmerist called upon the spirits of the dead beneath the cliffs. More drinks came round. He took a seat at a table alone, in the furthest corner from the entrance. The darkness of the room seemed to deepen, somehow.

"Like some company?"

His head felt cottony. There were broken pieces behind his eyes that shifted when he tried to lift his gaze. His leg ached. He must have been standing on stage too long.

"A simple 'no' is plenty," the woman who electrified his paper said. Up close, she was pretty in a weary, unhappy way.

"I didn't mean to ignore you." His words rode thick puffs of whiskey breath.

"Good. Now buy me a drink and save a few marks for whatever comes." She laughed, though Fleischl wasn't sure what was supposed to be funny. "Have somewhere to go?"

"Yes, but I don't know how to get back to it."

"You are a funny little boy, aren't you. Lucky for you, I've got just the place. You're going to get a show for your money."

★★★

She led him down a series of streets until they found what she was looking for, a small theatre. She rapped a soft, irregular rhythm on the door and he heard a chain unlatch on the other side.

The door opened and she ushered him inside like she owned the place. "Give me five marks for the house," she said.

Fleischl did as he was told. He had very little money left. August Bliekroder's entry fee was not insubstantial, and he never got his pfennig back from the waxed magician.

"Wait right there. No wandering off."

She went up a flight of steps. At the top, she slipped his money under a door. A few words were exchanged before she came back down.

He followed her through a set of musty red velvet curtains. On the other side, he found himself in a dark room. She navigated the path between seat rows like the nocturnal animal she was. The theatre, such as he could make out, was meant for twenty, maybe thirty people in all. She guided him to a middle row and pushed him into what felt like a roughly sanded chair.

"Will there be others?" he asked.

"It's past two, liebe. Only us. But there'll be company for you."

She lifted her skirt, followed by the loose fold of her belly. Her hips began to sway. Her free hand pulled down her slip and bloomers. In the murk, she pawed at the wild thatch between her legs.

A light sprang from a high point on the wall behind him to illuminate the dank room. Dust motes caught in the beam of light sparkled and turned in air. He smiled.

"That's my good boy," she said. "Like what you see?"

"Yes."

She reached for the belt around his waist. "Let's see what my good boy has for me."

The beam stretching above his head filled with new things. Flecks and movement. He looked past her gyrations to the screen. Words flickered by in blurry succession, filling the luminous milky square on the wall. Then a grainy shading began in the screen's corners. When it crept into the center, it tightened to an iris. Within it he saw a man in a white tunic. He raised his fists and moved in fits and spasms. An animal moved in opposition.

"Oh," Fleischl said.

"Yes, yes. Everyone loves the kangaroo. Get your pants off if you want some. I'm tired."

The man boxed with the kangaroo.

"I'll help you. Drunken dumbkopf."

She yanked at his pants impatiently. Onscreen, the kangaroo balanced on its hind legs, its paws raised in queer mimicry of the man circling it. They moved around a ring, and behind its ropes were people walking through a carnival.

She straddled him, blocking the screen. He shifted to his right.

"You're soft as butter," she taunted. "Maybe you'd rather shtup the kangaroo."

She reached down for his pants on the theatre floor and took out money. Then she took him in her hands. The screen ignited once again as she bent down. Another white backdrop, this time with words.

A fairy fable in shadow show

This iris was different than the boxing kangaroo. It was scalloped, like two halves of a clam shell. When it parted, an elegant and feminine hand took hold of a pair of scissors. A black blot appeared and the scissors carved at it until it had been crafted to the silhouette of a girl seated on a bench.

"That's more like it," she mumbled.

The scissors caught another black cloud and cut it into tiny beings. They danced on air, on shivering wings, bobbing out of the black into white space to tease the figurine on the bench until they reached the curled lip of the iris and disappeared.

It was joyous. The still figurine, the darting little winged beings. "My boy, I've done all a girl can do. My jaw aches."

His companion stood and dressed herself. He hadn't noticed that she'd removed her top.

On screen, the female figure stood as well. It moved like a marionette. It turned and there was a visible appendage on its back. A misshape, a hump. The hand appeared next to it, holding the scissors.

"Time to go." His companion had finished dressing. She straightened herself and sidestepped to the aisle. "Decent folk ought to be in bed."

The scissors finished their work. The figurine's hump, now wings. It set off for the top of the iris and slipped away.

"I'm staying," he told her.

She shrugged and left him.

After a moment, when the white screen didn't fill again, he

walked out of the theatre to the inside steps. There he climbed to the door at the top. "Are you in there?"

Rustling came from within. A whirring of some mechanical marvel. The tinny popping of cans, a steady ticking.

"Please, may I see it again? The last one. The figure with the wings at the end."

The only sound within was the striking of a match.

"I have a little money."

He fished the last few marks from his trousers and pushed them under the door. Nothing. No footsteps, no turning of good coin. Only the earthy burning of tobacco.

"It's all I have."

"It's late," said a man's voice, weary and corroded by smoke.

"Can you tell me how it was done? The images?"

"Gotte." A small chaos of dropped metal followed. "We've an artiste among the whores. Galeen made it. He made all of them. Pankow, here in Berlin. There's a hall there, the Wintergarten, where he shows them. It's nice. Leave now and you'll get there faster."

"I'd truly like to see it one more time. It makes me happy somehow."

"My sad and lonely friend, who has trapped me in this filthy hole, they're paper dolls made to move through trickery of light and shadow. Though the kangaroo was real."

"Very well. I won't trouble you any further."

"Do I hear tears?"

Fleischl walked down the steps, passed through the curtain and felt his way through the darkened theatre to his seat. Retrieving his coat, he trudged back up the aisle. He'd almost reached the exit when a dusty beam of light split the blackness.

A fairy fable in shadow show

The figurine came to her bench again. Her wings emerged. He turned to watch the light high on the wall. "If you like these so well," the projectionist called from the screening room window, "I've one more. Boring, if you ask me. Galeen just showing what he can do. I like where it is, though, if it's real. Never can tell anymore, can you?"

The light became a spacious gray. The screen filled with what Fleischl first took for a dusty old cartograph of a deep, brushy woods. The iris closed, then reopened on a tree. A holly tree, it seemed, by the weave of the brambled boughs that wrapped around a hut. The door was slightly ajar. The aperture closed again, to open on a spiral steps, down a dark, teardrop-shaped tunnel.

When it opened for the last time, Fleischl let out a soft sigh. A lake. The iris trained on its surface. Something at the bottom gave off light. It cast a cloudy glow that spread through the water. It possessed a form reminiscent of the piazza's rotunda-like rims and borders. It felt built.

There was movement in that light. A figure, grainy and far away, twirled in the light that surrounded it. It had wings. After a moment, it turned and ran out of sight as the iris closed around the dark water, taking it all away.

"All the lonely men like that one," said the projectionist.

★★★

In the early morning light, Fleischl located his pension door at last. He fumbled through his trouser pockets for the key. The door opened abruptly. "I've been up all night waiting for you," said a red-faced Rapholtz. "My first stop this morning was to be the kommissar. I thought something had happened to you."

"Please, Laszlo. My nerves."

"Come. Wash, dress in something that doesn't look like you died in it. A.B has asked to see you. Where were you?"

Stripping himself of his sweat-stained clothes, he washed himself at a basin. "Hasn't he ridiculed me enough? Why must I see him?"

"Young man, I told you. Did I not? Your ideas have no corollary in science and will be met with skepticism. Do you not remember me telling you that?"

"Skepticism? They all laughed at me."

"They laughed at you, yes. But if you truly think this is your life's purpose, toughen up, herr Berger. It only gets harder from here. If you need any additional proof that you're not half as smart as you think you are, consider this. August Bliekroder is not the A.B. you were corresponding with."

★★★

They arrived at a cozy café nestled in Potsdamer Platz where, by a well-kept fire, A.B. read a newspaper. The remains of boiled sausage and cumin-dusted rolls sat on a plate.

"So he's alive."

The newspaper dropped, revealing a freshly coiffed, smartly dressed woman. Given her expertly applied makeup, her swept, sandy hair, and chic, tinted glasses it was difficult to guess her age. Early forties?

"Herr Rapholtz," she said. "I don't believe he recognizes me." She folded her paper. "Waiter, coffee for my guests. Please, herr Berger, sit before you keel over."

"I'm well enough," Fleischl said.

"Well enough to withstand scrutiny without running away like a child?"

"We shall see."

"Good. Now tell me where you've encountered me before. Let me give you a hint. This was how I looked at you when you so thoroughly condemned the shortcomings of the galvanometer yesterday."

She gave him a withering glare.

"The woman on the amphitheater stage," he said. "In the lab coat."

"Very good. Let me introduce myself a bit more thoroughly. My name is Alice Bliekroder. A.B. I'm a scientist and engineer. I made improvements to the galvanic method you dismissed without basis."

"I apologize."

She dismissed his attempt with a wave. "I'm also the wife of August Bliekroder, the rather influential man you quarreled with."

"I suppose I've completely humiliated myself."

"Not completely. Though I expect you're about to." She sipped her coffee. "Explain this incident that you believe happened to you."

Fleischl began. In time water arrived, and coffees with cream poured from the rounded snouts of porcelain bears, and boiled eggs arranged in a circle around glistening stacks of ham slices. Spearing an egg, Fleischl put it on his plate. Its whitish hide was brilliant and unblemished, like the screen of the night before. Were there were constellations of light and dust hidden inside?

"I may not be a male scientist," Alice said when he'd finished, "but all that can be explained any number of ways."

"As can everything," Fleischl said through a mouthful of egg. "It's light out here right now and there's no shortage of ways to explain it if you've no idea why. Every one of the explanations unlearned men can create would be wrong. There's only one that's right."

"A valid point, if perhaps arrogantly spoken," said Alice. "Of all the possible explanations for what you say happened..."

"What did happen."

"Your explanation is the only one. You dismiss all other possibilities. Coincidence, prank, lie. There can be no other."

"There can't."

"Don't be impertinent," said Rapholtz.

"I believe the word you're looking for is cocky," Alice said. "Coming from one who lacks sufficient credentials."

"That machine of yours," Fleischl said, "the point of it as I understand it, is to chart electricity's course from the brain through the spine, yes?"

"And determine how the brain communicates its messages, *inside* the body it resides in, mind you. Which is the only place it can be found. That's the issue with your entire theory."

"No, madam. That's the issue with yours."

"I beg your pardon?"

"Have you seen any of the moving images made these days?

Like those made in Pankow by a Galeen, I believe?"

"August has investments in a few of them, if you must know. Personally, I consider them trifles and nonsense. They're never going to replace a good play. Really, a boxing kangaroo?"

"If you wanted to know how moving images happen, you wouldn't begin by studying the light coming from the wall. You go into the projection room and study the machine. I refer to the brain."

"I'm not an idiot, Berger. I know you refer to the brain. Better men than you devote their lives to studying it."

"They're only studying its generation of electricity within the body, as with the heart. I propose studying transmission outside the body. We already know the brain's capable of transmitting clear or twisted thoughts. Rational or fantastical. The world as it is or something that doesn't exist anywhere but in the mind. That it runs on electricity. My mentor here knows that as well. And if you've ever spent any time with the insane, you'd know it."

Alice Bliekroder smiled for the first time since breakfast began. "I spend my time with men who think themselves better than me, and like you they lack basis. Does that count?"

He reached for the ham slices. "I know a man who believes he's holding a document of names, except he really isn't. Do you know why he believes that? Because a trauma delivered decades ago burned so deeply into his brain that it changed him and the world he sees. Now his mind projects that figment to the exclusion of everything else, every day. I know another man whose life is lost but for a rope and counting steps to the sea. It's been two years since the wreck that damaged him. If the brain can muster sufficient energy to keep the same moving images going all that time, like a projector in a theatre that never turns off, surely it's capable in one terrible moment of doing what it did to me that day."

Alice picked up a spoon and stirred her coffee. She looked at Rapholtz as if they were parents of a wayward toddler. "At least he hasn't run away yet," she remarked. "Though he looks like he wants to."

Fleischl forced himself to remain in his chair. There was nowhere to go, anyway. The Bioscop wasn't even open yet.

"And the reason you ran," Alice said, "was because no one in that room took you seriously. Let me tell you, no one there or anywhere else takes a woman seriously, in the scientific arena or any other arena you can think of that doesn't involve sewing circles. Yet I remain."

"Actually," Fleischl said, "I saw your chair empty at the end."

"Someone had to cremate the monkey," she said.

It was his turn to smile despite himself. "Why have you shown interest in my idea when you find it so ridiculous?"

"I never said that." She pronounced the coffee tepid, waved a waiter over and demanded a fresh pot. "I'm tired of mediocre men doing mediocre things and being lauded for their mediocrity. If I see promise, I explore."

The waiter returned to fill her cup. She raised it to her painted lips and blew ripples across its surface. "I see your expressions, gentlemen. If I wanted to take a young lover, I would do so without a fuss. That much I've learned at the side of a highly lauded but mediocre man. That's not what moves me. You, Berger, are not what moves me. I'm no wounded old woman prowling for a companion on her jeweled arm to attend operas and Ouija parties. I care nothing for opera, nor for communion with the dead. Do you?"

"Once, perhaps." He poured himself some coffee. His head pounded mightily. He hoped he didn't look as bedraggled as he felt. "No longer. I want to treat this as a scientific inquiry. I've made an observation. I want to form a sound hypothesis…"

"Make a prediction," Alice interrupted. "Then conduct an experiment and analyze the results. If there are any. I'm familiar with the scientific method."

She considered Fleischl over the top of her glasses. "This is what I expect from you. You'll work tirelessly, without complaint and straight through failure and frustration. You produce a suitable paper. You present your theory and defend it. You will *not*, let me stress, run away."

"Agreed. But your husband won't allow me anywhere near the university."

"This will have nothing to do with the university. Not until you've a proper paper, at least, that you're prepared to fight for. You'll defend it there, and perhaps well enough to be admitted. Or perhaps you'll prove the impossible and have your choice of anywhere you want. Until then, I'll be your benefactor."

"If I may ask," Rapholtz said, "what do you benefit from this arrangement?"

"Likely nothing," Alice said. "Some credit for something as improbable as this, perhaps. I'm not in need of money myself, or did the two of you think these rings of mine were as fraudulent as those garish paste beads at Kabarette Bretl?"

She smiled at the surprise on Fleischl's face. "In case you were wondering, the cane is attached to his belt loop with horsehair and the omelet is in the hat the entire time. Don't look so shocked, Fleischl. I've been there. I know of night spots in Berlin that would stop your young and electric heart."

"Don't forget the wax on his finger to palm the pfennig," Fleischl said.

"I'll wager he kept it."

His coffee was cold, but he didn't mind.

"Your new scientific method," she said. "Work, paper, defend. If you can."

"I accept. But I still have to ask, why? Of all the people who must seek your support, why this? Why me?"

Alice stood, opened her purse and took out money to cover breakfast. "Mattering so much," she said, "that you were heard no matter how far away? I have my reasons for wanting to know how such a thing must feel, Fleischl."

CHAPTER Ten
Unter den Linden

Alice situated him in a clean, updated one bedroom apartment on Unter den Linden, overlooking the city palace. She filled the apartment with suitably utilitarian furniture. There was a circular kitchen table of walnut with four matching brown chairs, padded but not plushly so. Across from the table was a couch, also brown, finished in a slippery leather with recessed studding and a middle cushion that, when sat upon, sank fully below its two neighbors. There was a single bed, with a caftan and soft sheets. In the middle of the room, abutting the kitchenette—it was impossible, Fleischl saw immediately, not to abut the kitchenette— was another circular table with a glass top and two faded blue chairs. On the wooden pedestal beneath the glass, there were parts for constructing several batteries and a solid month's worth of writing implements. Pads of paper, fine lead pencils, pens, ink, envelopes. Written in Alice's hand was a note with directions to local shoppes and eateries, including a bakery that specialized in mohnkuchen, her favorite. He supposed he would be expected to have a stock of the sweet on hand for her visits.

One written instruction stood out from the rest. The address to the nearest telegraph office in the Stralauer Tor station.

"In your work," she had said upon his first visit to the apartment that would become his home, "I expect you to correspond
with leaders in their fields of thought. Letters are last century's
procrastination."

"And this?" he'd asked, for he'd spotted on the apartment wall
a perfectly stretched canvas the hue of bone. It was framed in the same
chicory shade as much of the furnishings, though it betrayed a hint of
red when struck by sunlight. The canvas itself was largely blank but for
five thinly written lines, each perfectly aligned with delicately hinged
panels cut into the glass that covered it. They made five little doors that
opened.

> *Observation*
>
> *Hypothesis*
>
> *Prediction*
>
> *Experiment*
>
> *Result*

"That's for you to complete," Alice said, "when you know."

In his first couple of weeks on Unter den Linden, Alice came
by almost daily, and always precisely at three. She was let out of a sleek
hansom by her chauffer in front of his building. Exiting in fine couture
at the height of the days' comings and goings was obviously purpose-
ful and more than a little intimidating. He didn't know whether her
display of wealth and privilege was meant for him, the neighbors, or
Berlin at large. But she was pleasant each time she came calling for
him, notwithstanding her grand dame glances at the glass frame, which
over the first weeks remained quite blank.

He supposed she'd endowed the work of others before him
and was accustomed to the fits and starts of men with ideas. Surely her
husband hadn't emerged from the womb fully capitalized and generating hearty returns. Given everything else women had to endure in this
world, he thought, a wealthy woman demonstrating a little patience
while a man fumbled his way to his destiny couldn't be too tall an order.

He was grateful for her support and her resolve, though he still wasn't entirely sure why his particular idea —lying in wait between the blank lines of one through five beneath little glass doors—merited her attention. She was, most of all, an intimidating woman who made him nervous. It had been a good long while since he'd found himself in the company of a woman, and he lacked a true north for how to behave. The only women in his life—both winged, both gone—had left no guidance.

He suspected that despite her denials, Alice liked him for something more than his ideas. Imagining how she might look winged or bathed in light, however, was a challenge.

I find my certainty about proving what happened grows weak in her presence, he wrote to Rapholtz. *It's one thing to fashion a theory in the safety of the library with you, and quite another to make it concrete, test it, and present it to the lab-coated world of science. I don't know if I can. Also, by writing this, I'm apparently a nineteenth century procrastinator.*

It's not quite the twentieth century, Rapholtz replied, *so you're forgiven. Don't try to prove the whole of this anomalous thing that happened. Just the first step. Observe. To wit, you lost sight, were unconscious, and someone heard, or you think they did. Your light dimmed as another's ignited.*

You are, among other things, a perfectionist, and perfectionists cannot take the first step toward something new without the fear of appearing a fool and a failure. You will fail and fail, and with luck one day succeed. Go fail, Fleischl Berger.

P.S. Don't forget what you did with Anton. You should tell Frau Bliekroder about that. Help with the galvanometer, perhaps, since you lambasted it.

Laszlo

For the first weeks, he spent his afternoons with Alice, and he discovered the quaint and the questionable pockets of his neighborhood. Alice was equally at home in the better cafes and fallen Kabarettes, and as recognized in both. It was enjoyable, but by the time spring's colors rose, he knew it was time to get to work.

In the mornings he studied the brain's hemispheres and made copious notes on everything from the nascent talking cure emanating from Austria to the most basic principles of electric current. Soon he'd created a rough schematic identifying where to place the galvanic electrodes. He would have a bit of lunch, a stroll past a nearby pond to watch toy boats sail and sink without a whimper from anyone but distraught children, and then get to work for the afternoon.

Observation: Mine was but one of many forms of transmission.

He wrote it on simple paper, not the canvas. First, he thought, I shall fail.

Making use of the telegraph office and August Bliekroder's files full of inventive and profitable men, courtesy of Alice, he opened a correspondence with an engineer at the Atlantic Telegraph Company who, in a series of telegrams, described the finer points of constructing a durable telegraph cable meant to traverse the ocean between Britain and India.

GUTTA-PERCHA STOP JUICE OF THE PALAQUEM GUTTA TREE STOP AN EXCEPTIONAL INSULATOR STOP WITHOUT INSULATION IT ISN'T TRANSMISSION BUT DESTRUCTION STOP

What sort of protection exists for an audible thought, he wondered.

A rather embittered assistant to a dead Italian sent him a parcel of notes and drawings that, per his accompanying letter, irrefutably established that said dead Italian, and not "that whiskered larder Bell," had pioneered the telephone. Fleischl had heard of the invention but had yet to see one. Alice, of course, had one of the first in her home.

"I'll show you how it works," she told him, "If I can think of someone compelling enough to call."

Signore Meucci did the telegraph one better, his correspondent wrote. *The voice rendered as a signal of electricity, carried over wire, turned back to sound and the receiving end.*

There were drawings of copper threads, magnets, vibrating diaphragms, the voice as current. The current, went the assistant's letter, is the electricity that moves the coil. Talk loud, big current. Talk soft, small current.

"And therein lies the issue with your work," Alice said one sunny afternoon in late May. She'd emerged from her hansom in chic, light clothing, invited him for a walk, and set an appointment for dinner the following week, at which time she expected to hear about his progress. She then invited herself into his building followed by her chauffer, who made several trips carrying boxes of files from the hansom's boot up three flights of steps and into the small apartment, where he deposited them in every available corner.

"You need to think ahead," Alice told him in his kitchenette.

"Ahead to what?"

"To whatever your experiment will be. It will have to involve stimulus, correct? Of a very loud sort, as this Meucci put it?"

"He's dead."

"A pity you couldn't have been in touch when that happened to see if anyone heard him."

"Dear God, Alice."

"Dear God nothing. This squeamishness only establishes my point. If you really want to prove this transmission idea, you'll have to test it on a living subject."

"I very much doubt a monkey could tell us much."

"As do I. Have a look," she said, gesturing to the boxes of files. "Start anywhere."

He opened the top box nearest the kitchen table. Selecting a file, he found a case history of a woman in the southern part of the country who, seemingly without reason or warning, had suddenly lost her hearing.

That one was followed in succession by others who had lost their abilities to walk, sleep, eat, speak and see.

One of the files was sealed with a wax stamp bearing August's chancellor designation.

"We're not to touch any file with that seal," Alice told him. "Those are August's private matters. It shouldn't be in there. He'd kill us both twice."

"What's in it?"

"I don't pry. Something to do with eye color. It's probably useless for our purposes. It was temporary, then it went away, so I'm told."

"Our purposes?" he asked. "What exactly am I supposed to find in all of these cases?"

"You're supposed to find a test subject," she said.

Alice had left a note atop the boxes. Directions.

Read this first – WHAT

The file was filled with an assortment of short papers on the use of water to break through catatonia, mania, and deep-seated, dark impulses. Ice bath immersion, scalding, even high-pressure water cannons.

He winced at water and cannon together again, and at the paper's closing line. *Results are promising, if harmful to test subjects.*

Read this next – Extremis

The methods grew darker. A Swede posited the introduction of hemorrhagic fever to burn away madness. A Frenchman hypothesized electric shocks applied to the testicles to control epileptic seizures.

Read last – WHY

Inside was a single brief paper.

On Human Trials: For The Sake of Man And State

A man enters a surgical theatre in hopes of cure. He awakens improved. He only awakens because many who came under anesthesia before him never woke.

A man is relieved of pain by precisely administered doses of codeine and morphine. He is relieved because many before him died from inexact dosages administered without knowledge.

We may say the same for fire, or the construction of our homes, or the navigation of the seas. Not everyone makes it. Still, it must be said: many die so we may forge ahead. We the intellectuals remember them. Society will not. Both are valid. It is how science and progress happen, and how capital finds its worthy causes. It has always been. For this simple, clear, historically proven reason, I support human trials. By the nature of our selections, those who die do so largely unremarked upon, yet they will improve the lives of our children and our nation through the eradication of mental traits that diminish us.

And so, among my holdings is a prison, location unimportant. What is important: in exchange for promises of leniency, there are men who will serve as subjects.

August Bliekroder

On the evening of their dinner engagement, he met Alice at Lutter & Wegner on Potsdamer Platz, in the verdant Charlottenstrasse. She sat at a center table, surrounded by a fashionable crowd of artists, writers and actors who'd left salons and stages for a chance to be seen at the right hour, by the right people. From the glances cast Alice's way, particularly those from men, it was clear everyone knew who she was. Heads turned and matches were kept at the ready should she bestow a look and with it, permission to approach her.

She wore a serene and satisfied expression. Waiters scurried past her, trays full of expertly balanced glasses of vintage champagne drawn from the cellar's exquisite stock. They made time on each pass to keep her flute full, and she sparkled as brightly as her glass of bubbly gold. She'd chosen a dress of deep blue, with rubies at her throat and cuffed lace on her wrists. Each time she moved, her jewelry caught the faint light of the chandelier above.

At the top of a short staircase to the restaurant's main floor, he felt uncomfortably beheld by a different sort of light. He wore the same suit she'd seen him in countless times. He'd neglected to shave that morning, and a fine if patchy stubble darkened his cheeks. He'd bathed and could at least be grateful for that.

Descending the steps, he followed the host to Alice's table

as practiced eyes studied him without subtlety. He was certain they found him lacking whatever qualities they were confident of possessing themselves. He was unworthy, and they far more deserving, of Alice's attention.

While he waited for the host to pull out his chair, Alice withdrew a compact from her purse and daubed at her face. Delicate clouds of talc rose into the light of the chandelier. He was certain she looked flawless from a few tables away, but sitting at her side it was not hard for Fleischl to make out the lines around Alice's tired eyes.

He set the files down next to a cheeseboard for two. She eyed them, then ordered him a champagne. "Your progress," she said flatly.

Over the cheese and a first course of lobster bisque ladled table side from a deep, silver taurine, he explained his idea for her galvanometer. He had a theory about dividing the hemispheres of the brain into a map of sorts, and a method for situating electrodes atop each section.

"Atop the skull of course. No more monkeys." He smiled queasily at how nervous he was and chastised himself for the number of times he looked at the files. Throughout his presentation, Alice consumed one champagne flute after another.

"I think," he said, "well, I believe, this method will greatly improve what the galvanometer can detect of the brain's currents."

She sipped quietly. He noticed her great boulder of a ring. The gift of a wealthy man to his wife. It was turned so that it almost cut into the skin of her middle finger, as if she'd been fidgeting with it.

"Oh," he said, "Laszlo asked that I speak to you about something I did for someone I treated." Through the main course, grilled squab on a bed of roasted root vegetables, he told her of Anton, the diorama in the library, and of giving Johannes back.

He kept Greta to himself.

"Interesting," Alice said. "Some promise there. Though not what I pay for."

No." He let the meat on his plate cool.

She waved down the waiter and asked for a brandy.

"Do you notice how people stare at us?" she asked when her glass arrived. "What do you suppose they think?"

There was a softly melting center to her words, owing to the headiness of all the alcohol he watched her consume.

"They think," she continued, "that August Bliekroder's wife is getting even at last. It's ludicrous, really. Ask anyone who thinks they know me. They'll tell you I've no feelings for anything or anyone. Just my work. You understand. I know you do. You're the same."

She tapped out a rhythm on the files. "He owns the galvanometer, you know. All my work and my name is nowhere to be found. Lost to history. No one will hear of me."

She applied another layer of powder to her already thickened face. He felt as if he was watching a magic act at the Bretl. A figment evaporating before his eyes, with only some dollops of makeup to show she was still there.

"I never asked you how you came to be married to August," he said.

"There's much to be found in what isn't said. Remember that, Fleischl."

"I will."

"I'd have thought by now you'd just know. August is the sort of man who keeps mistresses. Stupid girls who are easily impressed. I was one of them. The second. No, the third. It's hard to recall now. I do remember we married soon after his wife-at-the-time died. There at our wedding was his first wife's sister, telling me that she died from the broken heart I gave her."

"That was unfair of her," he said.

"There's no such thing as fair or right or any of that. Only the actions we take and the consequences they bring. If you can live with the consequences, that's all that matters. Remember that."

"I will."

An oddly somber tone had crept in between the congealing squab and the drained glasses. Alice was drunk, it was obvious, and elegiac, as drunks tended to be. For some reason he didn't understand, the dinner felt like something to be marked in a diary or commemorated quietly each year at roughly the same time of evening.

"Now August," Alice said, "can't be hurt. He possesses no heart to break. You may one day arrive at a place where you despise him enough to want to hurt him. You can't."

"I can't imagine being in his circles at all, let alone know him to such an extent."

"Remember that," she said.

He felt the need to comfort her, though he wasn't sure for what.

"I think you're a formidable, admirable woman who deserves credit for all you are. In any room where I've encountered you, you're unfailingly the smartest person there."

"And I think you're an idealistic dreamer, and something of a lost soul. Do you know what that makes us?"

"I don't."

"Impossible to love."

The waiter arrived with small wooden placards. Dessert, should they wish.

She paid the list of sweets close attention. "Tell me again," she said, her eyes on her choices, "about what happened to you at the army camp."

"You've heard it all," he said.

"Have I?"

She told the waiter to prepare a plate with one of each dessert for them to share.

"You don't ever speak of the one who heard you," she said. "Don't you agree, that's a crucial element?"

"It's irrelevant."

Her gaze grew steely. "You should welcome any interest in this thesis of yours," she said.

"Interest." Fleischl smiled.

"Is this mystery person who heard you male or female?"

"Female."

"Related by blood?"

"No."

"Marriage?"

"I've never been married, Alice."

"Love?"

"I don't understand your question." He tried to keep his voice low and steady, the way she would. "Love is not a condition of relation."

"You understand. Did you love this female who heard you, and if so, is this a necessary element to any experiment you think you need to perform?"

"It may be," he said.

"And since she heard you, would you say this love was reciprocal?" He hesitated.

"I suggest to you," she said. "I have a title for the paper that results from this."

She took a pen from her purse and wrote on the back of the dessert placard. Then she slid it across the table to him.

The Electric Love Song of Fleischl Berger

"This is obnoxious," Fleischl said. "You're drunk."

"I may be drunk, but I'm not wrong. Do you know why I gave you those files? Not because I expect you to choose a subject and go through with this. Because I know you can't."

"That's not true."

"It isn't? Excellent. Which man did you select?" She opened the top file. "Point him out. Tell me how you'll almost but not quite kill him. Tell me who loves them enough to listen for them. Or is that only true of you?"

"There's a way to prove this without subjecting anyone to what I went through. There must be. I just haven't found it. I need time."

"Do you still speak to this person who heard you?"

He hesitated. "No. Not for a long time."

"I already knew you didn't. I would have seen her. I would

have heard about her. The space she should take up in your life is a void. And there it is, Fleischl. The fact that you can have what no one else has and not do anything about it, just live alongside its absence, is all I need to know. You're too afraid to set the world on fire for what you believe, or for who it was who loved you like this. Like no one else, my young friend. That's why you'll content yourself with papers and nothing else. You'll live alongside this as if it was just an odd thing that occurred once."

She gathered the files and moved them to her side of the table. "That's not what I pay for. I pay for someone with the courage to be different than me."

"Where did you learn to be this way?" he asked.

"From men." Her point made, she closed the file. "I think you should stop, Fleischl. You'll never prove this thing that happened. This other, what you did for the old sailor, do that. The good work of a simple life."

Dessert came, but the artifice of the cakes repulsed him. With their dusting of crystalline sugar, they shone just like Alice.

"It seems," he said, "that you've decided I've failed."

She chuckled. "The sounds men make when challenged."

"I think it's time I left. My presence is unwelcome."

"Words for my stone," she said. "What will yours say, I wonder."

Something happened to me, he thought. "Get out," he said instead.

"Why?"

"I don't actually know."

"Take a walk. Get some air. Think about what I've said."

"What have you said, other than I should quit?"

"Goodnight, Fleischl Berger." She raised her empty glass. "I had hopes because of you."

He left the restaurant without meeting anyone's gaze. Not that it mattered. No one was interested in him. Unlike Alice, he could do nothing for them. Besides, they were all as drunk as she.

He was grateful no one could hear his thoughts careening

from indignation to anxiety. A high flame of humiliation raged in his chest, keeping company with his sour stomach. He could return to the restaurant and throw the dregs of her many glasses in her painted face. Or he could step aboard another ship and resume flax trading some- where, and no one would ever know that he'd been a man pursuing a greater purpose. Should he pass ten others on deck, odds were that at least one of them was no different. A man who was once, almost, something more.

His walk took him to the weathered door of the Kabarette Bretl. All along the way he catalogued the reasons why she was arro- gant and bitter and wrong. She was thinking of her own failings; she'd admitted as much. A powerful woman was what she wanted everyone to see. But she'd let him glimpse the aging wife whose husband took credit the way he took mistresses. Alice had taken it all out on Fleischl. She wanted too much from him. If she was ashamed to live alongside her failings, how was that his fault?

The entire way to the Kabarette door and inside, he wrestled with her note on the dessert card and her assessment of him. He took a seat in the back of the room, as far from the stage as possible, and like clockwork, his bravado gave way to the deep, unsettling suspicion that she was right. He'd never prove anything. He didn't have the will. What was he supposed to do, leap from a tower and hope a telegram arrived before he hit?

The worst of it was her proclamation about living alongside Greta's absence. With that dagger, whether she realized it or not, Alice had found his most soft and tender target. She must have spoken from painful experience, he thought. There was someone lost to her, too. Someone she lacked the courage to go after.

That makes us impossible to love, she'd said.

There in the corner he sat, feeling perfectly heartsick. I should just go home, he thought. In the morning, with a little coffee, I might even believe in myself again.

Hypothesis: I'm feeling more than a little drunk right now.

He ordered tea and watched the magician, Professor Lischke, rifle through his practiced patter for those few patrons still awake. It was simple enough to perceive the fraudulence in his mind-reading routine. A matter of puzzle and probability. Arrange enough guessed consonants and vowels, Fleischl thought ruefully, and you too can scratch a living from nocturnal Berliners desperate to hold on to their dearly departed. How people needed to believe!

The hour grew late. All he wanted was sleep without thoughts warring in his head. He returned to his apartment, where he found the door ajar.

Of course Alice has a key, he thought.

She lounged in one of the blue chairs, still in her evening finery. Her legs splayed in a crass manner reminiscent of the woman from the Bretl. Her head lolled back and her mouth hung open lewdly. Her hands steadfastly gripped the armrests. Then her body pitched fitfully forward and shook in vigorous denial of what was happening.

He saw the wires draped across the chair to the floor and back again to one of the batteries he'd made with the parts she'd left for him. There were electrodes at the other end. One attached to her neck, one to her lower back.

Wrong, he thought.

She was delivering currents of electricity to her spine and cortex. He pulled the wires from her, causing the battery to tip over.

He took her up in his arms and helped her slide out of the chair. They both ended up on the floor.

"Alice? Alice, wake up!" He slapped her until her eyes opened, then hoisted her back into the chair. She recovered quickly. Her breathing evened out. Daubing at her forehead, she apologized for her appearance.

You don't look all that different, he thought.

While she wiped her brow, he inspected the battery. It was small and not nearly powerful enough to kill her, or even harm her in any meaningful way.

"What did you think you were doing?"

"I wanted to know what it's like to be you," she said. "The only one in the world worth listening for."

"Alice..."

"Spare me your pity. I'm drunk. I can't go home like this."

He hefted her in his arms and carried her to his bed. Her heart beat impressively through her skin, into his. The body is a telegraph, he thought. We are all electric.

"You aren't the one I wanted to hear me," she slurred.

He was about to say that he hadn't heard her, but her eyes had already closed. She was asleep almost the moment her head touched his pillow.

He drew the caftan over her and began packing his things. When he finished, he composed a short note and set it on the nightstand along with his key. She never stirred. Her breathing was deep and sonorous. A dried tear had carved a pink path through her caked makeup.

He turned the note to face her, for her to find whenever she woke.

Perhaps this mediocre man will make something of himself yet, but it must be without your support, which I have deeply appreciated and can never adequately repay. I do hope it will be with your friendship, should you wish to offer it.

I don't know who it is whose absence you feel in your heart as I do mine, but I hope you recover them and never lose them again. And if anyone stands in your way, I hope you turn that impressive Alice Bliekroder ire on them and never let them best you.

You're well worth hearing, my friend.

Fleischl Berger

CHAPTER Eleven
The Ballroom

He left Alice's graces with no furnishings, only his clothes, his writings, and the glassed map of steps he didn't know how to take. With his humble savings, he managed to rent a pitiful apartment on a shaded lane just off of Kurfurstendamm. It consisted of a single room that held his cot, his books and papers, a counter for cooking that at night was overrun by ribbons of ants streaming from every crack in the walls—there were several—a small table, and two chairs he purchased on credit from a nearby thrift shop. There was also a radiator grill against the wall near the entry, which clanged and hissed like a steam train no matter how he tried to stop it. The gas lamps in the apartment's shadowy hallway cast just enough light by which to find his key though they also cast gusts of gas that conjured death by asphyxiation when he lay his head on his pillow and considered his current situation. He scarcely saw other lodgers. Those few he did encounter while passing them in the murk of the hallway seemed to be of the rough, nocturnal sort. He decided not to strike up any conversations.

He did have a window, for which he was grateful. It opened with a squeal and remained that way. Which was, all told, a perquisite.

Much of his view, of the skyline and a distant lush park, was mercilessly obscured by the construction that consumed the affluent parts of the neighborhoods along the Spree. With so little money left for any sort of entertainment, he spent a great deal of time staring out that window.

He renewed his correspondence with Meucci's assistant, and with the Atlantic engineer about his trans-oceanic telegraph. He haunted the library on the Babelplatz, where he perused the stacks in search of works on transmission of any kind. He sat on the wooden floor between the bookcases, studying and imagining a door somewhere nearby, and a sea tunnel beyond.

In the late afternoons he composed letters to Rapholtz, one per week, and he signed them all, "your nineteenth century procrastinator." He studied the relative brain pans of animals, looking for that sweet spot of semi-sentience between consciousness and unawareness, should he ever decide to experiment on something with the ability to stare back at him. He paced the apartment and imagined what it would be like to look out through his window and down to the street below to see Greta looking up at him like a lone, lit candle fluttering in the breeze. Come out, she would say. For dinner, or to run away together and see the world.

He made a point of attending all the late-night performances at the Kabarette. For a few extra pfennigs he became the favored assistant of several performers and a featured regular in the act of the Prescient Professor Lischke, mesmerist extraordinaire. One night, while waiting at the bar for their turn onstage, he asked the Professor how to terrify someone into believing without question that they were about to die.

"Without actually doing anything to them," Fleischl added emphatically, "that would hurt them in any way."

"Have you thought of hypnosis," Professor Lischke said. "A gentle bombardment, if you will, until the malleable mind silences to all but you."

Down the hypnosis path Fleischl went. He studied catalepsy,

lethargy and somnambulism before deciding that a malleable, placid mind was not at all what he'd felt at Kiel. But he'd made a friend in the Professor, one eager to please. So the Professor tutored him on the finer points of stagecraft as it applied to galvanism, magnetism and hydraulics. He taught Fleischl basic sleight of hand and even oversaw the construction of a rudimentary phantasmagoria from muslin. Together they cut out figures inspired by the scissors and the winged woman.

With Fleischl's help, the Professor debuted a new trick using a small battery built into his top hat, with wires running from the back of his head to the top of his buttocks. "A wave of my hand," he would exclaim, and a far candle—a small, curled bulb, really—ignited and then went out.

"It needs a name," Professor Lischke said.

While the Easily Lost Light pleased audiences at the Kabarette, it made Fleischl a little sad, and certainly didn't move him any closer to understanding what happened; it didn't magically return Greta, that so easily lost light of his own, and it certainly didn't afford him more than a few months' rent.

He tinkered, sulked, and mused during the daylight hours. On the evenings he wasn't at the Kabarette, he walked the avenues of Berlin in the deepening warmth of the late summer of 1898. The city was a symphony of comings and goings on the cusp of the new age. He took supper at the Cafe Baues on Friedrichstrasse, where he listened to his fellow diners complain about von Bismarck and the folly of Berlin as the capital of anything, let alone the empire. "Better it serves as capital to Brandenberg," was a typical sentiment. "Or Silesia. They're all coming here anyway."

They were bankers, members of insurance exchanges, engineers drawing the city's new skyline. These were fine men, quite unlike the red-eyed students and artists he encountered closer to home at Cafe des Westens, the bohemians who didn't speak of industry or Berlin's explosive growth, but of philosophy, theatre and, when their animated arguments turned upon the changes in their neighborhoods, the growing sense that Berlin was being taken away.

Poor men argue, rich men debate. For his part, Fleischl listened.

Nights in Berlin were heady. The stock exchange emptied out to waiting liveries surrounded by a throng of boys with red errand caps who held out their hands to receive messages and an unwaxed pfennig for their trouble, then ran to make deliveries to Siemens or Borsig before setting off to join the other wild boys sending word from Berlin's kaisers out to the reaches. An old waiter told him one evening that a man on foot was once able to traverse the city end-to-end in an hour. There had been a lovely area to picnic alongside a lake called Halensee, but it was a desert now. Good folk once lived and worked and ate in the vey place they stood, but no one did that anymore.

"Our city," said the old waiter, "paved under to make way for their city."

"Whose city?" Fleischl wanted to know.

"Theirs. The Grunewald men, the Lichterfelde men, the Charlottenburg men. The Bliekroders of the world, but mainly the Jews. The moneylenders. You know them when you see them."

Do you? Fleischl thought. The increasing frequency of remarks like that moved him to attend synagogue, but only occasionally.

One night, he stopped for something cold to drink at Pschorr's with thoughts of taking in an operetta at the Apollo —if he could spare the expense. His walks left him feeling increasingly lonely and directionless. Things weren't moving forward. In his apartment there was a poor battery with wires attached to nothing. He was in need, though he wasn't sure of what. So he passed up the Apollo in favor of the Orientalisch on a quiet corner away from the bright lights. The theatre was intimate, with heavy curtains that kept the sun and the elements out. Nothing but a kientopp, a room with chairs and a screen, and the contraption he'd seen in the theatre on Kurfurstendamm. Behind a white scrim he heard the whirring of turning wheels, and in the pale light beheld the boxer and the kangaroo, its paws held up like fists.

His eyes adjusted. The walls were decorated with sconces in the shape of gargoyles holding torchieres in their mouths. The flickering light picked up a bit of the deep red velvet drapes and cast it against the ceiling, imparting to the tiny kientopp a dark, decadent spirit.

Most of the seats were empty, with only two men sitting shoulder to shoulder. He took a seat two rows behind them, passing through the beam and the floating motes that glimmered like stars.
The screen emptied briefly, then opened on the path through the lush, holly garden, under the trellis.

He held his breath. The first glint of moonlight bloomed on the lake. What marvels, he thought. What unimaginable joy, to move to the mesh of stars reflected on the surface. There it was, the winged figure, small as the pit of a cherry, wandering into the frame of the camera's oval iris.

He began to cry softly without knowing why.

The figure twirled. It was so tiny and fragile as to be unreal. It shouldn't live. Such tiny twirling things at the water's very bottom didn't really have well-lit spaces in which to dance. If they did, they'd all still live.

The men in front of him held each other close and watched the screen. Once, as the little winged thing paused and ran swiftly out of sight, they kissed.

One of the men turned around. "Don't cry," he said. "It does no good."

"I can't help it," Fleischl whispered.

"Who among us can? We all come here to commune with secrets, don't we?"

When the water was gone, and the screen blank but for the harsh and unforgiving light, he went home. He didn't want company, or to walk any further. Just sleep.

★★★

A handwritten note arrived at his door the morning after the Orientalisch, carrying Alice's peculiar scent of citrus and spice. There was neither notation nor postage.

My dear herr Berger:

My conscience tells me, often, that I was harsh and unfair to you, and that I ran you off. Were I callous, I might suggest that you're no stranger to running off, but I won't give in to my base impulses so easily.

I'm fond of you, I suppose.

Please understand, it's not that I consider you an unmotivated crackpot (at best), or a liar (at worst), or that I suspect the thing that happened to you didn't really happen. What I said to you that night I would say again, though not as rudely, and not while drunk. It was for your own good. It was to encourage you to find the courage of your convictions or else go in a different direction. To that end, I want you to attend a dinner I'm giving. There will be some interesting people you might enjoy meeting. I'd like you to come. You can talk about what you did for that old man. Perhaps make it a bit more interesting than it sounds on paper.

A.B.

How might I possibly fit in with such people as you attract, he replied. *Not to mention your husband's antipathy toward me.*

Begin, she wrote, *by getting an appropriate suit. Then arrive by six at the very latest. After you've managed to accomplish those two relatively straight-forward things, stop thinking so much.*

★★★

August Bliekroder's home was like nothing he'd seen before. A villa carved from the forests of Wannsee just south of Berlin, it had been lovingly constructed during the Wilhelmine era and bore the year of the three emperors prominently.

Alice met him at the front door. "I already feel like I should leave," he told her. "It's simply not possible that someone like me belongs in a place like this."

"For now," she said, "I'm pleased you came. No running off."

She gave him a brief tour. There were seven bedrooms, two libraries, four studies, three banquet rooms, including a dining hall that was nearly as large as the university's lecture amphitheater. There were

servants' quarters, oak floors, and white-washed walls as clean as clouds.
Far behind the house, obscured from view by the darkness of nightfall,
there was a private woods, she said, and even more that, curiously, she
wouldn't elaborate upon.

"I'm sure he'll show it at some point tonight," she said as they
returned to the grand foyer. "He always does."

"Show what?"

"The lake." She smiled inscrutably. "What's in it. One of my
husband's many excesses. The wealthier the man, the less comprehensi-
ble the appetite. Remember that, Fleischl, should the day you succeed
come at last."

She was nervous and already a little tipsy, having consumed
three flutes of champagne since his arrival. She was one of the more
stoic Teutonic people he'd met, so the sight of her ill-at-ease made him
anxious. He gulped down a flute himself and accepted another from
a passing servant. He took that glass to the rear window of the foyer.
Beyond the mansion's lights, everything outside was darkness.

"My guests don't see anything I don't wish them to see."

August held out his hand in greeting, but Fleischl hesitated.
For the briefest of moments, he'd seen August's approach in the black
mirror of the window, hand held out, and imagined it was Anton Lautin
returned from the ravages of grief. And then his father. And then the cliff.

He wished his mind could simply lie still.

"Don't indulge too much before you've had the opportunity
to amuse my colleagues." August clapped him on the back. "Alice, your
young hobby demonstrates an appropriate degree of anxiety around
your husband, and like a good German he calms himself with a drink.
I might even come to like him slightly better, if he can avoid making a
fool of himself."

With Alice's arm slipped through his, he entered a cavernous
dining hall dominated by a slab of a wooden table adorned with ornate
candelabras, loose sprays of wildflowers, and seasonal sprigs of laurel.
Platters of food were crowded one against another. Heaping bowls of

kartoffelpuffer and sauerkraut vied for space next to wooden blocks laden with carp and trout mousse. He counted thirteen fully roasted geese, one for every four seats, bread dumplings, braised cabbage, and short ribs in a thick brown sauce. Gloved butlers seated guests beneath the game trophies.

He and Alice sat together. August sat on the opposite side of the table, which divided itself into quadrants of theory, polite argument, and ribald humor. August navigated them all. Alice drank.

"A healthy union requires distance to survive," she told Fleischl in a low voice. "From that distance, flaws are indistinguishable from virtues."

The philosophical stage of drunkenness had arrived. Soon, he thought, she would sing. Or cry.

"Before we commence the argument portion of our evening," August announced over the din, "let me say a little something about the new face in our midst. Berlin crawls with spiritualists, mesmerists, and doggerel religions. I should know, I employ some of them. Perhaps this 'preeminent psychiatrist' will rise above all that. Perhaps he can't, owing to his disposition, heritage and preoccupation with the fantastical. I'll let him speak to that. I give you Fleischl Berger."

August beckoned Fleischl to stand. He did, as a cold trickle down his back moistened his shirt. "After such comments," he said, "I hardly know where to begin."

He gazed around the room. "My name is Fleischl Berger. I've a bit of ability with psychiatry. I also have ideas for improving the way we treat patients who are otherwise presumed…"

Alice nodded encouragingly.

"Lost," he said. And here he briefly described his work with Anton. "There's some promise," he concluded, "in using visual aids to reach people like him."

"Perhaps we can discuss that further," August said.

"I would require a salary," Fleischl told him.

"I certainly didn't mean to suggest…"

"And a share of the patent," Fleischl said, "for any mechanism

I create. It will be known as mine."

The table grew quiet.

"My, how lean times and a wealthy woman change a man," August said, to even greater laughter this time. "Provide me a proposal, herr Berger, and perhaps something will come from it."

"Visual?" asked a gaunt, wiry man about Fleischl's age. "Such as a photograph?"

"Or even the capture of motion," Fleischl said. "A way to provoke to the mind."

"Fascinating. May I ask how this idea came to you?"

He looked down, but only for the moment it took to bring his father in, and his mother's grave, and Thalhammer on the bluff where home once was, and the sea one thousand, seven hundred and two steps away.

He felt the old telegram in his pocket. Always with him, always there.

"Something happened to me," he said, and left it there.

★★★

Late in the evening, a roaringly drunk Alice argued with August in a rustic anteroom, before a hearth the size of the burghemeister's guild hall. Though he tried not to listen, Fleischl did manage to overhear Alice spit, "You should just hear without me having to say it."

Then came a gaggle of men in rapid succession. Ties loosened and more effervescent drinks swept in on trays. Cigar coals flared. The mansion's many rooms became speakeasies full of bawdiness and drunken jokes.

Gradually, Fleischl drifted away to a window made red with firelight. He rested his throbbing head against it and considered leaving without saying goodbye.

"I imagine this is a lot to take in."

It was the man who'd asked how he'd come up with the notion of using moving images in psychiatry. They stood together at the window. "I'll admit it is," said Fleischl.

"August told me a bit about you. About what you say happened."

"He made it sound perfectly credible, I'm sure."

"Not even a little bit. But I'm interested in your story anyway, and your hesitancy. Do you not think of what happened to you as something worth pursuing?"

The man's voice possessed a warmth and melody that put him at ease. "No one believes what happened, and I don't know how I'd ever prove it."

"These are all fine, accomplished men here tonight. Fine German men. But never fear that there isn't still a place for dreamers in the colossal engine that is Germany. Dreamers do the things that last. Always, they're the ones who are laughed at, shunned, or worse for having the chutzpah to do it anyway."

"You're a Jew?"

"As are you, if I'm not mistaken. Mishpucha."

"I'm not terribly religious, I'm afraid."

"Nor I. Proud of what I am? Yes. But do I dedicate myself to a thousand-year-old health law? I like my schweinebrauten."

"It's true."

"Let me tell you about the rich Jewish history of arguing with God, my friend. Do you know the Kabbalah? The mysticisms of our people? Something as easily understood as the number eighteen actually means life. There are always smart, practical, powerful men, Fleischl. Always. But look among them for the dreamers like us who see what else there is. You'll find your place. And when you do, invite me over. I'm tired of goosefat and cognac and talk of Prussian greatness. I far prefer chasing the divine."

"How drunk are you?" Fleischl asked.

"Wildly so. We're men of clay. Think about this now. Clay over time becomes dust. It's too short a time. So we should spend it trying to touch the divine. Maybe no one will believe us if we manage to. But we'll know. We should die trying, don't you agree? Belief in something wondrous fuels every discovery, every art, every science."

"So do accidents," said Fleischl.

"My long-winded way of saying, don't let others stop you from believing in what you know. Once, there was ridicule for the idea that we could hold a moment of life still. And now? Daguerrotypes. Cameras. Even images that move. Have you by chance ever seen some of the moving pieces of film at the Orientalisch?"

"I have. It was the most beautiful thing. I can say it's what caused me to consider pairing it to psychiatry. There was one in particular. Water, and something below the water. My God."

"My good new friend, I hope you don't think me a braggart. But I'd like nothing better than to see your face in a moment's time. Follow me."

Fleischl did, and a veritable museum emerged around every corner. August Bliekroder had assembled the most magnificent collection of art he'd ever seen. The man's appetites ran a wide gamut, from trophies of kills to fine Persian ceramics. The display of wealth was staggering.

"Nothing is as tragically beautiful as folly," his companion said. "This Victorian assembly we walk through is testament to that. I'm usually not this pompous, but I am drunk and am happy to hold forth. The next time we meet, I'll be quite boring."

They passed beneath a bronze head so large it filled the upper part of the room. "Dolphin," his companion said. "Workers had to quite literally lower the road just to pass it under a bridge on the way here. Imagine! Ah, we're coming to my side of things, as it were."

"I'll never live such a life as these people," Fleischl said.

"I was just thinking the same thing. Perhaps you heard me."

"Funny. I'm quite certain we can attribute that one to simple intuition. It's impossible to walk the halls of this mausoleum without marveling. Or retching, depending on your frame of mind."

"You sound more in the latter camp."

"And you?"

"I'm betwixt, herr Berger. On the one hand, I don't appreciate ostentatiousness. I find it wasteful. What I manage to earn with my work goes right back into my work. That's passion, I suppose. On the other hand, he and Alice are patrons whose funding makes my work possible. Why, I've used this very property for some of my projects."

"What is it that you do?"

They arrived at a surprisingly understated door of simple, weathered wood. His companion found a switch on the wall and flicked it up. Outside, a string of tiny lights ignited. They formed a delicate path into a canopying tunnel of thickly intertwined holly boughs.

"Oh," Fleischl breathed. "Oh, it can't be."

"I make moving pictures, Fleischl. I'm so pleased to meet you. My name is Oliver Galeen."

The lights flickered on in succession, away from the house, until the furthest ones lit, far down the tunnel.

"I've seen this," said Fleischl.

"It seems you have."

"Is it here?"

"I believe I know what you want to see. Come. Ah, Alice! Join us, won't you?"

Alice approached the door, drink in hand.

"But of course she will," August said. "Sooner or later, she's always out there."

Fleischl followed Oliver through the quaint door, then a garden, and into a ramshackle woods. The lights strung were through the trees overhead. He glanced back to see Alice pass under a pale circle. Her face was taut. She appeared nervous.

August brought up the rear, the coal of his cigar burning in the dark.

Ahead, Fleischl saw the dappling of moonlight across an inky, rippling surface.

"What is that?"

"Four lakes' worth of water," said August.

A knot of limbs had grown around a door near the edge of the water, next to a wooden dock that stretched forth from two rough-hewn stone pillars. The dock reached a few dozen meters into the water. There was a rail along the dock and a gazebo at the end, and he saw that the enormous lake was surrounded by forest.

"I promise, it's quite stable," said Oliver, setting a foot onto the first slat of the dock. The muffled report of heel on wood reminded Fleischl of Stralsund's docks.

He followed Oliver onto the lake. Spatters of stars cast faint light out to the tree line. The lights of August's house glowed warmly behind them. The buzzing of crickets echoed through the cool night air. Occasionally, a splash would interrupt the silence.

"Carp," said August as they walked to the gazebo. "They come to the light."

Fleischl kept his hand on the rail. Ahead was the silhouette of a small outbuilding resembling a tiny observatory, rounded like a pastry, constructed on the dock. A thin needle poked out of the top, toward the sky.

Oliver paused on the pontoon. Fleischl joined him at the rail. "There," Oliver said. "That's precisely one hundred feet down. Am I right, August?"

"That's correct."

"In my camera, I made it look even further and smaller. Do you see what it is? Can you tell?"

At the lake bottom, there was a great dome of glass. Its light rose through the water in an oily palette of yellow and heather. He could see an open space, parquet flooring, torchiers on the walls like the lights strung through the trees.

"It's a ballroom," Fleischl said.

"Entry and exit back there," Max said, pointing to the rustic door they'd passed on shore, on their way out of the garden path. "I love it best from here. It's…how shall I put it? Creamier. More a dream than a physical space that can be occupied. Here is where I stood when I made the images you saw."

"I saw a figure," Fleischl said.

"Yes," Alice said quietly. "You did. I'm going back to the house. I feel a chill."

"Fleischl," Oliver said, "would you like to see the entrance up close?"

"If it's quite all right, not yet." He lingered in the honeyed glow of the underwater ballroom.

"My friend, may God bless you for saying that. Never let reality ruin your imagination, not until it absolutely must." He allowed the others past. When they were on the shore of the lake, he told Fleischl, "that happens each time August inflicts this on his wife. There's someone who frequently stays down there. August's ward. I say 'ward.' The truth is, she's most likely his mistress. An extraordinary girl, I should emphasize. I find her a bit of a muse myself, though not in a prurient way. That's who you saw in the ballroom. I remember vividly the day we filmed her. Odd, to say the least. Come back to the house when you're ready. I'd like to talk about some way we might work together on your ideas. Two dreaming Jews, staring at the cosmos and believing the cosmos stare back."

"I will. Thank you for this. It's more than I could have imagined."

"I don't believe that for a moment. You're capable of great imaginings. I can tell these things."

In a moment he was alone, with only the far footfalls of his new friend passing into the trees near August's estate. Movement below caught his attention. He looked down and saw a figure in the ballroom. The water made a dream of it. The light rippled around it, bent and distorted it. Nothing of it was clear, and yet he felt distinctly that it was gazing at him.

In an instant, the figure's arm rose, reaching for something. Then the light of the ballroom disappeared.

He crossed to the shore, then made his way to the rustic entrance atop a slight dune of grass. It truly was something out of a fairy tale, the way the wood of the entry seemed to grow out of the thick ivy that framed it. He tried the knob and found it difficult to turn, as if the years had rusted it in place.

There was a thin seam between the wood and the jamb. He could just make out a bit of wall, and the beginning of what looked like a steep staircase down into the dark. He waited there a long time.

When Oliver came back out they passed pleasantries. He told Fleischl to take care around the Bliekroders, particularly Alice, and particularly now that he'd been brought in as far as he had. "She's a fierce advocate," Oliver said, "until she isn't. She's capable of turning on people quickly."

"I understand," Fleischl said.

"You don't. And it's best that you don't."

They passed a few more quiet moments, then Oliver left him alone. He thought about what his new friend said. He wanted to stay near the door, just to see if anyone climbed up from the bowels of the lake. He didn't know why it mattered, only that it mattered enough to remain.

After an hour, when the house and the lake were perfectly dark, the door finally cracked open.

"I never come up until I know I'll be alone. I'm not welcome in the house, nor do I want to be there. But I came because I saw you."

He couldn't speak.

"If you're wondering how, so am I. I suppose we were bound to find each other. Just not the way we think."

There was a buzzing in his head and it could have been the electricity in the wires of lights.

"I know," she said. "It's too much. Shall we start simply? A hello."

He nodded dumbly. The mere motion made him dizzy. "Hello."

"Hello, Fleischl Berger," Greta said.

CHAPTER Twelve

The Glass House

"He lets you live down there."

"She does as well. In some ways more so."

The morning sun was beginning to blaze through the tree line. There was a paling of sky between the leaves. A heavy mist descended to frost the still surface of the lake. Where it had been quiet all around him at the moment she'd emerged from the ballroom, now he was aware of birds and splashing fish.

"I come when I want." Greta smiled, and it spoke of the silent life she'd known without him.

"I suppose it's preferable to being seen in public together," he said.

"I'm a friend, Fleischl. A muse is what I hear people call me most often. I'm only a secret to those who don't know."

"Are you a muse to Oliver as well?"

"Yes, I'm his mistress and August's mistress, this one's mistress, that one's. I'm no one's, Fleischl, whether they like it or not. You of all people should know what it takes for me to be with someone. It takes more than most have ever shown to me. Perhaps all."

"I suppose that was meant to hurt me."

"It's been quiet between us for a long time. If all you want is to discuss the details my personal life since I last saw you, perhaps it should stay that way."

"I've much to apologize for," he said. "I know that. But I had to leave. Everything I loved was gone by my own hand."

"No." She shivered in the cold dawn air and he offered his coat, but she refused it. "Not everything. Just me. The rest? By life or God or whatever you choose to call it."

"I'm sorry. I've wished on my life to take it all back since I left. I was empty without you, and then that day."

"Empty is a good word. Fill it with what you can. For me it's the stage. Oliver's film. Others."

"Please tell me what happened to make you send the telegram. Did you actually hear me? Was it real?"

"When someone else tries to put their hand where yours once was, is that real? Do you hear me?"

"Go ahead, then. Do my voice. Make me a coward who ran away. But I beg you, tell me why you reached out across the distance. No one believes me. I don't believe it myself, sometimes. But I have to know what happened to make you come back to me after everything. On telegraph wires, Greta."

"I didn't come back to you," she said. "And I won't have this discussion here."

"Where?"

"Where you are for me. Below the surface."

★★★

He followed her down a twisting stone staircase that plunged them deeper into a darkness illuminated only by soft green phosphorous. As the space grew narrower with each turn of the steps, he grasped a metal banister and tried not to panic.

"I know," Greta said. "It's different, yet not."

The tunnel was narrower and far longer than the library tunnel they were both thinking of. It was shaped like a spade drawn from a deck of cards. Its old stone walls were slick with condensation. The floor was carpeted with patches of dead algae. Here and there he saw the pinnacles of lake vegetation poking through cracks in the limestone foundation.

She led him down the long corridor toward a dim golden light. He heard water outside the walls. When he placed his hand on the damp stone, he felt it churning on the other side.

"It's always different," she said. "The lake, the way it sounds. I can hear when it rains. The echo as it hits the surface of the water is just like bells."

The golden light ahead took on a greenish hue as they drew near. It filled a larger room beyond, empty and domed in glass that bled tones that hearkened to air before a storm. The dome's center stood forty feet above. It was curved like the backbone of a whale and was composed of hundreds of small, square panes of glass. Light refracted in the water and filled the ballroom with an iridescent, shifting color palette of green, yellowish gold, and hints of mauve. Every few feet of the ballroom's parquet floor held a new season.

"Alice told me once when she was drunk," Greta said, "that the architect didn't intend it to be lit this way. It's because of the sun, even the moon if the water isn't stirred up, and the way the plants in the lake absorb and reflect the light. The way the stones bend it at the bottom. She said it was the same with me in her life; I'm, here whether she wants it or not. Things you plan for don't happen and the world turns colors you couldn't have imagined. Isn't that sad? The rich wife of an old man, pining for a different life. I suppose it's no different with you and that day. It wasn't, and then it was, and here you are. Trying to understand what color the world is now."

She put her hand on a doorknob. It was odd, the way she lingered over it.

"What's behind there?" he asked.

"Just a closet. Nothing too mysterious. I keep some wine."

"You seem nervous."

"Don't do that, Fleischl."

"I'm not doing anything."

"You're like you were. Trying to figure things out from the voice."

"Tell me what you heard."

"This needs to stop," she said. "I didn't hear anything. Nothing happened. It's a coincidence, that's all. I was thinking of you and how long it had been, and a silly feeling came over me. A bad phrase, and I shouldn't have sent a telegram, clearly."

"To Kiel. To exactly where I was at exactly the time."

"Stop it. I remember your father's map as well as you. I stared at it for hours, you bastard, because that's where he was going to take you away to, and that's how long it would have been. It had been a year. Kiel was the last place. There's nothing else to say."

"I don't believe you."

"You don't want to believe me. That's different."

She sat down and folded her legs like a yogi. "I was part of a theatre troupe when August and Alice came to see us perform. An old folk tale, Der Golem. A Jewish story, you'd be proud. We went through Europe with it. The Bleikroders came to see us in Berlin. Our little troupe was out of money by then, and along comes a daft folly of a man. Wealthier than God. An industrialist, an investor, a Chancellor. What didn't he do. A tycoon, and in our audience. And his homes! One in the city, one in the country. He had one in Paris he said he would take me to. He says it to every woman he encounters, young or old. He needs to. Alice told me early on, people are either to be pitied or profited from."

"Which are you?"

"He's mentioned you. He knows nothing of us, obviously. Neither does she. He calls you a lying Jew his wife fancies. He thinks you're a fraud after her money. Which is his money, after all."

She was right about one thing. It had been a long time since they had been so close. He felt his heart's original ache at the sight of her. She was near enough to touch. But she was also terribly far, and something about her was wrong. The high, assured brightness in her voice. She wouldn't look at him. He'd hurt her, true, but the Greta he knew would have held his eyes with her own. She would have opened his hands like a book so he could read what he'd done, forced him to see what she saw. This Greta was hiding.

"It's you in Oliver's moving picture," he said. "You wore wings."

She didn't look at him.

He gazed up through the ballroom dome. Only a bit of the greenish light permeated the glass to dapple the floor. The ballroom disappeared into waves of shadow. "Sound carries so strangely down here."

He walked to the closet door. "You ran here in the end. You were dancing, you wore wings like the library, and then you just ran. Jesus, Greta. It happened here, while Oliver was filming you."

He leaned against the wall as the realization fell upon him like a coat of lead. The film that fascinated him was the very moment he'd almost died, transmitted from hundreds of miles away to nitrate and to her.

"Nothing happened," she said. "I ran because I didn't like feeling what I felt. It made for a good ending, Oliver said."

He could see her body quivering.

"Why are you so obsessed with this idiotic notion?" she asked. "Aren't you selling flax? Or working at Thalhammer?"

"Neither."

He told her all of it. All the life that moment had brought him, from the camp to the Kabarette to his first glimpse of a figurine the size of a pinhead.

She studied him. That much hadn't changed. She could evoke the truth with her eyes. It was different from Alice, who placed a pit in his chest with such looks. Greta's eyes were candles, beckoning him to come out.

"That's what I was doing until your telegram. You were gone to me until that day."

"I'm still gone to you. Look up."

He waited for the shimmer of the water to settle. It was full of moving light which he knew to be the carp catching the sunlight on their scales. Above it was the muted white of the pontoon and a grey smudge.

"Is that a person?" he asked.

"Someone's watching us."

"August? Alice?"

"Maybe Alice, or a servant or a visitor. Perhaps they can't see us. Perhaps they're just admiring the water. Understand this, if nothing else. You're looking for what doesn't exist, just like your father. If you choose to spend the rest of your life trying to prove this, you're choosing to live with death every day. Again. That's your business. I'm not a part of it. I'll never be a part of it."

He looked up at the pontoon. Whoever had been there was gone.

"Go home," Greta said. "Go set fire to the Electric Love Song and everything you think you've wanted since that day."

★★★

Oliver Galeen's studio was ideally suited to Fleischl's state of mind, filled as it was with sound and, especially, light.

Located in the rear of a modest country wood and stone cottage in Rathenor, about fifty miles west of Berlin, the studio was a glassed greenhouse and a wonder to behold. It stood forty feet high and half as wide. It featured a steepled roof and windowed walls with not a bit of hindrance to keep the sun from filling its interior from dawn until the last bit of twilight.

Thanks to the capacious light, Oliver maintained a schedule as diurnal as the days. He tinkered with his contraptions and outlined his stories, filmed all midday while the sun was high, and by nightfall he was cloaked in a corner, developing prints.

Two days after seeking Greta in the ballroom, Fleischl stood in the middle of the glass house, his head in a whirl and his heart struggling to make sense of where it all left him. The simplest answer, he'd heard it said, was often the right one. Greta's answer was above all, simple. Nothing happened. A coincidence. Unfortunate timing, perhaps. Even if she had intended to be cruel, it didn't mean she was somehow prescient. Words took on terrible shape from the violence at his end, but there hadn't been violence at hers.

And yet there was something in Greta's eyes and in the way she refused to look at him, and in the way she spoke, as if every word plummeted down from somewhere high. That was what brought him to Oliver's storied glass house with his arms full of pads and pens, to see the man's newest mechanism. Over the course of the morning, he filled pads with notes on celluloid nitrate, chemical dousings, sixteen frames per second. *Each frame held by claws, turned by gear teeth until the image leaves where it was in the world and arrives in the cinematographe housing.*

Next to that note, he wrote a word he hadn't used in a while. *Transmission.*

"There's precedent for what happened to you," Oliver said. Tucked comfortably in a bright corner of the studio, he smiled at Fleischl while inspecting the guts of a shiny, black, rectangular box on a small table. Its black finish was polished to a high sheen. All manner of odd appendages studded its painted skin. A curled tube, a handle, a smooth cylinder like a candle pierced through with a rod.

"If there is," Fleischl said, "I've certainly never run across it. And I've looked."

"It's called p-energy," Oliver told him. "Psychic energy. It's a subject of study and debate in certain circles."

"Dear God, Oliver. For a moment I thought you were serious. That's not exactly scientific."

"Hear me out." Oliver closed the box and rested his hand on it. "The camera obscura didn't sound scientific, nor the cinematographe I use. Nor this device I'm about to introduce you to. You're acquainted with the telegraph, obviously."

"Obviously."

"One day, someone thought of adapting the oldest form of communication across distance, signal fires and shadows, by adding electricity. That sounds highly unscientific. Have I told you that I attend the occasional meeting of the Pansophic Lodge?"

"I hesitate to ask."

"It's a loose affiliation of occultists, magicians and specialists in the hermetic and alchemic arts. Don't look at me like that. It's great fun, a wonderful source of story ideas, and they serve excellent refreshments. I've met some interesting people, people with money, Fleischl. And I'd be happy to make introductions for you."

"I think it best not to describe my experience as occult," Fleischl said.

"Oh, they believe in all sorts of nonsense. Ectoplasm, levitation. One story I heard there did remain with me because it wasn't told by a believer in psychic energy, but the young man it happened to. Have a seat near this unscientific contraption, enjoy a glass of Reisling and let me tell you about the widow."

Fleischl sat next to the device. Oliver was a gregarious, warm and generous host, and he didn't doubt the sincerity of the story, but in the days after Greta appeared from nowhere he was confused enough. He didn't need an occult affiliation to muddle things further.

"This young man, Albin, went to see a spiritualist on a whim. He simply noticed a stenciled sign on a window in Hamburg, stepped inside, and spent the next hour with a man who told him he heard the dead. Albin thought it a sham until this man said someone was speaking, someone Albin knew who'd died years before. He spoke of a story Albin had written. This dead friend knew precisely where Albin kept it. A middle desk drawer. He knew so many things no one could possibly know. At the end, he told Albin that his dead friend warned, beware the widow."

"Who was the widow?"

"That's just it. Albin didn't know any widows. The next day, he was hosting a party for his uncle when someone almost fell into a spider's web."

"Ah. A black widow. Clever. An effective story for the Kabarette."

"It's also transmission, Fleischl. If you believe it."

"The problem," Fleischl said, "is that people hear my story and respond in precisely the same way I'm responding to yours. A fanciful little tale that can't be proved, only believed. And no one believes me. Greta says nothing actually happened. A moment's thought of me and macabre timing. That's all, and that makes the most sense. Yet I can't shake it."

Oliver's eyes met his, then skittered off to the far corner.

"What is it?" Fleischl asked him.

"I shouldn't say anything that might only make your predicament worse."

"Please."

Oliver drew a breath. "I wasn't in the ballroom with her that day, as you know. I was filming her from the dock above. But I know what I saw and I know how she was. She was terrified. She screamed, and it was chilling. I heard it through the water. It all came from nowhere. None of us knew what had happened down there. She was alone, just a girl in wings, and then she ran into that little closet with her hands over her face. She wouldn't come out for the longest time. I could hear her sobbing. When she finally opened the door and rushed out, she wouldn't say anything. She wouldn't talk about it. To this day she won't talk about it."

The sound of footsteps drew their attention. Alice was walking through the manicured garden that separated the main house from the studio.

"Ah, she's here," said Oliver. "I invited her to see this machine. She did underwrite it, after all. My friend, you look stricken. I should have said nothing. I don't want to reopen a settled matter."

"Far from settled. Even when I left that dinner with Alice, it was all I thought about. Then Greta reappeared. And now this."

He rubbed his eyes as Alice opened the glass door. "I thought I could leave it."

"It obviously can't leave you," Oliver said.

They stood. Alice greeted Oliver with a firm handshake, and Fleischl with a proffered cheek for him to kiss. "You don't seem pleased to see me," she said.

"Of course I am. Things on my mind, is all."

"You've been rather distant."

"I'm sure I have. But I'm here now, and apparently we're to see something wondrous."

"Hear something wondrous," said Oliver. He adjusted the cornucopia. "Who's ready for the remarkable?"

"What do you call this beast?" asked Alice.

"It's a soundwriter," said Oliver. "Can you believe it? A marvel to mark the century's end."

"Is this your invention?" Alice asked.

"God no. See the signature on the side? Herr Edison came up with this. But I have thoughts, Fraulein. Improvements, always improvements."

"Which will require funds," Alice said with only a hint of amusement. "Always funds."

Oliver leaned over the cornucopia. "Watch the needle."

Slowly, loudly, he recited their names into the horn. As he repeated them several times, the needle quivered across the surface of a wax cylinder. He turned a crank handle as he recited, rotating the cylinder and cutting grooves into the wax. When he'd finished, he replaced the needle down at the beginning of the first groove and cranked the handle again, setting the cylinder spinning. The needle slipped into the string-like divot, bobbing up and down along its path.

Oliver Galeen. Alice Bliekroder. Fleischl Berger.

"Remarkable," Fleischl said. "Isn't it, Alice?"

"But what do you do with such a thing?" she asked.

"I'm thinking about the combining sound with moving images." Oliver spoke loudly, to be heard over the tinny rasp of his recorded voice caroming from the walls. "Sound, light, and image in harmony? I don't know much yet. But it's fascinating to consider, isn't it?"

"So repeated sound creates a pattern," Fleischl said, "one that can be followed. Like a map."

"Just like a map. Implications for your own work, perhaps. Alice, don't you agree?"

Alice had stepped away without them noticing. She was holding Fleischl's notes and reading. "Explain," she said curtly.

"Along with the sort of work I did for Anton," Fleischl said, "I'm…revisiting transmission."

"And subjects?"

"I recognize the need."

"Things seem to have changed for you since the dinner party at my home. Perhaps making Oliver's acquaintance did it."

"They're just thoughts, Alice. I remain intrigued."

"I trust you're not one more pathetic man trying to impress an ingenue," Alice said. "I saw you talking to her."

"She's from Oliver's moving picture. I was interested in what it was like to be filmed. I've no interest in impressing anyone."

He had learned to stand his ground by watching her, and he hoped he in no way resembled a man thinking of a candle flickering in a long-ago window.

"I hope that's the case," Alice said. "When someone lies to me, they're something more than dead to me. Far more. It's laughable if you think you're the only one who's ever looked at her, on my property or off. Even now she's on a stage, in a play we paid for. A revival of some Jew tale. A merchant, of course, and a Muslim and a Christian knight. Or some such."

"*Nathan Der Wiese,*" Fleischl said.

"You know it?" Alice fixed him with a withering look.

"I saw it once."

"Shall we see it?" Oliver asked, excited as a child. "It's been ages since I saw a story alive in the room with me rather than from the inside of a camera, waiting to be pieced together. Come, let's make a night of it."

"Go without me," said Alice.

"I can understand how you feel," Fleischl said.

"You don't even begin to understand how I feel."

"With your permission, I'll accompany Oliver."

"You certainly don't require my permission."

"But I do ask for your peace of mind."

"Well, thank you, then, for caring enough to say that."

"May I say one more thing before you go?"

She waited by the glassed door.

"Please don't lose sight of the fact that I'm Jewish," he said.

"I know that," she said, as her expression fossilized. "Don't be hyperbolic."

After she left, Oliver turned to him. "There's more like them, you know."

"We're to be pitied or profited from, so I hear."

"So we pity and profit from them right back. Now, let's us two Jews go see some good Germans onstage, pretending to be us."

"I'd like to ask a favor before we go. I want to see the film of her in the ballroom. Please."

It didn't take long, such were the wonders of Oliver's many machines. The soundwriter and the cinematographe held promise. But as he settled beneath the long black shroud Oliver situated over him, the old phantasmascope began turning like the pistoned wheels of a train and the first flicker of incandescence appeared against the glass wall before him, a grainy image of the only thing he cared about played across what any sane person would have called a window.

The little winged figure came to a halt exactly as he'd seen before. But this time it felt violent. *What's happening to you?* She ran, covering her face with her hands. *Why are you lying to me?*

He watched her leave. Moving closer, he was tempted to believe he could reach the same closet door and save her from himself.

Only scared, lost boys put their stock in belief.

Oliver asked him if he was all right under the shroud. He didn't answer. He remained near the iris of light that spit from the phantasmascope until the last frame crawled past a boy who didn't die.

★★★

He found the troupe's rendering of *Nathan Der Wiese* surprisingly moving. Out of balsa, plaster and curtains, they had invoked a shtetl, a series of cottages, a small tavern, stone-paved streets, villagers in schmatta and nobles in finery. He felt nostalgic. There was a moment when the merchant, learning of his daughter's near death, touched the Star of David pendant on her chest, Fleischl felt a queer longing for the world on that stage, where no one was profited from or pitied.

They remained after the production had ended and the curtain had dropped. He wanted Greta to know he was there, that he saw how she still could disappear. Her every moment was a figure behind a sheet the length of a library, wearing wings and trailing lights.

It was late when a trio of women walked onstage with mops and buckets and set to scrubbing the hardwood. Greta emerged from behind them, accompanied by a lumbering, half-dressed monster. Gray from the face down, the creation looked every inch a stone sculpture.

"I saw you," said Greta.

"You were extraordinary," Oliver said. "Truly. And you, sir."

"I'm grateful." He extended a hand. "Paul Wegener. Forgive the appearance." He worked his fingers beneath a thin skin running the length of his forehead. "It sticks. I lose a bit of hair every time I remove it."

"What is it?" Fleischl asked. "It looks as if you're tearing your own scalp free."

"Excellent!" Wegener held a flap up for Fleischl to inspect. "It's for our next production, *Der Golem.* Greta showed me. She's been experimenting with makeup, prosthetics. She's quite creative."

"It's not difficult," Greta said. "A mold. I took a plaster cast of his face and head, and then poured a hot, liquid plastic into it.

When it cools, it's like skin. I painted it and sewed hair into it.
Then I packed wax into it to make his forehead look more prominent."

"You're quite versatile," Oliver said.

"Indeed," said Fleischl. "You've mastered the ability to hide who you are."

She eyed him coolly.

"All the small things you did onstage. The way you spoke suggested that you were used to the harder lot in life. You seemed weary. You weren't sure what to do with the attention of men."

"How closely you observed me," said Greta.

"There is truly no better patron of the arts," Wegener said, "than one smitten with the magic. Bid her farewell, gentlemen. She leaves us tomorrow for a while."

"Indeed?" Oliver asked. "Don't tell me you're going to be filmed by someone else? Not those scoundrels Lumiere and Melies!"

"Nothing like that, dear Oliver. Just going home for a brief time."

Fleischl studied her freshly washed face. "If I may ask, has something happened?"

"Something is always happening somewhere," she said. She walked past him, up the soft slope of the theater toward the exit.

"Rehearsals in a week," Wegener called after her.

"I'll be back."

"Who will you be in the next one?" Oliver yelled.

"That's always the question," she called back.

Fleischl excused himself and caught her at the theatre door. "You're going back to Stralsund. I didn't know you visited home."

"I haven't. But now I need to."

"I want to talk to you. I have things to ask. I need answers, Greta."

"I've no answers to give. Your questions don't concern me. My father's ill."

"Is it Serious?"

"He no longer knows who anyone is. Including himself."

She stepped into the lamped glow of the street, and soon she was gone.

★★★

When he returned home, he found a letter beneath his door.

I apologize for my tone. I ought not visit my feelings toward my rather interesting life upon you. I suggest a dinner, just us, to talk like the friends we are.

I admit to some confusion as to what you're doing. If I'm to return to a benefactor's role, I'd like to know what I'm paying for. Are you again pursuing transmission, and if you are, do you truly appreciate what you need to do in order to prove it?

A.B.

He wrote a reply and arranged for its delivery to the mansion.

Dinner would be lovely upon my return. For now, I'm going to visit home. I've been thinking of my friend Rapholtz. He's been like family to me, especially after the loss of my father. I shall return soon.

As for your question, I'm discovering a newfound need to at least explore it. Why, just tonight I was studying the circumstances of that strange day.

After packing hastily, he burrowed beneath the covers and waited for sleep. He thought of seeing Stralsund again. It was a sheet of a city when he imagined it, and somewhere behind the sheet was a girl he once knew.

In the morning, there was another letter from Alice. He read it on his way to the train. *I envy you a home you wish to return to, and a city with memories of loved ones. Yours will always be as they were. We who live, though. We don't remain the same as we thought we'd be.*

CHAPTER Thirteen
Wake

After arriving in Stralsund, he located a suitable pension, changed into a fresh set of clothes, and walked to the piazza. He could count on the market remaining as it was. A thousand ancient languages still rang between the tunnels. The crisp air still smelled like a soup pot: fish from the outer straits blended with beef slaughtered in French meadows and cockles scraped from the hulls of trawlers arriving from New York and Nippon. The notion that he'd ever actually lived and worked within it felt surreal.

It was nearing the supper hour and Gert's shoppe would soon reopen for vendors hungry for a tongue sandwich. He went there first but found it dark with no one waiting outside.

He tried the door. Unlocked.

The shoppe was musty, its shelves empty. The copper tang of blood and the heady aroma of open carcasses were gone. The place felt discarded.

He went around the counter to the charnel room where Gert and Greta worked. Every tool was gone. A coat of dust lay upon the butcher's table.

The cartsman at a nearby stall told him over the salted vapor of roasting roots that Gert had been ill. "No one's seen him in a while," he said.

Thanking him, Fleischl walked to a bench near the center of the piazza. From there he contemplated the shoppe and her home above it. It was dusk already. Soon there'd be little left to see of his old places.

When the little light flickered to life in her childhood window, he went to her.

★★★

"I've been sending them money for over a year," Greta said.

Gert lay on a couch in their front room. Fleischl took his pulse and listened to his steady, quiet breathing.

"One day," she continued, "he didn't remember how to get to the shoppe. My mother finally wrote me and told me how bad it was. By then they were almost out of money because he couldn't remember who he bought meat from. He didn't know where the money went and she knew none of it. Not a woman's business. I sent as much as I could. The burghemeister was kind. He's a good man and never foreclosed. I've agreed to sell him the shoppe in exchange for a small allowance for my mother. After everything, that's all that's left. His life was for nothing and he doesn't even remember it."

The close air stank of unwashed skin and dry piss. It was too much for one beleaguered woman to keep up with.

"He wanders off," Greta said. "He doesn't remember how to find home."

"Domence senile," Fleischl said. "So I've heard it called. Or the inevitable decay of time. I'd like to bring him to Thalhammer and spend some time with him."

"I'll speak to my mother about it."

"She's rather quiet."

"She's been that way since you first met her," said Greta. "She just lacks a jam jar."

For the next week he spoke to Gert. He took the frail man outside and talked about sausage. Simple, small words, over and over. He bathed Gert and spoke of Greta's mother. Occasionally he brought Gert to Thalhammer's library, a foreign place for a butcher, and there he spent all day repeating Greta's name into the ear of a broken man. For at least an hour each of those days, the library sounded with the sorrowful echo of single words repeated. Fleischl at one end, saying Greta to Gert at the other. Sometimes Gert would say *Jurgen* or *Elegy* to the unresponsive ghost of Dowid, ever at the window.

Fleischl made notes. He sketched the beginnings of several dioramas in which to situate Gert. There was the kitchen where he took meals and complained of customers, and the counter where he greeted customers he'd later complain of. He drew simple sketches of the library and the couch. But before too long he found himself drawing Greta, draped in a blanket and little else, and then a version of him lying next to her that day. And he was mumbling to himself. *Don't leave her. You won't find anything.*

In the evenings, he and Greta walked their old paths. They crossed the cemetery as the sun fell. Each time, they stayed for a moment at the graves of his parents, and at the headstone for Anton, who'd passed peacefully the summer before. He'd been at the library window with Dowid when he slumped over. And that was it. Rapholtz said it was all very quiet.

Of course it was, Fleischl thought. Thalhammer's library will always be home to the quiet ones.

The sun and air felt different in Stralsund. The way they filtered through the masts in port. They could be touched and they responded. They made way. He was surprised at how much he missed the place, especially the ocean, and perhaps the memories.

They always ended at the docks. He wasn't sure if she chose that, or if the place exerted a pull on them despite it looking out over all profound hurts of their lives. But what did people do after all, when they hurt in so unreasonable a way, except gather the hurts close as kindling and set them ablaze.

On only one walk, on the first true summer day of 1899, he asked her to tell him what really happened. "The truth," he said, and he tried to sound gentle when he said it. But behind his words was her, running with her face in her hands and wings on her back. Behind her was his father, going down and hoping to take the truth of his mother with him. He was sick of those who said they loved him but told him nothing. They should all go live in the library with the other quiet ones.

She walked away. When he tried to follow, she waved him off. He sat on the bench and waited for her to return. She was further down the docks, her hand to her face again.

Eventually she returned to the dock path and walked silently alongside him. She didn't say a word until he brought up something else.

"I'm sorry that this is happening with your father," he said.

"I'm afraid the last of me he still remembers, I was young. I was his little girl and he was here, and whole. All I care about is making myself feel better that I didn't break him when I left."

"That's not selfish. You told me once, we all deliver each other hurts. But we persist."

They sat by the sea and the ships, and for a moment he thought he saw Anton far down the docks. It was nothing, a play between the sparks of lamplight setting off the water and a sapling growing along the path. Its frail branches resembled outstretched hands.

He thought of those hands, and then the hands that fashioned wings and the hands that reached down for him in the tub. Something began to take shape in his mind, but he said nothing. Instead, he brought her close.

She studied him. No one knew him like she did. No one ever cared enough to make a story of him.

She smiled as tears came to rest on her cheek, where they remained as thin stripes of sunset. "I know where we can go," she said.

"You'll be missed."

"I'm not missed."

"But I left you."

"Yes, you did."

They went to the piazza. Cart men passed them on their way out of the market. None paid any mind to the figures slipping inside the old sausage shoppe.

"Our lives have run alongside one another's from the first day," she said as she undressed him, "yet it's been a series of leavings. We've gotten too used to saying goodbye."

He took off her coat and didn't stop until she was naked in the shaft of light from the new moon bisecting the slaughter room. He lay his clothes on the floor and kissed her as they went to their knees.

Their lovemaking was both fevered and patient. It was new and eternal. He pushed hard inside her and her hips rose to meet his. Their mouths fed oxygen to each other. All was silent. Their sighs folded one into the other. He felt her suck him in deeply and hold him, her fingers pressed into his back, pushing through to his spine.

He closed his eyes and a great falling came over him. It was endless and not quite dark. It fanned open and there was a color he couldn't quite see. He couldn't breathe and didn't want to.

"Come back," she said, and he did.

When he rolled off her, he lay by her side and feared that it was already happening. The next distance between them. There she would be, on a screen or a stage in a theatre, or on a street in a city somewhere.

"I love you," he said.

"I know you do. I've always known."

He wanted to put something right for her. And he wanted to know. Both felt strong enough to save him or kill him, and he didn't know which he deserved more, because he was thinking of something incredible. He knew he couldn't do nothing. Maybe he would fail. The decay of nature. Maybe all he could do in the end was no more than a frog's leg set to trembling. Maybe she'd hate him for it.

Later, after he walked her to her door, he roused the burghe-meister from his table at the bier haus and sent a telegram to Oliver.

PLEASE COME TO STRASLUND STOP BRING CONTRAPTIONS STOP SOUND AND VISION STOP I'VE AN EXPERIMENT IN MIND STOP

BUT HOW STOP came Oliver's reply.

I'VE FOUND A SUBJECT STOP

In the morning he told Greta that he wanted to try reaching her father. He said it could certainly fail, would likely fail, but he wanted to try, for her. He told her he intended to build something like they'd built for Anton. Then he asked for her help.

"I don't understand. Help him how?"

"It's all a puzzle in pieces, but I think with the right stimulus, we might reach him."

"I can't do anything for him."

"Yes, you can," he said. Sound came from the piazza. The new day's early work, already beginning. "You can tell me about the day you left him."

★★★

October 1899

With an architect named Til and his young son, Fritz, Fleischl and Oliver spent several weeks reconstructing a bit of Stralsund life in the glass studio behind Oliver's home. The sausage shoppe, the counter, the butcher's block, the bell on the door. Alice (meaning August, Fleischl supposed) funded all of it. Each day as the sets grew, Alice came with files full of documents for him to sign.

"You're like children playing with model trains," August said on his one and only visit. To his wife he said, "I hope I've something to show for it in the end besides a make-believe shoppe."

Alice kept them company in the glass house, moving through the day to evade direct sunlight. "I don't need to look any older," she said. To occupy herself, she catalogued the conflicts their country was involved in. "To assist my husband," she explained tartly, "in determining his next investment. Besides you two and…this."

There were plenty of opportunities for August Bliekroder to make money. Good German men marched over the grasslands of the fondum of Baful. They deployed their superior skills in putting down rebellions by Hehes and Boxers.

"Brave fighting men are hammers to the nails that build the world," Alice said one morning while setting out more documents for signature. Fleischl assumed it was a sentiment she'd heard August say. He knew her to be strong, frequently cold, but not nationalistic.

"I don't quite understand the reference," Oliver said. He, Fleischl and Til worked on a sign that would be hoisted above the false shoppe door. "They strike at things in order to build them?"

"Well, sparks," Fleischl suggested. "Maybe they make showers of sparks. Isn't that what happens when a hammer hits a nail?"

"Some Jews actually understand tools," Oliver said.

"None that I've met," Alice remarked, thrusting a pen into Fleischl's hand. He signed. She shuffled the papers into a folder. With a glance around the sun-dazzled room and the facade of the sausage shoppe, she left.

"She seems a bit more sour than usual," Oliver said.

Fleischl poured himself some tea. The constant light kept it pleasantly warm. "She's angry," he said.

"Clearly. How did you address it with her?"

"I told her we spoke to Greta briefly after the play, learned of her father, and here we are."

Across the garden, Alice climbed into a waiting hansom. They watched it disappear behind a neighboring house.

"She knows who Gert is to Greta," Fleischl said. "She knows

nothing of who they are to me."

"Let's hope it stays that way," Oliver replied. "I'd like to avoid having to search for a new benefactor."

They sat together in the welcome shade of the shoppe frame, sipping tea and enjoying the quiet. On the table beside schematics of the set were all his notes, organized into two piles. He'd seen Oliver stealing glances at them with the same air of anxiety that informed Alice's glances each day, past the glassed walls and to the garden as she waited for the inevitable moment Greta came.

Oliver, he knew, was looking ahead to the day Gert was behind the shoppe counter, and what would happen after. It wasn't sitting well with him.

Observation, on the top sheet of one pile. Below it were blank pages waiting to be filled once the experiment began. He'd already added a sentence to the top sheet of the second pile.

Prediction: it's not enough

Oliver's mind, he could tell, occupied itself with the work to come. "Alice is certainly making me pay for her support," he said, hoping to ease his friend's worry. "I'm signing away God knows what. Contract after contract. I fear what it is I've agreed to."

"She and August easily own half of all I do," Oliver said distractedly. "More, probably.' He drained the last of his tea. "Best not to think about it. She's more like her husband than she'd care to consider. And they call us avaricious."

★★★

When the day came, Fleischl picked up Greta, Gert and Rapholtz from the depot in the city and brought them to Oliver's studio. He could see Alice through the glass walls, watching their arrival. Dawn was still an hour away and all was still dark in the garden, but Oliver had strung little lights through the trees to illuminate the path, and in the glass house, candles lit up his studio like a cathedral on Christmas. It should have been peaceful, but Alice's expression was chilly and calcified. Greta's was pinched with anxiety.

Greta took steadying hold of her father's arm. Rapholtz took the other. They entered the glass house. There, Greta let go of her father and stayed back in the garden. She avoided Alice entirely, focusing instead on the black curtain drawn across the width of the studio.

As he introduced Rapholtz to Alice, Fleischl kept an eye on Gert. The man had no sense of where he was. When he glanced at Fleischl, his eyes betrayed no recognition.

It had been the same in the weeks he'd worked with Gert, speaking his name and Greta's, walking him back and forth in the piazza. Gert's mind seemed to have retreated back into itself.

Fleischl and Rapholtz helped Gert into a chair. Alice maintained her focus on the curtain, and on the night stars still visible above, on anything but Greta in her garden.

"She's a bit dour," Rapholtz said.

"She is," Fleischl said. "You're not the first to make that observation."

"Does she make you nervous, being here?"

He smiled. "She is of many moods."

"That's not what I meant."

"I know."

Rapholtz chuckled. "I believe we'll talk more about this rather piquant quandary of yours."

"It's not a quandary. She's a sponsor and a generous patron. Nothing more."

"Perhaps."

"You're just an incurable romantic."

"The scientist who chases the soul is calling me a romantic."

"It's just about time," Fleischl said.

"Go."

He approached Alice. "We're about to start. I'll just let her know."

Alice stood. "I'm leaving," she said. She allowed Fleischl to place her ermine wrap over her shoulders. "I don't need to be here. This isn't where my interest lies. Excuse me, Fleischl."

He watched Alice walk out of the studio into the garden. "It's starting," she said to Greta as she left.

"I'll be right back," Fleischl told Rapholtz. He went to join Greta beneath the garden lights. The sky laced itself with slow moving auburn. The wind was calm and cool. The breeze tousled her hair as she managed to light a cigarette. He didn't even know she smoked. He looked at her and watched the red coal glow in the twilight as she took a drag. *Of course she does*, he thought.

"How are you feeling?" he asked. They were easy words. Another part of him wanted to say, *Get out. Take your father and get as far away from here as you can. You don't know what I'll do for you.*

She drew in smoke and let it curl from her lips to rise over the glass house. She wore no makeup and was dressed as he'd asked. She looked as young as she'd been when she left Stralsund and her father, and how could a man lose whole years of his life? He couldn't bear the thought of losing pieces of himself and not even knowing they were missing. Forgetting that he was forgetting, until everything was gone. Even her.

"What if he carries that day with him," she said. "All of it locked up in him, replaying it over and over and he can't do anything but watch?"

"What day?" But he knew.

"The day I left."

"I don't believe the brain works that way," he said.

"But you don't know. That's the whole reason for this. August wants to make money and you want to know. So you'll do what you did with Anton and you'll find me in there, breaking his heart."

The last of her cigarette dimmed. She flicked it onto the garden stones, where the wind took it away.

"If it was me," he said, "I'd want to see you even if it meant pain. Beneath all that, it would still be you. It's still love. That's what it is, to carry who you love wherever you go."

"Is it?"

"Isn't it for you?"

"I don't know anymore."

"This may take a long time. We might be at it for days. Longer. But just maybe, we might pull him from dementia. Isn't it worth trying, to have just a piece of him back? Or maybe I fail and nothing changes at all. I don't know. Just try to promise me, when you think of this, of what happens, know that I had to try."

Movement in the studio caught their attention. Gert was growing restless.

"Oliver's with the actors in the house," he told her. "Can you let them know it's time?"

"I'd like to be in there with him."

"Of course. You should be the first thing he sees."

"Thank you for this," Greta said. "For trying."

Get out Greta

"You're welcome."

★★★

Fleischl led a docile Gert behind the cloak and stood him at the counter. Had he the awareness, he would have seen that he was in the shoppe where he'd greeted Stralsundians for decades. On the shelves behind him, fresh cuts of meat hung as they always did, courtesy of Alice, her order submitted to a fine butcher in the city and retrieved by her loyal chauffeur.

When the bell Oliver had installed above the studio door rung, Fleischl pulled on a cord, and the curtain dropped. Gert came face-to-face with a half-dozen men dressed as seamen and cart sellers, along with one portly burghemeister.

Greta lingered at the rear of the group, watching as the actors stepped to the counter and placed their orders. Oliver had given them ample caution not to ask where Gert had been, where he lived, or why he appeared unkempt. Ask him for a good sandwich of black bread and tongue. Ask him, are you trying to get me fat with that wurst of yours? Ask him anything but where did you go that you can't come back from?

Fleischl didn't know what to expect or what Gert might do. But now he saw. Gert didn't do anything. His make-believe friends ordered food that should have been as familiar to him as Greta's face or his wife's preserve jar.

On the bright morning, Fleischl wrote while Gert stared dumbfounded, *when the shoppe opened, there was a crowd. Gert's customers greeted him but he couldn't remember what to do, and then the men tried to engage him in idle conversation. And there it was. The dimming. You could see it happening, and there was nothing to be done. Nothing but wait to see what came next.*

After a suitable time, he and Oliver conferred. The curtain fell. The actors were paid and dismissed.

Fleischl and Rapholtz sat in the garden with Gert, under the bright sun of mid-morning. "I'm sorry, my boy," said Rapholtz. "A lot of creative effort for nothing."

"Not for nothing," Fleischl said. "It shows me what doesn't work."

Greta lingered by the studio door. "See to Gert's comfort," Fleischl said to Rapholtz, and went to her.

"Let Laszlo take you to rest," he said. "There's nothing left today. We'll all get some sleep and see what tomorrow brings."

She hesitated.

"He'll be looked after," Fleischl said. "Go on. Laszlo will meet you out front."

She was exhausted, pliable. "All right," she said. She kissed his cheek and he felt his heart crack open.

Rejoining Rapholtz and Oliver, he asked, "is the other set ready?"

"It is," Oliver said.

"What other set?" Rapholtz' hand was on Gert's shoulder. Gert's face turned toward the sun.

At least he knows that much, Fleischl thought.

"I asked you a question. What other set?"

Fleischl met his friend's gaze the way Alice would. "Go with Greta," he said, "and watch her."

"Oh." Rapholtz' eyes welled up. "In case she hears something."

"Gert won't come to any harm," Fleischl said. "I swear it. Say nothing to her."

"There's nothing for me to say. Not a damned thing."

After Rapholtz joined Greta in the front of the house, a carriage picked them up to bring them to their hotel. When they were safely away, Oliver went to Fleischl and asked, "you're sure about this."

"A man once told me about hypnosis," Fleischl said. "He called it a gentle bombardment of the mind until it silences. I'm trying to reach someone who's lost, and I've tried gently. I'm also trying to prove what happened. So I need to do the good Professor Lischke one better. An overwhelming bombardment of the mind. Sound and vision, Oliver, until the mind's anything but silent. Until it screams like mine did. Loud enough to be heard. I'm not even trying for hundreds of miles. Across town will do."

"I won't be a part of anything that hurts him," Oliver said.

"Neither will I. I'm not going to hurt him. I'm going to wake him."

★★★

Gert sat at what they hoped he would recognize as his kitchen table. There was an empty chair across from him, pulled out as if his wife had stepped away momentarily. An open jar, a napkin left alongside.

The facade of the kitchen occupied only a corner of the ball-room. At its center was a table where Oliver's soundwriter waited. An array of canisters were stacked alongside it. His phantasmascope rested atop a tripod.

August and Alice sat in chairs outside Gert's line of sight, near the entrance. August leaned over occasionally to mutter something to his wife, who made notes. It was easy enough to see how jaded they were, how eroded their connection.

Fleischl took his place behind the shoppe facade. He nodded to Oliver, who inserted the first wax cylinder onto its dowel.

What had the weather been, Fleischl had asked Greta when they talked in Stralsund.

It was raining, she'd said.

The ballroom filled with distant thunder, running groundwater, a rain-pattered roof. It was loud but not overly so. It took up space in the ballroom without reverberating too loudly. They'd worked to get the volume just so.

Where were you, he'd asked Greta, *when you told him?*

I'd come down for breakfast. I usually waited for him at the shoppe, but not that day.

Lights rose in the kitchen to cast a soft glow across the table and beyond, to the entryway that in Gert's actual home led to a short staircase. The sounds beneath the rain grew louder as the lights grew brighter. There came footfalls on wood. The distant turning of cart wheels across the piazza's paving stones.

When did you tell him, Fleischl had asked.

I was afraid, she'd said. Soon customers would come. I wanted to wait until midday, but there was the noon hour meal. And *then I thought perhaps before supper. We would clean the shoppe together, just the two of us. Mama knew that was our time. But I couldn't do it to him then. I had to get it over with.*

The actress Oliver had selected came into the doorway of the kitchen. She held a small travel valise.

She went to the table, took up a cloth and wiped it from end to end. She moved as slow as a dream.

How did you leave? he'd asked.

"On a ship." The actress' voice rose from the sound writer, alongside a distant steam whistle. It wasn't exactly Greta, but mixed with the whistle and the rain, it was enough to suggest her.

Oliver wheeled the phantasmascope over.

"Quickly," Fleischl said, and together they bent Gert over and bound him with a strap around his head. Each pull of the belt forced Gert down to the phantasmascope, until he was immobilized against it.

His eyes were pressed to the frame. He whimpered.

"Start it," said Fleischl.

Light spilled out from the slit between the lens piece and Gert's face, across his forehead and stubbled cheeks. As Gert watched, his whimpers became screams.

"Fleischl," Oliver said.

"Keep going."

They both knew what Gert saw over and over. They'd made it, then watched it. It was Greta. And then images breaking open over her grainy silhouette, over the kitchen table and the walls of the room they'd built. An ocean, its surface dappled with waves. A delicate hand upon a rail, wet with ocean spray. A ship's horn bellowed as if they were all standing beneath it.

What did you say to him? Fleischl had asked Greta on the floor of her shoppe. His heart had thrilled at the feel of her and at the knowledge of what he would do in her name.

"Poppa," said the actress' voice from the wax cylinder. "I'm leaving."

Oliver brought the soundwriter to Gert's ear. Fleischl held the horn and felt it reverberate. Oliver kept the sound and the phantasmascope endlessly turning. Alice remained stoic, her hands resolutely folded atop her notes.

For an hour into two, Gert knew nothing save his child at the kitchen entry, and waves and rails, and her telling him over and over, *I'm leaving.*

None of it, not the rail, not the sea, nor the words, stopped. Fleischl made them louder. The ballroom shook with them, to the point that Fleischl glanced up to see if the dome would crack.

There were figures on the dock, watching.

Gert's hand rose from the armrest. Fleischl loosened the restraint.

The figures were gone when he looked up again.

Gert's gaze found the actress. His lips moved, but nothing came. Gradually, his eyes searched the room and found the entryway, where

Greta stood with Rapholtz.

"Greta?"

The look on her face spoke to something unutterable, but there would be time for it. For now, Fleischl thought, let me linger over this. The ocean giving a father back for a change.

★★★

It only lasted a short while. Fifteen minutes, perhaps. The lightening, Rapholtz dubbed it. Gert's window opened a crack, then slid right back down again. By then the darkness deepened above the surface of the lake.

August pondered how the wedding of sound and image could be put to commercial use, and what profits might be made. Alice took notes. Oliver sketched potential improvements to the soundwriter.

Fleischl wanted to be among them. He wanted to be considering ways to push the brain further and increase its sensory capabilities. Surely the window could open wider and stay open. He wanted to be caught up in the wonders they'd created, crossing the ballroom floor in a mad dance with it all. But Greta cradled her father's head as his light dimmed. Before, Gert had looked up at her and seemed for all the world to recognize his child. It showed in his eyes. But now he couldn't be sure what Gert knew.

Greta stared at Fleischl with tears falling on her cheeks.

"Did you hear him," Fleischl asked. He had to know.

The others turned from their work at the sound of his voice. It was the first sound since the storm died away.

"Please tell me," Fleischl said.

"No."

She brushed her father's hair from his eyes. "I heard you in the glass house garden," she said. "Lying to me. I knew you were going to do something. But not this. How could you put him through this? How could you put me though this?"

"You heard me," he said.

Alice looked away from her notes and her husband's stunned

face, to the two of them.

You see us, he thought.

"The telegram…"

"What do you want from me?" Greta screamed at him. "Do you want me to say I heard you down here? That I heard you *die?* If you cared for me, you'd stop this madness. You have *no* idea how horrific this thing of yours is. Look at my father."

"I helped him," Fleischl said. "You saw. He knew you."

"And now he's gone. You used me to cut him open and you didn't care who it hurt. Only about what you so desperately need to believe. You're sick. I hope it never happens to you or anyone else, and on the day you die I hope I don't hear a goddamn thing."

★★★

By midnight Fleischl was alone in the ballroom. Gert and Greta were gone with Rapholtz, bound for the depot and the train back to Stralsund. Greta wouldn't look at him as they left.

"I pray you got what you were after," Rapholtz said. There was more kindness in his voice than he deserved. "It came at a high price, my boy."

He wasn't sure when Alice and August had left. He'd been intent on the figures standing above on the dock. He thought one of them might be her, watching him through the water, perhaps wishing the lake would come crashing through the dome and end him. Perhaps she was listening for that.

It was time to leave. His head pounded. His leg ached, out of nowhere.

Climbing the steps, he emerged in starlight to see Alice waiting in the garden archway.

"I heard every word," she said. "I saw. So did August."

"Alice, I'm tired. May we talk later?"

"She's the one, isn't she."

He stood quietly as it all came down.

"Of all the people in the world, she's the one who heard you."

"She is."

Her face hardened. He knew how hard it could get.

He left her for the dock. She followed him to the middle of the lake, where he leaned against the rail. She lit a cigarette. Its coal tip glowed dimly in the dark.

"We may begin," she said, "with the contracts you signed."

"What of them?"

"It's mine. Sound and vision. Transmission. Whatever you manage to make of this. All the patents, all attendant rights."

"You can't do that."

"Sue me, as you people are so fond of doing. Find the money in a city where I fully intend to ruin any ability you have to earn a livelihood. Find an attorney who can stand up to August Bliekroder and his wife and sue me. Understand, I'm not the least bit emotional about the money, and he's not emotional about you breaking Greta's heart. She's a plaything to him. What I am emotional about is you taking something that belongs to me. Something precious. My faith, which I placed in you above many others. You lied to me. You've lost me. You're in a very dangerous position with me. And the only reason I let you walk out of here in one piece is that you lost her too."

She passed him on the way back down the dock toward the house. "I leave you with nothing in this life but a telegram from her and whatever it tells you about a day long ago. Don't ever let me see or hear from you again. And woe unto you, should I ever find her with you. Men looked at her all the time. You were the only one I ever saw her look back at. And none of you ever, ever saw me, no matter what I did. You son of a bitch. You don't get to keep any of this. Today is the day you lost everything."

She crossed the lake to the shore. There she stood in the glow of her mansion. She was as small as a figurine. A shape cut from dark paper.

A loon cried out. Crickets, the carp breaking the surface, the mad watertop scramble of a bird skidding across the surface. All of it hidden in the dark, but they spoke their existence, so he knew they were there.

Alice hadn't yet turned off the ballroom lights. It was just a dull glow, and in its center was a small shape he recognized. An empty chair.

Only a life as empty as that chair, he thought, could hold all this.

CHAPTER Fourteen

The Elegy

Sometimes, in the years following the debacle of Gert's brief and jarring moment of lucidity, Fleischl told prospective employers that he was the fourth in his family's storied line of psychiatrists. In more desperate times he told them that he was the true author of Freud's talking cure and was directly or indirectly responsible for any one of the dizzying number of theories on the mind's mysteries *(you're aware of the ability to recall traumas to consciousness so they may be discharged. I did that).* Sometimes, he even told the truth: he was trained in psychiatry, had a hand in bettering the placement of galvanic electrodes, and co-authored a paper on external stimuli. "One might say I continued in that field," he would add.

It had all been taken away, he had no choice but to disclose, by a powerful couple he couldn't name, through a course of legal maneuvers he couldn't discuss, and a whisper campaign that by the winter of 1903 seemed to have reached every sanitarium, clinic and asylum in Germany.

The replies he received, whether in person or by post, were astonishingly consistent. *We checked your references, and were directed to Chancellor and Mrs. Bliekroder...*

So it was that after the incident in the ballroom, he scratched out what living he could, in any way he could, whether he was "qualified" or no. By day he wrote pseudonymous columns on psychic energy for the pittance royalties paid by fly by night rags that ran his work alongside photographs of ectoplasm. Almost every night he assisted the magicians and mesmerists at the Kabarette. Under their tutelage, and in the cause of generating tips of his own, he became adept at sleight-of-hand tricks like The Obedient Dime, The Prisoner Released, and The Juggler's Joke. Through him, the nightly acts were introduced to feats of chemistry and magnetism. He taught them the static paper trick, which was soon given a fresh name, The Sparking Demon. He and The Prescient Professor Lischke co-created The Merry Iron Filings, The Dip of The Needle, and The Metamorphosed Knife. Fleischl steadfastly refused any participation in the Professor's favorite, The Seafarer's Compass.

"Shouldn't you be working as a psychiatrist?" the Professor asked him one night.

"There's no money in it. Who knows? I might find myself in need of these skills one day."

He managed to pay some, but certainly not all, of his bills. An additional income came in fits and starts from an unexpected and occasionally troubling source: the slender fame he enjoyed owing to a drunken Alice. She'd ill-advisedly commiserated one night about the experiment to the wife of a journalist. Which was why he also received personal overtures to see individual patients, though not as a psychiatrist.

"As some sort of miracle worker," he told Oliver.

The overtures came by letter and contained money for train fare, ships' passage and what equipment they thought he would need. Restraints, said one. *Electrodes,* said another. *An actor,* one wrote, *made to resemble our dead child.*

"Dear God," Oliver commented on that one. "What do you do with such things?"

The letters all ended with the same plea. *Make pictures move. Record the sound of screams. Just bring them back to us.*

"I'm ashamed to admit," he told Oliver, "it depends on how hungry I am. But I won't do any of those things. I go. I talk. I try, and I always leave them just as I found them. Because to treat them as a psychiatrist takes years. They don't want years. They want bombast, and they want now."

"You won't do for them what you tried with Gert?"

"No."

"Why?"

There were plenty of nights he wanted to cry "why indeed?" Was it so horrible? Wanting to know whether there was any hope, however slim, that something happened? Why was that wrong? Who wouldn't want to know? Every day he had to force himself not to think about whether or not it really happened, or whether it could happen again. Or whether she was right. That it was nothing more than a coincidence best forgotten. On those days he felt no better than a morphine addict. He craved, he justified, the need to know. And thanks to the need to know, he'd given Gert the sight and sound of a daughter he'd forgotten he had, however brief.

Why indeed?

Then there were the nights when he lay in bed or sat at a table in the murk of the Kabarette and old feelings took him. *Something* had happened, alright. They'd been torn from each other, he'd been set on a path he never asked for, and he'd lost her forever. Maybe himself along with it all.

Love, the hardest light to extinguish, snuffed out because of his need to know. That, he thought, is truly the Thing That Happened.

Why indeed.

"Because the ones who write to me," he responded to Oliver's question, "love the ones they're writing to me about. I can't do to them what I did to her."

Occasionally, he received legal papers from the fine attorneys

at Haxthausen & Lommer, counsel for August and Alice Bliekroder,
with injunctions against activities he wasn't engaged in, or suits seeking
damages he couldn't pay in two lifetimes.

*Cease and desist from marketing electrode placement for the mechanism
known as the galvanometer (Patent Pending). Foreswear any and all usage
of the "sound and vision method" (Patent Pending), or derivatives thereof.
Maintain no impermissible associations.*

He knew who that last one referred to.

Oliver offered financial assistance, which he steadfastly refused.
"I'll find my way," he said, and though he'd traded his apartment on
Kurfurstendamm for a hovel, though he often felt hunger, worry,
loneliness, and regret above all, he generally did find his way, to the
Kabarette, to the occasional psychiatric patient, and to the cinema
when he could afford it. On those nights, he looked for her. The
Bliekroders' blacklist extended to her, so Oliver told him. "They've all
been warned," he said, "not to give her parts."

"It won't matter what they do," Fleischl said. "She'll always
know how disappear."

Behind the stars, embedded in the background of each film,
he honed in on crones cleaning taverns, imps playing flutes, hands
spinning webs. Her, disappearing into an imagined life. On those nights
when he found her, he went home to his hovel, filled his tub, climbed
in and held his breath while poking at the underside of the surface.
He would think of his father and of Greta, and he would stay until he
could feel his consciousness evaporate.

It always took so long to get there.

On a November night of light snow in 1903, he met Oliver for
dinner and a proposition. "Do you recall the story I once told you of a
young man named Albin?"

"I recall the name."

"The widow story."

"I remember. The occult group."

"The Pansophic Lodge. Albin is a writer and has met with some success, as have other men affiliated with him. They've decided to pursue their interests in the form of short reels. And Albin has an interest in you."

"More millionaires," Fleischl sighed.

"He's highly intrigued by oddities like p-energy."

"It's getting dreary being included in such company."

"I mentioned you. He'd like to offer you a paid consultancy. Plus, he'd indemnify you against lawsuits, should August or Alice hear of it. At least think about it."

When he returned to his apartment that night, a telegram lay against the door.

DOWID SLEEPWALKS STOP HE CARRIES THE ROPE AND SOMETHING OLD FROM YOU STOP BALSA WINGS STOP LAST NIGHT HE SPOKE STOP YOU NEED TO HEAR WHAT HE SAYS STOP

In three days' time he was at Thalhammer, enjoying a welcome supper of roast chicken and potatoes and waiting for night to fall. Rapholtz recounted Anton's last days. Sunlit windows onto the Baltic. A final glimpse of the tunnel. Rapholtz also offered a list of his own ailments.

"A bit of gout. My ankles swell. I can't sleep these days. But I shouldn't complain. Tell me of you."

Fleischl spoke of his last days with the Bliekroders, of his tiny apartment in Berlin. He said he sensed possibilities. He just didn't know what they were yet.

"Are we as we were?" he asked Rapholtz. "After the ballroom?"

"I did warn you."

"I know. I had to."

"Are you done with all that now?" asked Rapholtz.

Fleischl smiled. "Yes. But ask me again tomorrow."

Into the night they called up memories of Fleischl following Anton to Thalhammer and all the offshoots of Anton's life. A discovered name. A brother. A ship. A master roll. They spoke of how good it was to be known in the way Anton was at the end. All the while, Dowid slept peacefully in his chair at the library window.

Just past one, Fleischl noticed a change. "Laszlo." He nudged his old friend.

"Umm?" Rapholtz sat up stiffly from Anton's couch.

"Look at how he lists to and fro."

Dowid leaned left in the chair. His eyes remained closed. He'd clasped the rope to his chest. Over the course of thirty breaths—Fleischl counted each one—Dowid's body slowly centered itself, then tilted right.

"It's starting," Rapholtz said. "There he goes."

Dowid stood up from the chair. His eyes opened, but Fleischl saw the emptiness. His body continued to list gently from side to side as if the room was unsteady. He didn't follow a straight line, but Fleischl didn't think it was haphazard either. "I need paper," he whispered.

Rapholtz handed Fleischl a pen and a piece of Thalhammer stationary. They followed Dowid's every step while Fleischl traced dashed lines on the paper. He drew boxes and labeled them. Couch. Window. Table.

Dowid circumnavigated the library five times in all. His path varied. He eventually found his way through the door and out. He held himself and shivered. He rushed along the corridor, crying. One hand extended out, fingers sifting the air.

Is it dark where he is, Fleischl wrote.

They followed him to the washing room. There Dowid paused with his face pressed against the little window in the door. He held one end of the rope up to the small window as a look of anguish came over him.

"Jurgen!"

And then Dowid was awake.

Fleischl's hand shook as he crossed out *washing* room on the map and made note of where Dowid truly was. *Elegy.*

They brought Dowid back to the library. He took up his seat and asked how many steps to the sea.

"I think it's the storm," Fleischl said. "I think it's the last day."

"Your father's name," Rapholtz said. "Awful to hear it like that, but I felt you should know."

Dowid didn't move from the window. For the rest of the night, Fleischl kept vigil over him, Stralsund and the Baltic. He let his mind wander as best it could, to the intricacies of card tricks, to Greta's last hiding place on screen, to anywhere but *Jurgen.*

Once, near four in the morning, Dowid mumbled something unintelligible in his sleep. It could have been the last thing he ate or the first of one thousand, seven hundred and two steps, or Jurgen tucked away in an addled mind that replayed a storm and the deaths of men day after day.

His restlessness roused Rapholtz from his spot on the couch. "I can see it in your eyes," Rapholtz said worriedly. "What will you do, strap him to another contraption?"

Fleischl gazed out over the brilliant, onyx sea beneath the bright moon. "No," he said. "Something else."

He made one more entry on the map. *Roundhouse.*

If you're in there, he thought, it's time to get out.

Back in Berlin, Fleischl called on Oliver. "This man you mentioned. Albin."

"Albin Grau."

"He remains interested?"

"I'm certain of it."

"There's something I want to do. I need to. If he can fund it, and if indeed he'll indemnify against anything Alice or August slap me with, you and I have an extraordinary endeavor awaiting us."

"Ah, a film to wake someone. What's it to be this time?"

"We're going to build a ship," Fleischl said.

★★★

In the temperate spring of 1904, Stralsund's residents added a new attraction to their Easter parade route.

There was the carnival, as always. The burghemeister presided along with his new son Willi (thanks to the latest in his succession of wives), and lucky Willi assumed the coveted post in the piazza manger. There was food, drink, frolic, and of course the parade behind the angel. It was there that the newest element made its appearance. The parade left the piazza altogether to travel down the sea-facing tunnel to the docks. There it turned slightly north and stopped at the open gates of the shipyard, where the people of Stralsund could see a different sort of birth. The second coming of the *Elegy*.

Its hull was reconstructed atop sawhorses at one-half scale length and two-thirds of her depth. The hull itself was thinner to an astonishing degree, but as Fleischl explained to an indefatigably curious burghemeister, "it's only meant to float, not to voyage, and it'll only float for as long as it takes."

"As long as what takes?" the burghemeister asked.

"To get out," Fleischl said.

When it was completed in early May, the *Elegy's* topside possessed a patchwork of square decking, a ladder, and a narrow walkway spanning its length. Oliver could lash a camera and shoot all that happened below.

"Does this vantage point remind you of anything?" he asked Fleischl.

Fleischl nodded; he had already thought of the ballroom.

Below the walkway, Til, Fritz and several crew members constructed a long, dark corridor to the precise specifications of the map Fleischl had sketched in Thalhammer based on his father's diagram of the ship. It recreated every twist and turn Dowid might have taken, ending at three possible doors. Beyond them were those rooms aboard the *Elegy* where his father may have met his end.

The galley, Fleischl wrote, *cooking for them. The forecastle, gathering them. The roundhouse, reading to them when their hope was all but gone.*

Wherever he was, Jurgen Berger didn't get out or I would have found him. I think Dowid found him that day, in the roundhouse.

Their Pansophic benefactor provided funds with which to build the boat, assign a cameraman to each room, and construct a facility in which to process the footage. *I cannot provide you a storm,* Albin Grau wrote to them. *Though I shall provide you protection from the elements, including Alice and August Bliekroder and all their accursed attorneys. Fraternitas Saturni!*

"Brotherhood of Saturn," Oliver explained. "He's fond of the phrase, whatever it means."

"He's an occultist," Fleischl said. "Maybe he meant to invoke Satan."

"He and the rest of them are paying for all this. Hail Grau, hail Satan, hail whoever we need to hail."

At dusk on May 22 the almost-but-not-quite *Elegy* slid from a framing track into the shallows of the Baltic. By then Fleischl and Oliver had a visitor. Albin himself, a young man scarcely ready for the razor. He arrived at the dock dressed in a black wool suit and fedora at least one size too large. He carried a book filled with misshapen symbols. "Alchemic," Albin said as Fleischl gazed curiously at the strings of odd characters. "Some Enochian as well. Oh, and some Hermetic."

"You're quite young," Fleischl said.

"I'm twenty. Old enough to appreciate the stuff of a man's vision, I promise you. This undertaking is something I have to see for myself."

For the next hour, the *Elegy* anchored in the shallows, where it was tied off with three thick ropes per side. Nothing of the crew's equipment, the cameras or soundwriters, were loaded. Fleischl walked the ship's bottom for another hour after that, searching for leaks while Oliver and a nervous Albin followed along on the walkway above. Pronouncing it fit, they proceeded to shock the burghemeister and the gathered Stralsundians by running thick, insulated, electrical lines from every telegraph pole along the edge of the sea.

"Through the water," the burghemeister said to Fleischl, near tears.

"I know, my dear friend. And I have to trust, she knows as well."

When all was ready, Til, Fritz and the others covered the *Elegy* with tarps. Fleischl sent the crew to supper and to rest. It would begin at four that morning.

"One last thing before we get some sleep," Fleischl said. "Though you may think me insane. Or a hypocrite. Is there a prayer for a ship that's not really a ship?"

By ten that night, Rebbe Bernhard stood at the dock in answer to Fleischl's question, his teffilin and yarmulke in place, his prayer book open. "Will you all pray with me?" the rebbe asked.

"I'm afraid I don't know many words," Fleischl said.

"Nor I," said Oliver.

"I'm a Satanist," Albin said cheerily.

"Minyans come in all shapes," the rebbe said. "I'll take care of the Hebrew words. Send your own thoughts out with them."

Rebbe Bernhard bowed and chanted. Albin found a suitable page of hieroglyphics and muttered to himself. Oliver closed his eyes. "I just like the melody," he said.

"So do I, my friend," said Fleischl. "I guess there's nothing hypocritical about taking a chance that what you believe in believes in you. Isn't that why we're here?"

"Amen," the rebbe said.

"I called down the ancient pagan sea gods," Albin said.

"How nice for you." He shook their hands and departed.

"I was kidding," Albin said. "I just listened to the sea. But I do wish this extraordinary venture the very best. I think it might lead us on an interesting path."

"How about you?" Oliver asked Fleischl.

"I kept it simple. I prayed that no one gets hurt."

★★★

At midnight, after Albin and the crew had gone to get what little sleep they could manage in the time they had, he sat with Oliver on the walkway listening to the tarps flutter in the breeze. There was a light on in Thalhammer's library, and a figure at the window. Fleischl wondered what Dowid might be thinking about the extraordinary sights in Stralsund's harbor, or whether he'd recall them at all come the hour when Rapholtz was scheduled to slip laudanum into his tea.

As passersby stopped and stared at them from the dock, Oliver set out three plates with a chop, a sprig of bloomed rosemary, some apples minced with walnut, and sweet wine divided into three cups. "Such is our compulsion," he said, "that we let Pesach slip by unnoticed."

"To the empty chair," Fleischl said as they raised their glasses.

"L'chaim."

"Indeed."

"I do wonder what Grau will do with it after," Oliver said. "The film of what happens. Not the *Elegy*. I still cherish the hope it will find a permanent place here. Only fitting."

"Perhaps there'll be nothing worth his trouble," said Fleischl.

"Do me the courtesy of looking down at what we've done."

"It's a marvel. I don't mean to suggest otherwise. But what if it leads to nothing at all?"

"Certainly Rapholtz would welcome your services at Thalhammer. You'll always work in the interest of healing the mind. It's who you are. This is no different, just larger."

"And the other," Fleischl said.

Oliver refilled their glasses. "To the other. Let it be what it's supposed to be."

They drank.

"I suppose I could always headline at the Kabarette," Fleischl said. "Fleischl The Mysterious, conjurer of ship parts, here to fill your papers with static."

He thought of the last time he'd been atop the water at night.

Gert, the lake, and her. The last time he'd seen her on a screen some-where, what had she been? A Roma, casting spells in a deep wood. He didn't remember the name of the picture. Nothing about it worth remembering, save for her.

He felt Oliver's glistening eyes upon him.

"I was just thinking," Oliver said with an apologetic smile. "I've never said what I ought to. I'm not much good for certain things. But I wanted you to know, I'm sorry you feel so alone that you're doing this. All of this. It's extraordinary, and it's heartbreaking."

"I'm well loved by at least one truly good person," said Fleischl, "That's extraordinary."

"There is another besides me."

"There was."

"Well, now that I've taken a perfectly peaceful night and made something maudlin of it, I suppose I should try to get some rest. Hard to believe it's tomorrow at last."

"Go. I'll be leaving soon."

He watched Oliver walk along the docks, and he let his thoughts slip beneath the Baltic. Over his shoulder was a light in a library, and soon the laudanum would have its way with the man who cried his father's name.

Just before dawn, the docks were already teeming with people. They came from the guild hall, the sea tunnel, and in Albin's case, Thalhammer, where he'd insisted on staying the night. "Think of the stories in those walls," he said, sounding like a boy primed for adventure.

The crowd held lights and huddled together in the predawn chill. Their murmurs traveled across the shallows to the *Elegy* and the walkway, where Fleischl and Oliver waited. Fritz and his fellows took hold of the ropes and pulled gently, then harder, noting the degree to which the mock *Elegy* tilted from side to side. They positioned a camera at each door and a soundwriter in each hallway, checked that the cables were dry, and cleared sightlines to the walkway above.

The last thing they did was carry a deeply slumbering Dowid into his cabin, where they lay him in a bunk some thirty feet below the walkway and Fleischl's vantage point. "He looks like a corpse," Albin remarked with some interest.

"How much laudanum did Rapholtz put in his tea?" Oliver asked Fleischl as the hour of six arrived.

"Enough to approximate what passes for a night's sleep aboard a working vessel. He should stir soon."

By six-thirty, Dowid showed the first signs of stirring. His fingers spread slowly, coming into contact with the bunk wall.

"Pull," Fleischl said, and four of the assistants pulled on their ropes until the *Elegy* swayed port to starboard, back and again, a cradle on the water.

"He's opening his eyes," Oliver whispered.

"Start filming," Fleischl said as a lone bell sounded from a wax cylinder. Dowid seemed to remain in a dream state. Oliver held up the script for everyone to see. He pointed halfway down the page. *Roughening seas.*

Each man set to his ropes. They held up fingers illuminated by small candles and counted down from three. Then their arms grew sinewy and the water beneath the *Elegy* churned with the ceaseless sway of the hull.

Dowid tumbled from his bunk onto the floor planks, where he curled in on himself. Another cylinder spun out voices. *"Tide's rising! Storm due west!"*

Oliver waved his hand before his candle. Once, twice. The men at the soundwriters reset their cylinders. There came the sound of rope thudding against wood, timed perfectly with the slap of boards against the side of his cabin.

"Water's getting in." Oliver pointed from the walkway down to the corridor outside Dowid's cabin. "It's not holding."

Dowid's lips moved silently, and it took a moment for Fleischl to understand. "He's counting steps. He's still at Thalhammer. Pull harder. Make it violent."

The screams of men rose grew louder. The soundwriters' cables were now in half an inch of sea water. Til and his men pulled the hull almost all the way to port, then back to the starboard. Oliver had lashed himself alongside the camera, but when he looked up from the eyepiece, he saw Fleischl clinging to the walkway, dangling freely.

"He's going," Fleischl said. "Be ready."

"You can't go down there."

From the hollows of the *Elegy* a soundwritten calamity careened through the thin wood walls: men screaming at their fellows that the ship lay on her side, that death waited below decks. *Cling to anything that floats, some are trying to swim but the sea is swallowing them. You can't get ashore. You can't get anywhere.*

From the cylinders came the terrible sound of weeping, the cries of the men who were too weak or too afraid to climb up from below decks, or to swim, or to do anything but pray for the storm to stop.

The ones who needed bedtime stories from a father.

The sounds of a story rose from the soundwriters then. With it came Dowid weeping below.

"I know where he's going." Fleischl said. "Don't stop filming, whatever may happen."

He let go of the walkway and dropped to the deck. Pain shot through his leg as he landed. Ignoring it, he found a ladder and descended below the planking to the hull's bottom and the corridor. Oliver was little more than a black bird against the grey sea sky.

Fleischl pointed in the direction he was going and ran for the roundhouse.

Oliver unlashed the camera and ran along the walkway, calling out to the camera operator outside the roundhouse door to make ready.

Fleischl arrived at the roundhouse just as the ship turned hard to port, sending him and the camera operator sprawling. He scrambled to his feet, opened the roundhouse door and went in. "Don't let him see you," he said while the ship pitched. Then he closed the door behind him.

"How close is he?" he called up to Oliver.

"Moments."

"Play my voice next."

The *Elegy* filled with the sound of him repeating: *Elegy, Jurgen*

"Drop his rope outside the door," Fleischl called over his own voice. "Pull the hull onto its side. Hard."

He took in the room as the ship turned, sending him into the wall. He could feel its flimsiness. It was as if the hull's ribs bowed and breathed. The sea pressed against the port side, looking for a way in.

Til's crew had left some tools in the corner, a hammer, an awl, and a spike suitable for separating beams.

He took up the spike and thrust it into the slit between two of the beams, then struck it with the hammer, loosing a spray of water. He hammered again.

"What are you doing?" Oliver screamed.

"Bringing him in," he said.

★★★

He counted the steps.

It was too dark to see. Frigid water rose to meet his forearms. The screams of his fellows echoed from the walls and he winced. Water rushed in as the ship foundered. There were so many ropes in the water with him. Some of them hummed. Some of them put his hands to sleep. But he found one that didn't do anything. That's the one, he thought. The one he made me.

Ahead was the roundhouse door. He thought he saw a face there, so he counted steps as the man had told him to. He'd always suspected that the odd sights he'd been seeing were wrong. The far ships, the sea below him as if he was aloft. Now he thought he understood, he'd always been here in the rising water. He'd never really gotten out.

By the time he waded down the dark corridor, rope held high, Dowid saw the man inside the roundhouse, the water up to his neck. He tried the door but the bobbing man in the little window shook his head.

"Jurgen," Fleischl said.

Dowid's face came near the glass. He held up the rope. "I can't reach it," Fleischl told him. "Dowid, do you know where you are?"

But Dowid just stood in stuporous regard of the door and the water. It occurred to Fleischl, as the water crossed his lips, what his father must have done for the one boy who hadn't yet drowned. Because surely there were boys in the roundhouse with him who weren't getting out. The book he'd read to them to keep the storm from frightening them might have floated alongside him. Out the door was someone from his son's village who was still able to live and who held a rope he'd made.

"Dowid," he said, "get out. Hurry. One step at a time. Turn away and go, one step at a time. Count steps, Dowid, until you're out. Start with one and don't stop until you're out."

The water in the roundhouse enveloped him. He had time to draw a quick breath and shout to Oliver to keep going before slipping under, with Oliver's pleas for him to get out.

It's actually sinking Fleischl.

His eyes welcomed the exquisite sting. Dowid was a blur. A dream of a man behind glass. Dowid's mouth opened. He talked as the ship tossed them both.

Fleischl's feet left the floor. He floated. The room was slanted. It was like he was on the low end of a seesaw. Above him was a blot on the pontoon, which could have been Oliver, or someone else, or just the camera, as everyone abandoned the sinking ship. Almost everyone.

Dowid remained.

Fleischl's eyes seared but he refused to close them or pass out. If Dowid was saying something, he wanted to be seen until it was done. He hoped it was heard and held. The blackness that covered him was strangely comforting.

He felt hands. He was vaguely aware of the roundhouse door giving way under unrelenting weight of the Baltic. He felt himself carried along the edge of the ship to its corner. He found the hole he'd made, and was pushed through it against the great flow of water coming in. Then he drifted somewhere far away.

"Remember?"

He opened his eyes. He lay on the hard, warm wood of the docks. Salt caked his eyes and made a painful blur of the faces surrounding him, but he found Oliver, Albin, Rapholtz, the burghemeister and closest of all, Dowid.

"Remember?" Dowid said again.

He held up the rope, then gave it a tug. Fleischl felt a constriction around his chest. His hands went to it and felt the rope tied around his torso.

"You made this for me," Dowid said and smiled.

"Someone help him sit up," the burghemeister ordered. Oliver and Til took him by the arms.

"I'll kill you myself," Oliver said. "Lunatic. Mind the cable. It's right next to you."

"I see it," said Fleischl, staring at Dowid's placid face.

★★★

He sat on Anton's couch beneath a thick woolen blanket. Its wiry threading itched a bit, but it felt agreeably heavy across his legs. His chest throbbed less dramatically, and the brandy Rapholtz served him went down warmly.

He held a notepad and pen atop his lap. He hadn't written much.

Dowid looked out the window. "It's quiet," he said. He clutched the rope to his chest. "I dreamt I saw your son. I'm so tired."

"Sleep a while," Fleischl said, and Dowid closed his eyes.

When he wakes, Fleischl thought, he may well be gone. Yes, I'm sure he will. Nothing lasts.

Rapholtz refreshed his glass while Oliver set up the sound writer and mounted the cylinder. "It's ready," he said. He settled on

237

the couch alongside Fleischl while Albin and Rapholtz took up chairs across the library.

"I couldn't hear him," Fleischl said as Dowid's body twitched. Sleep had come so quickly.

"I could." Oliver held the needle above the cylinder. "Be sure before you listen to this."

He hesitated only a moment. "It's okay. Play it for me."

Oliver lowered the needle onto the cylinder. After a series of pops and hisses, Dowid's voice emerged from behind a rush of water, the real and false cries of men, and the sounds of a storm brought back.

I can't reach you.

It's locked I can't.

Stay above the water Jurgen.

Jurgen get out!

I'm listening.

I'll tell him, smile if you can hear me Jurgen.

I'll tell him you've been mad at him your whole life and now it's you under the water.

You don't deserve this Jurgen, don't say that.

I'll tell him his heart was a drowned heart and you lost them both, but you saw her light and he came back, he was the angel, it was always him, I'll tell him.

I think I can reach you, take the rope.

The needle reached the end of the groove in the cylinder and the sound ceased.

They sat in silence. Fleischl felt a different sort of hollow carved out of him. He couldn't name it. One day, a proper name might suggest itself.

"I don't know what you might hear in this," Oliver said after a while. "Let me just say what I hear. You've wanted something of him all the time I've known you. At the end he wanted to give you back your life. To the very last breath, my friend."

"May I suggest," Rapholtz said, "that what happened to you

long ago was not meant to happen and may never again. You didn't hear your father that day and you didn't hear him today. What you did hear, what you'll now carry with you, is what he lived with."

Fleischl gazed down at his scribbled notes. The stricken title he'd decided to keep, and the first words.

The Electric Love Song of Fleischl Berger.
Observation: We are all electric.

Hypothesis: It needs a path to us. It needs things to be in place to work. It can go in the wrong direction, and it can never find us. For nearly all, it never finds us. But one day, maybe it did.

Let us consider our life if it finds us.

"I remember once," Rapholtz said, "you almost threw yourself from a ship. Today you sank one. I need to know, Fleischl. All of us who care for you need to know. Will you ever do anything like this again?"

They waited for an answer. He waited for it as well while the room grew still but for his paper crinkling. Dowid snored blissfully. Somewhere in the world, Greta roamed the background of a fantastical silent life, his father turned in a deep tide, and his mother's blue light would never reignite.

He sat with all of it, and with people who loved him there and then. In a quiet while, the right answer seemed clear enough.

"No," he said. "Never again."

Oliver rose and hugged him first, followed by Rapholtz and even Albin. "Perhaps now you'll see how good it can be to stay among the living," said Rapholtz.

They took supper late, drank, and went to bed. Fleischl peered in on Dowid and on Rapholtz, and found both asleep. Taking a bottle, he went to the docks. The last bits of the *Elegy* poked out of the shallows. It hadn't been constructed to last in the best of times, poor old wreck, let alone withstand a madman Jew wielding tools. Much of it had broken apart under the force of the incoming water, to float away or settle at the bottom. Pieces of it would no doubt wash ashore for months. He could still make out a bit of hull in the dock lights, with half its name still poking up above the waves. *El,* it said.

Good for you, he thought, then raised the bottle. "To you. I promise to do my best not to die in the water. The Berger tradition ends with me." He laughed. "Sorry. I'm drunk. To you, Momma. I'm sure I would have really loved you. To you, Poppa. I really did love you, even the day you left, when it might have felt like I didn't. I hope you knew."

He took a healthy swig. "Those boys were lucky they had you at the end. You deserved to come home. You all did."

He threw the empty bottle into the Baltic and went back to Thalhammer and his rest. He didn't bother to glance down the sea tunnel to the piazza or her window as he passed. She was gone. There was no point waiting for a candle to light.

CHAPTER Fifteen
Sound and Vision

On an unexpectedly warm day in the early fall of 1907, two attorneys sat idly in a Juterbog courtroom as the judge read their briefs. The judge was an elderly man who had been called to the *amtsgericht* all the way from Dantzig. The only thing counsel could agree on was that Judge Twesten had appeared quite blissfully asleep throughout their oral arguments. There was little the attorneys could do but hope that, since the judge apparently didn't care about what they said, perhaps their written submissions would prove dispositive at last of the noisome legal battle styled *Bliekroder v. Berger.*

The litigants themselves had been barred from appearing in the same room together by prior rulings over the previous two years. Every presiding judge cursed with having to oversee some aspect or other of the litigation in all its permutations quite clearly saw who the aggressor was, and saw as well how wealthy, connected and intimidating that party could be. And so they blamed everyone equally in the interests of fairness.

After three stifling hours in the airless little courthouse, Judge Twesten finally roused himself from the papers. "Jews," he began, sending a sharp cramp through the already irritable bowel of the attorney representing Berger F. "Counsel for party Bliekroder, your clients are not Jews, correct?"

"That is correct, your honor."

"Then I continue. Jews, famously, know little to nothing about building things. Mechanically, of course. About wealth building, and alliance building, they excel."

Fleischl's attorney made mental preparations for the telegram to issue following the judge's ruling.

HERR GRAU STOP I REGRET TO ADVISE YOU AND HERR BERGER..

"Men of great wealth are even less inclined," the judge continued. "They hire others to do such things for them. They think themselves too lofty to bother with nuts and bolts. And so, as between the wealthy man and the Jew, I am presented with a quandary when it comes to ownership of these two…what do you call them?"

"Sound and vision, your honor," said counsel for the Bliekroders.

"And the ten-twenty method," added counsel for Fleischl.

"One is easy," the judge said, "one is harder. But this matter has gone on long enough. Today I rule. As to the ten-twenty method, I find by preponderance of evidence that Berger created it and therefore his claim of ownership is valid. Those improvements to the… what do you call the contraption?"

"Galvanometer," said the Bliekroders' attorney.

"That. Improvements made by Herr Bliekroder and his associate, identified in moving papers as 'A.B.' are theirs by preponderance of evidence. Neither party can demonstrate that they created the machine itself, and not a French engineer previously identified. Neither party owns it. We so rule."

The judge peered at the empty courtroom over the top of his bifocals. "To the harder issue. The rather poetically named sound and vision. It's ephemeral. It's vague. And as far as has been demonstrated, neither party has truly done anything save litigant Berger, who…" He checked the papers scattered across his podium. "Sought to drown himself?"

He removed his glasses and sighed deeply. "Enough of this, all of you. I order that you each leave the other to his own. There ought to be room in a country like ours for your ideas to compete, or coexist, or whatever the hell it is they do. Set aside your differences. Go make sounds and visions. Any agreement binding the parties ended, as I understand it, above a ballroom on a lake. So ruled."

Which was how, after patent applications, hearings, suits, and amendments to suits, Bliekroder v. Berger had reached its muted end.

HERR GRAU STOP WE HAVE PREVAILED STOP YOU AND HERR BERGER FREE TO DO WITH MACHINE AS YOU LIKE STOP

Albin made a centerpiece of the attorney's telegram at the finest table at Zur Lezten Instanz, where on a celebratory evening in late September, he, Fleischl, and Oliver held court. Arrayed before them were generous platters of chopped herring and onion, sausages of seasoned veal, a beef roulade over perfectly poached cabbage, an assortment of thick breads, and as much wine as two Jews and a Satanist could put down.

"A fitting spot to toast our victory," Albin said as he gazed around the room at Berlin's upper class. "Did you know it got its name from an incident involving two farmers. They fought for years in court over water rights or some such, and only after they got good and drunk at a tavern on this very spot did they settle their differences."

"To the farmers," said Oliver, hoisting his glass.

"To the lawyers," said Albin.

"I can use the method in psychiatric work," said Fleischl, who raised his glass to meet his friends'.

"We don't have to edit anything out of the footage," said Albin. "We can make sound and vision the main attraction of the stage show."

"Stage show?" Said Fleischl.

"I'm sure he's contemplating something tasteful," said Oliver.

"A tasteful Satanist," Fleischl said. "Everyone's heard of those."

"A tasteful Satanist patron," Albin corrected, "who underwrote the entire legal campaign."

"But what do you want to do?"

"A stage show with you." Albin paused to applaud the rowdy gentleman at the next table who'd ordered monstrous steins of ale, which they were busying themselves balancing on their heads. "A scientific presentation of your work," said Albin. "But with entertainment. The film, some acts, a lecture, the machine."

"I'm not allowed to use the machine," Fleischl interrupted.

"You're not allowed to use Alice's machine," said Albin. "So we use an old model. Hook up some paying customers with your ten-twenty hemispheric constellation."

"My what?"

"Entertainment," Oliver said.

"You're in on this too?"

After the restaurant they stopped at an arcade to watch one of Oliver's shorts on a kinetoscope. From there they proceeded to a series of cafes, watering holes, and questionable dives. At each one they drank to the legal defeat of Bliekroder, August and the mysterious—to the bench, at least—A.B. Over each shimmering glass of champagne or Night Sky Bier, Fleischl said things like, "perhaps we can discuss this further," and, "I'm a psychiatrist, not an entertainer."

At one a.m. they found themselves at a table in the back of the Kabarette. While Professor Lischke produced two eggs to the groans of the sparse audience, Oliver and Albin took turns reassuring Fleischl that he could indeed be entertaining.

"Don't think of it as a lecture," said Albin. Onstage, the

Professor promised an omelet. "Think of it as storytelling. The stories of people you help, with a bit about how you did it."

"Alongside an extraordinary piece of film," added Oliver, "and the machine. Oh, we could give audience volunteers a chance to have their minds read."

"You must be joking," said Fleischl.

"Not literally, of course. But they could take the machine's results home with them as a souvenir, couldn't they? Doesn't it scribble something?"

"Lines," Fleischl sighed. "Waves. It wouldn't mean anything to them."

"But it will," said Oliver. "It will represent what they were thinking. You of all people know how that notion can spark the imagination."

"I'll never make claims I can't prove," said Fleischl. "No talk of transmission, ever."

"Fair enough," said Albin.

"We could have other features with you," Oliver said. "I saw a sextet once, some harmonists. A little comedy, maybe some light music. It warms the audience up."

"Either of you could do this far better than I," said Fleischl. The idea of turning his work into some sort of stagebound revue was enough to twist his innards. That it would certainly invite the Bliekroders' scrutiny and, no doubt, legal action, turned his nerves up another notch.

"Now, a suitable name for you," Albin said.

"That's all I need to hear. I can't do this." He spied the Professor on stage segueing into a new trick. He seemed unusually ill at ease.

"You'll reach far more people than you thought possible," Oliver said.

A sad expression flitted across Professor Lischke's face as he fumbled with a kerchief and thread. He'd turned his back to the audience. His brow was knitted in fierce concentration. He glanced repeatedly back over his shoulder to a corner of the room across from where Fleischl sat, listening to his drunken friends cackling at the ludicrous names they came up with.

"He Who Is Not Very Entertaining," suggested Oliver. "No, wait! Fleischl Berger, The Electric Love Singer!"

"He Who Died Twice," Albin said.

"Melodrama," said Fleischl.

He was getting concerned about the Professor, who seemed to be in some distress. "And you're incorrect," he said. "I died once, at birth. One dies when the heart stops. Kiel was a fright, not a death."

"Have more brandy while I go over the finer points of entertainment for you," said Oliver. "Where are you going?"

"He needs some help. That's what I'm good for around here."

Fleischl rose from the table and approached the stage. He stepped over a sleeping patron on his way. "My friend," he said to the Professor. "What's wrong?"

"Is it that obvious?" said the Professor. "I'm forgettable, my boy. Don't bother with me. These are silly sleights anyway."

His hands trembled. It wasn't like him. Though his tricks were worn and workmanlike, they never failed. When he glanced up again at that corner, Fleischl followed his gaze to a noticeably tasteful looking woman of about sixty, tucked elegantly into a seat against the wall. She wore a smart suit, a man's fedora, and a loose tie, and she smoked through a long, ivory cigarette holder. She smiled and nodded when she saw Fleischl's attention.

"Who is she?" Fleischl asked Professor Lischke.

"An old flame. I haven't set eyes on her in almost a decade, and now here she is. I'm nervous."

"Here, put that trick away. Do you have what you need for ring conjuring?"

"Well, yes, but…"

"Through a drinking glass. It looks best under the light."

He climbed onto the stage and made sure to catch the woman's gaze. "If any lady will kindly bestow her ring, the Professor will be overjoyed to exhibit the electric action of metallic substance upon diaphanous bodies by demonstrating to you the imperviousness of ligneous products!"

"What in God's name did all that mean?" Professor Lischke asked him.

The woman rose from her seat and came to the stage. She slipped a large ring from her finger.

"It means you'll do something just for her," Fleischl said.

Professor Lischke smiled. "You always know, Fleischl."

"I'll help you."

The woman gave her ring to the professor, and he took it into his hands like the delicate and stunning gift it was to him.

The trick itself was a simple deception, smoothly executed. The professor held the ring in his left hand, pretended to pass it to his right, then pretended to place it in a napkin Fleischl took from the lap of the sleeping patron. Laying the cloth and its supposed contents across a full water glass, the Professor made a great flourish with his right hand that took the woman's attention with it while his left hand slipped the ring into the water as the kerchief settled. The reveal, her smile, and done.

Fleischl returned to his table, leaving the Professor and the woman at the edge of the stage to gaze upon one another.

When he got back to the table, he announced to his friends that he'd come up with a suitable name.

"And you say you can't be entertaining," said Oliver. "What's the name?"

"He Who Listens."

Albin nodded thoughtfully. "It speaks to what you do, without referring to what you won't do. It conjures the film. I like it."

"As do I," said Oliver.

Fleischl nodded to the Professor, who was leaving the stage

with the woman on his arm. The two of them settled at her table, in the shadows of the Kabarette.

"On more thing," Fleischl said to his friends." I think I've found an opening act."

★★★

Over the weeks leading up to opening night, Fleischl and Oliver worked with prop masters, panorama painters and metallurgists. Oliver's small office overflowed with lists for set designers, carpenters, tailors, and metal workers. Each such list eventually grew large enough to cover an entire wall and then trail across the floor. They read like bills of fare at the corner coffee room.

Scene One: Lights warm but not bright. Favours for volunteers. Talc and kerchief. Top hats, stick for spellcast. Three chairs and a knife.
Scene Two: Books, spines out. Shelving. Hearth, fire red. Desk, chairs, couch, panorama through window.
Scene Three: Corsican trap.

"Corsican trap?" Fleischl asked.

"Just you wait," Oliver told him, and because there was so much to do, he did wait. He considered what to cover in his lecture, or as Albin insisted on describing it in pamphlets that went up throughout the city, "an aural journey into the greatest of liars: the mind, that master of secreting the truth into the dark coves of memory!"

"Must I?" complained Fleischl. But Oliver and Albin preached the virtue of convincing people to go toward what they didn't believe.

"You promise them something no one else can have," Oliver said. "And you dress it in finery so they absolutely must have it."

It wasn't the verbiage that troubled him so much as what lay beneath them. In *master of disappearing*, Greta. In *dark coves,* his father.

He considered, as well, the task Professor Lischke had in front of him. During rehearsals he frequently found the intimidated old man staring helplessly at the sheer riot of activity unfolding in the theatre.

Cantilevers and counterweights, set and lighting changes, rainfall from the riggings, and most unsettling of all to a close-up sleighter accustomed to serenely inebriated audiences of a dozen or less, the number of seats in the house.

"An omelette in a hat won't do," said Fleischl. "Certainly not past the first row."

While preparations for the premiere whirled around them, he and the Professor adapted some handy magnetic standbys for a larger and more distant audience. They opted for a simple trick relying upon the Professor's beloved top hat. At Fleischl's request, the metallurgist fashioned wire filaments, thin as hair, which were bent around frames, and then fitted, one each, to the cards in a standard deck. Magnets were secreted in the Professor's hat, so that when carts went into the hat, they darted immediately to its sides and stuck. When he sprayed the cards into the air with one hand, toward the hat he held in the other (and said a few words of "magical" gibberish), the cards were swallowed into the hat. And when he turned the hat over to dump them onto the floor, none appeared.

"Easy and elegant," said Professor Lischke. "The Vanishing Deck." The trick was decipherable even from the balcony as long as the Professor remained beneath the theatre lamps.

The Professor practiced it diligently. On the night before the premiere, he was running through it when his declaration of "the vanishing deck!" was rudely interrupted by a violent trembling of the stage.

"Dear God, what is that?" he cried.

"That, my dear ingenue, is the Corsican Trap." Oliver took his place center stage with Albin, the metallurgist and his crew.

"We're including Les Freres Corses in the show?" the Professor asked.

"Not quite. It's a glide trap, but it's named for an English production of the Corsican Brothers at the Kean's Princess. A feat of engineering."

"To what end?" asked Professor Lischke.

"To the end of swallowing whole anything I have to say," said Fleischl.

"Entertainment," said Albin. "Must we remind you?"

The metallurgist showed them wooden laths set close to one another, running the length of the stage. "We've modified it. Typically, a counterweight will deliver an actor onto the stage from below, like an elevator.

"This daemon trap is something no one's seen before," said Oliver.

"What's it deliver?" Asked Professor Lischke.

He pointed and said, "That beast."

From behind an upstage scrim came a mighty reverberation that shook the backstage array of ropes and wheels. Down an inclined plane of rails it came, starting from somewhere in the heavens, it seemed, along a gentle slope of ledges to a semicircular trap, where its triangular nose halted.

"I don't know what to say." Fleischl stared at the construct. It was far smaller than its sleeping sibling in the shallows off Stralsund. It was just a bow with the name emblazoned upon it for the audience to read.

Elegy.

His crew behind him, the metallurgist enthusiastically described the trap's mechanics in words that flew by Fleischl just as Albin's alchemical symbols had. *Scruto, wound around drums, passes a groove, turned by a rope onto a windlass.*

Most of it meant nothing. Some of it, though, the name, and especially the rope, made it clear just what he'd be sharing the Wintergarten stage with.

"I know," said Oliver, as he wrapped a fraternal arm around Fleischl. "It seems overwhelming. Let me just say this. I think you're the most extraordinary man I've ever encountered. Berlin deserves to meet you properly."

"I'm afraid," said Fleischl.

"Of what? Tell me."

"That being amongst all this will make me want to try again. That I'll never stop."

"I didn't know you when Kiel happened," said Oliver. "But it cost you the love of your life. It led you to truly, finally face your father's death. There's only so much a man can take. I think you'll never try again just for the sake of curiosity. It would need to be something you can't imagine. Something impossible. No, I say you'll remain among we who care about you, helping patients and now, entertaining audiences with remarkable stories. And my astonishing reels, of course."

"Of course."

All around them, people scrambled to settle the last bits of business for the following night's premiere. Oliver's reels ignited across the scrim. The Professor sprayed magnetized cards into his hat. Scenery shifted on the fly. Sandbagged curtains rose and fell.

Late that evening, Fleischl would practice what he planned to say, and not say.

For the moment, arm in arm with Oliver, it was enough to watch the spectacle unfold. The descent of the *Elegy's* bow, the first thundering soundwritten notes of the storm, Dowid's voice, the place where he would stand amidst it all. He promised himself, there on stage, that whatever happened, whatever the audience's reaction, he wouldn't watch Dowid's film. He couldn't see himself nearly drown as Dowid gave his father's last moments back.

"A penny for your thoughts," Albin said as he came to where Fleischl and Oliver stood.

"I hope I don't sink it again," Fleischl said.

★★★

In the fall of 1908, *He Who Listens* presents *Under the Waves* premiered at the Wintergarten. It was one of the few significant theaters in Berlin not owned in whole or part by August Bliekroder.

The professor's card play was performed, as far as Fleischl could tell from the wings, primarily for the Kabarette woman who sat in the second row. But the rest of the audience applauded too, and Lischke left the stage beaming.

Next came some short Holmesian reels Oliver had fashioned from two of Doyle's lesser stories, projected from the cinematographe backstage onto the gauzy scrim that stretched from the rafters to the floor. While stagehands moved the last props to their places, the audience watched *Sherlock Holmes Baffled,* a trifle of a film only seconds long, in which the detective sat in his kitchen while a burglar appeared and disappeared. That was followed by *The Adventure Of The Beryl Coronet.* Between the films, Albin announced that beneath one lucky patron's seat, the title crown lay hidden. An excited woman stood and waved the trinket up for everyone to see just before the house lights plunged.

A soft glow rose behind the scrim. There was a hearth fire of muted red thanks to the lighting man's rig of tiny kliegs wrapped in tinted foil. Through the sheer fabric, the audience saw Fleischl seated at a desk littered with papers, open files and his own personal touch, a battery with wires. The painted backdrop depicted bookshelves running along the wall, broken in the center to make room for a map of the brain's hemispheres. At Thalhammer's library, which was the basis for the office set, that spot between floor to ceiling shelves was broken by the tunnel door.

The staging included an end table and a couch. It was meant as a nod to the evolving theories of psychiatric analysis, but as prop masters in either wing made ready with barrels of dry ice, Fleischl could think only of how Greta felt in his arms that long gone day on Anton's couch.

The dry ice did its work. Though he tried to maintain his pose—a serious man at his desk, lost in serious thought—he couldn't help but peek as tides of dry ice cloud flowed from the barrels secreted behind the roped curtain on either side of the stage to coalesce in front of the scrim. As it thickened to a minor fog bank, Oliver ignited his cinematographe once again. The still image of a man's anguished face projected directly onto the fog.

The audience gasped at the haunting specter of a disembodied head on clouds. Fleischl tried not to smile. The actor who'd sat for the image was an artist's model and, as Oliver put it, his outsize facial gestures were intended, "for the back of the theatre across the street." It was the face of a man beset by troubles.

"Illusions," Fleischl said loudly. He stood up from the desk, parted the scrim and strode through the dry ice cloud and the man's face, dispelling both in a breeze of chilled air. The audience applauded. In the wings, a props man sealed up the dry ice barrels. Soon the clouds thinned to wisps, leaving him alone under the lamps. The office lighting snuffed behind him, rendering the scrim opaque. He heard frantic skittering backstage as the stage was cleared to make way for the *Elegy's* entrance.

It was all on him now. His mouth felt sandy. The high collar of his shirt felt as tight as a vise. For a moment he feared forgetting the entire lecture. Then the men he'd witnessed up close came to mind and with them their peculiar, crushing burdens. Anton, Gert, Dowid. All of them carried one way or the other by the sea. Always the sea.

"To the addled mind," he said, "illusions are real. They are the world. Such people are lost to us. We try talking to them, but we can't get through. We try showing them things they ought to know. Their wives, husbands, children, homes, even their own reflections. It's as if they see something we can't. Or else they see nothing at all. Our sounds and visions are no longer theirs. How can we reach them?

"I have found a way. We give them a gift, a piece of them that's been lost. We pry open the window of their mind. I have seen it work."

An unwanted thought intruded, of Greta leaving as her father's own window closed. He grabbed hold of his next line as if it was a rope.

"It can be terribly difficult to see them leave us, and it can be strangely difficult when they return, knowing they may not stay long. But this work will help those we think we've lost to injury, to infirmity, to psychosis. I believe in this work with all my heart. And I'm here, with your kind permission, to demonstrate. The louder and brighter the sounds and visions, the wider the window."

Down came the *Elegy*. It rode the glide trap mechanism accompanied by thunder both soundwritten and real. The ledges shook and the stage felt as if it might give way. The ship's bow parted the scrim and astonished the audience. Fleischl thought the entire orchestra section might leap from their seats for fear of being crushed.

"There's no danger," he said. "Not to any of you, at least."

In the wings, Albin grinned at that. He nodded encouragingly.

Entertainment, Fleischl thought.

"This idea began with a man named Anton." He began the story, pausing at the building of the diorama, "in a room very much like the one I was sitting in a moment ago," because high in the balcony, he thought he saw a small light blossom open. A little flicker, perhaps a flame, fine as a faraway star. "I suppose," he said, "that's why I wanted to help him so badly. I understood what it felt like when the sea takes something precious. What I managed to do for him, the sound and vision, was all that a young man with nothing but odds, ends and someone helping me--someone extraordinary--could manage. It wasn't much. Yet it gave Anton a little piece of himself back."

Whether there had really been a light in the balcony or whether his mind had put it, he couldn't be sure. It was gone now.

"May I have a volunteer," he said.

A few hands went up slowly. He selected a sturdy-looking man of about thirty with thinning hair, a waxed mustache, and a skeptical expression. Egged on by his mates, the man came onstage and waved to the audience. Fleischl escorted him to a chair and a stagehand wheeled out a table on which sat the galvanometer and its electrodes.

"Nothing to worry about," Fleischl said.

"I'm not worried," said the man. "But what do you intend to do with that thing?"

"Read your mind," said Fleischl with a studied nonchalance.

The audience laughed, but the man whispered to Fleischl, "will it hurt?"

"You won't feel a thing," said Fleischl while he attached three electrodes, enough for the most basic of results. That the man's hair was noticeably thinning was the primary reason Fleischl selected him.

"You won't feel a thing," he told the man again. "And if you do, remember, it's most definitely not my machine."

After the electrodes were in place, he circled the man. Pausing behind him, Fleischl clapped his hands sharply. The man jumped to the amusement of his fellows.

"What were you thinking just then?" Fleischl asked.

"That it was a mistake coming up here."

The audience roared.

Fleischl said, "may I suggest that you weren't thinking at all? Whatever your brain did in response to the stimulus, it was spontaneous. For that instant, your thoughts were interrupted. Everything in your mind went dark and you had an involuntary reaction. Let's see what that instant looks like."

He tore the ribbon of paper spewing from the galvanometer and held it for the crowd to see. It was an empty gesture, as the waves traced from the machine's strings were so frail as to be invisible to anyone beyond the first row. His subject freed himself from the wires and came to look.

"That part there," said the man, "that little triangle. Is that when you gave me such a start?"

"Very good. That's your mind, crying out."

In the wings, Oliver feigned a swoon.

Fleischl escorted the man back to his seat to a round of applause. He gave the man the paper with waves on it as a souvenir. When he returned to the stage, the lights dimmed. A clap of thunder, magnified by several well-placed soundwriters, rocked the room.

A voice filled the theatre and Fleischl winced.

I remember.

Dowid's words trailed away as the footage of Stralsund opened across the scrim. Fleischl moved to the wings on one side of the stage, and had a clear view of Albin and Oliver, standing in the wings on the other. The first scene was a slow pan from sea tunnel to Thalhammer and back again. Fleischl turned away and wandered behind the backstage curtain to the inside of the *Elegy's* false bow. From there he stared up at the rigging, the rafters and planked walkway, at the pulleys and wheels, at the props men high above who stood ready at the curtains and lights. He looked anywhere but the scrim, where in a mirror of what the audience saw, the *Elegy* bucked, broke and sank, and somewhere inside he floated, tethered to life by a rope his father made. Being in the false bow brought him back to his days at Stralsund's shipyard, standing in the bones of wrecks, trying to piece together the puzzle that was his father.

The light was extinguished and the iris closed. The film was over. A stunned silence filled the Wintergarten until, row by row, there came applause. It didn't stop. It rose to a crescendo as Fleischl listened backstage.

Albin and Oliver waved at him to go back out. When he finally did, there came a fresh swell of clapping, shouting, and raised hands. The house lights came up. When the applause finally died down, Fleischl paused for a moment and said, "Are there questions?"

Hands went up. Before he could choose, someone stood in the tenth row and shouted, "I've heard stories about you."

As other voices rose to join in, Fleischl held up a hand for silence. "Let me just say this once. I imagine there are plenty of you who have heard things about me. As a smart man and dear friend once told me something: if you ask someone whether they believe in God, they can answer you; if you ask for proof of God's existence, no one can answer you. All they can do is believe. I'll leave it at this. Something happened once. Sometimes I believe it. Other times I dismiss it and try to forget it. But I can't prove it, so I make no claims about it. I simply hold it."

A voice called from the balcony. "I have a question."

"Yes?"

"The man in the ship, the one you were in the water with. How is he now?"

He tried to think of what to say. Rope. Steps to the sea. A pair of balsa wings.

Oliver and Albin watched as Fleischl walked to the very edge of the stage. He wished the little light would ignite once more, if it was ever really there to begin with.

"He's no longer silent," he said, "and I bid you goodnight."

Fleischl left the stage to more applause, made his way past the the crowd gathering around the Corsican trap, and went to Oliver's office. He sat with his head in his hands and wept. When the last of it had left him, he reached for Albin's new addition to the production office: the telephone. Holding it to his ear, he asked the operator to connect him to Thalhammer. Rapholtz came on the line. They exchanged pleasantries. Rapholtz asked about the premiere and promised to attend a show soon—if there were more to come.

"I expect there will be," said Fleischl. "May I say hello to him? Is he awake?"

"Give me a moment."

He heard Rapholtz set the receiver down. After a short time, he heard breathing.

"Hello, Dowid," said Fleischl.

It took a moment. Rapholtz had told him that Dowid was distrustful of the device.

"Do you know who this is?"

"Sometimes I think about you," Dowid said.

"Do you?"

"I don't like thinking about you."

"Still have the rope, I assume?"

"It's right here."

"And how many steps?"

"One thousand, seven hundred and two."

"Do you recall the ship, Dowid?"

The connection grew quiet.

"Or seeing me, perhaps?"

"I think I saw him," Dowid said. "I think I told him. I don't always remember things right."

"I'm grateful to you, Dowid. For trying to remember."

"When will you come back up?"

It was Fleischl's turn to be quiet.

"I'm tired," Dowid said. "Here's the man who came to get me."

Rapholtz took the receiver and asked Fleischl if he was well.

"Did I hurt him?" Fleischl asked.

"No, doctor. Did he hurt you?"

"I should say goodnight. It's late and I've kept you from your rest."

"He's the same, Fleischl. Don't worry about him. It's as we've discussed. I don't believe what happened is still within him, and if it is, it's settled at the bottom of Apia Bay. He's content counting steps. There has been no somnambulation since that day with you. Did you do something? Perhaps. But perhaps it's best to let men keep what they create. Maybe when all's said and done, it's not such a terrible thing."

They ended the call and Fleischl went to accept the congratulations of his friends. They planned a celebratory party for the following evening, drank, and went home.

He was exhausted, and desired nothing so much as his bed, but before he turned in, he went to his desk and withdrew an old file. He opened it, turned to the last, yellowed page of his thesis, and began to write.

Forget all the rest of this. It shouldn't have happened. It happened. It never happened.

Just live, Fleischl Berger.

CHAPTER Sixteen
He Who Listens

What began as an event became a sensation and a fixture at the Wintergarten. *He Who Listens* took up residence for the duration of the year. It garnered glowing notices and a faithful audience, many of whom returned for the spectacle, Fleischl suspected, more than the lecture. They came again and again, brought friends and relations, all despite the relative sameness of the shows. Only the volunteer and the manner of stimulus varied.

Professor Lischke's opening act garnered a brief mention in Tageblatt's review of opening night. Tucked a couple of sentences before the end of the piece, the critic wrote, "as a warm-up, the magician billed as The Prescient Professor pleased with a card trick." So emboldened was he that he added to his repertoire. Over the ensuing weeks he tackled levitation, a variety of egg-based sleights, interlocking rings, and self-shuffling cards, all to warm receptions. He won the favor of his lady friend and his colleagues at the Kabarette who came as frequently as their funds allowed.

Following the Professor's act and the always dramatic entrance of the *Elegy*, Fleischl continued soliciting a volunteer at the beginning of each performance. Word had gotten around regarding the electrodes and the chance to take home one's own brain waves, so there was never a shortage of raised hands. He repeated the same joke at each show: "You won't feel a thing. And if you do, remember: it's most definitely not my machine."

Once attached, he subjected the volunteers to soft stimuli. A clap of hands, a subdued yell from behind them, a touch with something cold. He varied the stimulus each time at Albin's insistence.

"These people talk," Albin said. "And the reviewers. They give things away."

Once, he used a hidden pot of powder that flashed when lit. Once, he struck a folded sheet of metal with a hammer. They all produced a minor, but reliable tick on the galvanometer. He revealed the bump in the readings to the audience member with a bit of fanfare. Wide, newly believing eyes, applause, and the finale that Fleischl continued to turn away from in dread.

The first few moments of the film portrayed a flurry of behind-the-scenes activity. A bit of set construction, the docks, and Thalhammer's hill in silver nitrate pieces.

He would take nightly refuge in the *Elegy* and listen to Dowid leaving his cabin. Dowid arriving at the roundhouse door. Dowid holding the rope. Dowid speaking.

Everyone said it was beautiful. The audience went wild for it. They wanted to know what happened to the man in the film. They wanted to know who it was he was supposed to find, and whom he was supposed to tell. Above all, they wanted more.

It made for elegant theatre. Fleischl's natural reticence translated as suspense, his quiet demeanor as a mystic's aura. So went the reviews.

There were always questions. Always, someone asked, tentatively, whether the rumors about him were true. He deflected their efforts to learn what happened, had it happened before, could he make it happen again, here, now. He told them it was pointless to ask.

Once, he said, "if a thing like *that* thing ever actually happened, it would take away far more than it would give."

He studiously avoided saying a word about cannons, death or telegrams. Always, he left *her* out of everything, despite the fact that everything taking place was drenched with her. And he succeeded admirably, at least until the final show on New Year's Eve, when the Bliekroders made their presence known at last.

★★★

Final show? But you've succeeded so admirably peddling fraud to decent Germans! Why stop now?
Anonymous

Oliver set the edition of the Tageblatt down on his dining room table so both Fleischl and Albin could see the full advertisement. It was directed to the attention of *Berger F, He Who Listens (to your pockets jingle)*.

"Who do they think they're fooling with this tripe?" Oliver said.

Albin set aside his writing. "You think it's August?"

"Or both of them," Fleischl said. "It must be."

"It can be no other," Oliver agreed.

"For what reason, though? Do I need to resurrect the attorney retainer again?"

Fleischl gave a full account of his dealings with the Bliekroders that went well beyond a simple, if nearly immortal, dispute over the rights to sound, vision and electrode placement. He left *her* out but for a few precious pieces. *She was close to me once. She was something that August coveted and Alice despised. She's lost to us all now.*

"The one who heard you," said Albin. "Where is she now?"

The last time Fleischl had seen her, she was a pageboy flitting madcap across the Orientalische screen, taking a globe of the world away from chattering, ineffectual men in search of something impossible. He couldn't help but smile at the irony.

"I don't know," he said. "What do we do about this? What if he tries to ruin the finale?"

Albin's was a thin smile, and it had taken Fleischl a bit to get used to finding the joy in it. But their occultist friend and patron seemed quite pleased at the provocation. "I'll tell you what we do," he said. "We reply."

To our privileged correspondent Anonymous

"I like the privileged part," Albin said. "A nice touch."

"That was Fleischl's idea," Oliver said. "He can be quite sarcastic in his stealthy way."

Greetings,

Rest assured, we concur wholeheartedly that fraud runs rampant in our society's finer quarters. Scientists pretending to be entertainers. Bankers pretending to be scientists. Where does it end? Why, we're even aware of a theatre pretending to be a dock!

We'll happily save you a seat, on the house. Perhaps you'll volunteer. While the machine is old, the electrode method is quite modern.

Management

"It's a bit antagonistic, isn't it?" Fleischl asked.

"There's a long and storied Jewish tradition of using humor to loosen the shackles of the oppressor," said Oliver.

"That's a bit dramatic," said Albin. "But, to Fleischl's point, does anyone believe this is the final word?"

"Only someone unacquainted with the Bliekroders could think that," Fleischl said.

"I'll have the attorney ready," Albin sighed.

Fleischl sighed as well. "And so we wait for the other shoe to drop, as they say."

★★★

Now It Can Be Told!

On December 2, 1909, a reply appeared on the second page of the Tageblatt. Its eye-catching proclamation that *now*, not later, *it* ("whatever *it* is," Oliver said cheerfully) *can be told* ("because I wasn't allowed to tell it before?" Fleischl asked) appeared above a rather artfully composed photograph Oliver had taken in the fraudulent sausage shoppe.

"An empty chair," said Fleischl.

"Keep reading," said Albin. And Fleischl did.

At each show, during which Herr Berger thrills with his presentation of the mind's unknowable landscapes…

"I suppose that's their idea of entertainment," Fleischl said.

"Of the purest kind," Oliver agreed. "How you've learned, meshpucha."

"…unknowable landscapes, there has been, unbeknownst to all, a chair left empty for the one who heard!

"No there hasn't," Fleischl said. "Has there?"

"Of course not," Albin assured him.

Fill it if you dare, oh anonymous listener, lest you not remain anonymous for long! The truth will always out. A sum of twenty-five marks to the audience member that successfully challenges, cajoles, or shames He Who Listens to prove that which he is too afraid to speak aloud. TRANSMISSION. Ask him! Demand it of him! Or is he a charlatan?

"I just hope this doesn't devolve into some sort of child's game," said Oliver. "Everyone trying to fill an empty chair when the music stops." He was a little tipsy.

"We're not putting what happened to you in the spotlight," said Albin. "It's good for us to have a bit of intrigue. Controversy, even. We can certainly reply to keep this going, but this man isn't prone to violence, is he? We can post guards."

"No," Fleischl said. "The Bliekroders are only dangerous in the way bitter, rich people have been for time immemorial."

"To more litigation!"

Fleischl's and Oliver's glasses met Albin's above their plates. They settled into their meal, and as Oliver and Albin exchanged ideas for putting new, dark pleasures before the camera, Fleischl stared at the many couples dining around them. "If we do reply back," he said, "I'd like to be prepared."

"Are you thinking he'll actually come to the Wintergarten?" Oliver asked.

He thought of the ad's empty chair, and of a pageboy spiriting a round blue world off to the vanishing point of a taut white screen.

"He's not the one I'm thinking about. I'm going to add a little something to the finale. I'll need plenty of wire."

★★★

It wasn't quite the game of musical chairs Oliver envisioned, but on the closing night of *Under the Waves,* a capacity audience buzzed pre-curtain, woozy with anticipation of a scandal that didn't involve them and could therefore be enjoyed much like the swooping *Elegy.* Which chair? Who heard? Were they in attendance? What of Anonymous? Would there be trouble?

They didn't have to wait long.

The Professor's act ended, Oliver's Sherlockian reel snuffed, the lights dimmed, and Fleischl appeared at his desk behind the scrim. The stagehands scarcely had the barrel lids off before the first audience member stood some dozen rows back.

Fleischl saw him rise but held his pose.

"What happened to you that day?" the man called loudly. There were scattered hoots and cries for him to sit down.

"Is it true?" cried a woman, "that you sent your thoughts one hundred miles?"

He couldn't help but look up. Through the gauzy barrier, men and women were standing. He counted a dozen by the time he left the office set and parted the scrim.

From the wings, Albin and Oliver watched with growing alarm. Fleischl nodded to them as he walked to the edge of the stage.

In the first row, an elderly woman stood with the help of a nurse. She held a slip of paper.

They all did, he saw.

"Is it true," the woman asked nervously, "that your transmission burned down a telegraph office?"

Now the questions came rapidly. The catcalls died away. For better or worse, the audience awaited his answers.

"Is it true that your transmission lit the sky with lightning?"

"Is it true that you were heard by an entire neighborhood?"

"I heard you married the one who heard you."

"I heard it killed the one who heard you."

That last one drew gasps, and Fleischl decided that he had had quite enough.

"Tell me," he said sharply, "who it is who supposedly occupies the empty chair if I killed them with my magical mind? Come now, don't simply repeat words given to you by this Anonymous without any thought of your own."

Albin gestured frantically to the stagehands on the scaffolds to drop the curtain.

Fleischl snapped his fingers and got Albin's attention. He shook his head and mouthed the words, "It's ok."

"Just do it then," a man cried out from the balcony.

"Do what?" Fleischl called back. Behind him, Albin and Oliver came onstage along with a few hands and the metallurgist.

"You know," the man shouted. "Transmit your thoughts! Be heard!"

"You hear me right now, do you not? There you are, then. Do I get a share of the bounty this Anonymous promised you?"

That earned a bit of laughter. It was still difficult to judge just how many had come to hear him and how many to see who else might hear.

Fleischl knelt to address the elderly woman and asked to borrow her paper. He read her question. It was written in an elegant hand.

He tucked it under his arm and rubbed it vigorously.

"I'm a psychiatrist," he announced before removing the paper from beneath his arm and letting its static charge adhere to the woman's head. The paper clung to her hair at a daft angle.

"Not a magician," he finished.

"So you refuse?" a voice called out.

"To prove it?" Fleischl asked as the audience quieted. "I've tried that. I can't. I don't think it's possible. To demonstrate any aspect of it for the purpose of entertainment? To sell more tickets? Yes, I refuse. For those of you who came to see that, we'll gladly refund your price of admission."

"What?" Albin said behind him.

"Now, if we may continue."

At the rear of the theatre, the exit doors opened and a figure entered. A young man strode down the aisle holding an envelope high above his head. Fleischl recognized the uniform; it was a telegraph delivery boy.

"Herr Berger," he said, out of breath. "My instructions were to deliver this to you if you refused."

He held the telegram up for Fleischl to take. "I was instructed to tell you, it doesn't ask if you died."

Fleischl opened the envelope, turned to Oliver, and said, "Entertainment, I suppose."

Oliver winced.

"I'm instructed to read it if you won't," said the young man.

"I'll do it," said Fleischl.

The undersigned calls upon the scientific community to attend a gathering at a date to be determined, at which the concept of transmission will be assessed, debated…

He paused.

...and demonstrated. If it is, the undersigned owns all rights. If it is not, Herr Berger is called upon to defend his assertion or face charges of fraud, as is she who heard him.

But the letter didn't actually say, "she." It said Greta's name, and it was underscored by hand.

"Signed by Anonymous," Fleischl announced. He gave it back to the delivery boy. "First of all, I assert nothing. Second, something's been bothering me since your advertisement, Anonymous."

Heads turned. Murmurs rose as the crowd searched their ranks for signs of Anonymous' presence.

"Do you remember," Fleischl said, "what you called the idea of transmission when we first met at your university?" He waited for the audience to hush. "You banished me and my sad little story, as you dubbed it, to the nearest ratskellar. You laughed me out of the auditorium. Yet now you do this. You want to claim it for your own, as if it meant something to you. Why? The answer, of course, is that you didn't take the advertisement out, August, nor did you author the message or these questions. The empty chair, Alice, was a bit heavy handed."

There was a small metal plate installed at the edge of the stage, next to his left foot. At his instructions, the metallurgist had implanted it in the wood, along with the hastily connected quarter mile of wire flowing from its underside through the theatre's basement, up the walls and to several fragile lights hanging in the dark above those seats that, despite the advertisements, remained unsold and empty.

He stepped down on the plate. Throughout the theatre, soft lights rose.

"Ah," he said. "There you are."

In the first row of the balcony, a soft circle of gold cast down from the dangling light to ignite the baubles sprayed across a woman too distant to see clearly. But he could guess the sour expression she wore.

"Not to worry," he said to the audience as they gasped. "That's not the one who, legend has it, heard me. That's Anonymous. Please,

Frau Bliekroder. Join me."

She left the balcony and soon appeared in the aisle. August was with her, and he didn't look pleased.

"Do you expect me to perform like a trained animal?" Alice asked him as she approached the stage.

"I don't expect anything," said Fleischl, "I'm just curious as to why you're doing this."

"I can't abide liars," she said. "I told you that before."

Albin and Oliver approached. "Perhaps we should drop the curtain," Albin said, but neither Fleischl nor Alice paid him any attention. They stared each other down.

"Ladies and gentlemen," said Albin, turning to the restive crowd, "if you'll just be patient with us, we'll start in short order."

Alice's eyes were full. He wondered when anyone had ever seen her like that.

"Why does any of this matter to you?" he asked.

"Because I wanted to believe…" Her voice cracked. "I don't forget. You've succeeded in at least one thing. You sent away the love of a lifetime and in the process, made it clear how little I matter to anyone. For that, you don't get to keep this. You can keep your trivial photoplays and your loud noises. Stick to shabby theatrics. It's all you have the courage for. Those idiotic little lights. What do you call that trick?"

"I haven't thought about it. Perhaps I'll call it The Electric Love Song."

"Fitting."

She stormed off, down the aisle and out of the theatre. To their surprise, August lingered at the foot of the stage.

"She'll fail," Fleischl told him.

"There are precious few things she fails at," August said.

"It's not worth what she'll go through. If you love her at all, you'll stop her."

"My love or lack of it has never been her concern. Nor have you, in case your ego has convince you that was a jilted woman pining for you."

He left.

"She's certainly pining for something," said Oliver.

After August was out of the theatre, and Oliver succeeded in coaxing the audience back to their seats, the show began anew. Fleischl didn't take his place in the library. It wasn't simply that Greta was everywhere now, as surely as if she'd appeared bodily from the dry ice cloud. It was that after all that happened in front of an audience who'd come for a fight, and instead watched three pathetic people compare old wounds in the shadow of a twice-sunk ship, the sheer fraud of it all drove him mad. So they went straight to Dowid's footage.

When it was done at last, there was only one question from the audience.

"Is it at all possible," asked a woman, "that she who heard was here tonight, in one of the empty chairs?"

Later that evening, over supper at the Adlon, the three of them talked about what might come next. Albin poured cognac and admitted the entire night had terrified him. "And I'm a Satanist," he said.

Oliver allowed that while he couldn't be certain it qualified as *entertainment,* he was certain the evening was assuredly not the last show.

"It wasn't?" Fleischl asked.

Albin agreed. It made for riveting theatre, and it opened new possibilities. To emphasize his point, he revealed that he and Oliver had concocted an idea for a new reel. And they wanted Fleischl to serve as the lead.

"A mystery to solve," Oliver said, "a damsel to rescue. Just an ordinary day for He Who Listens."

"Who on earth would want to watch me, of all people, in something like that?"

"Who on earth," Oliver said, "would want to watch you speak of helping troubled men. Quite a few, as it turns out."

"That's not why they come. They come for the near deaths and the ribbons and the debate, at least they did tonight. They tolerate my lecture at best. It's incidental."

"And yet they come away having heard it." Oliver pushed a script over. "There's room for what you do, what you truly do, in the story. We'll write those cards together."

"Albin," said Oliver, "talk some sense into him."

"I think it's a fine idea. Let the people see something extraordinary, in about six minutes on a short reel."

Fleischl turned the paper over. *He Who Listens,* or *The Man from Beyond*

"That title," Fleischl grumbled.

"I can think of a worse one, *Electric Love Singer.* "

They laughed because they knew Fleischl would try it. They understood that much; Fleischl Berger was an ordinary man whose ordinary days, alike as two drops of rain in a storm, held extraordinary things. Even the occasional impossible thing, if one were prone to believe. There was certainly room for one more thing.

They ate, drank, enjoyed each other's company, and through the evening Fleischl thought not of the Bliekroders but the woman and her question. *Is it at all possible that she who heard was here tonight?*

"Whether she's among us tonight or not," he'd replied, "I do believe she heard."

CHAPTER Seventeen
Blue

His ears ringing with the whistles of plummeting bombs, the ominous hum of Fokkers flying overhead, whizzing bullets and of course the screams, Fleischl removed the electrodes from his head and lifted the stylus away from the diamond disc. Oliver's recording wouldn't do. It was far too violent and too close to real life for the audience.

Closing his eyes, he listened to the last of it reverberate down the aisles and over the back rows of the Wintergarten. He'd been tinkering with ideas for the show as usual, all the while thinking that it was past time to give it a new name, a new opening act (now that Professor Lischke's age was overtaking him), some new banter, and a fresh coat of paint for the hoary *Elegy*.

He felt a considerable headache coming on. It was no wonder. He'd been barraging himself for six straight days with sights and sounds. He pressed the knuckles of his thumbs into his temples until bright little nebulae swirled in his vision. His back ached and a familiar throbbing returned to his leg. He craved fresh air and a cold drink.

It was nearly noon on a Sunday in July 1919. *Under The Waves* was into its tenth year. Echoes of the war still gripped the country in a merciless vise of fear and failure. He spent his free time studying the many ways men had concocted to change the minds of others. He was ever on the lookout for things to say or stimulus to try that would make people feel like the sun shone over the Rhine, there was enough food for all, and there were still reasons to dance. All for a Wintergarten audience who, though smaller now, and arriving with discount coupons clipped from the Tageblatt, still came for a chance to sit in the volunteer seat and relive a bit of the old days. An evening of talk, phantasmascopes, and short reels starring He Who Listens, or 'HWL' as he was called in the trades.

To Fleischl, the *He Who Listens* shorts had grown more out-landish. But the audiences enjoyed them. They were a comfort in com-fortless times, so he shouted *I hear you!* (his trademarked catchphrase) through a succession of flickering mysteries. In *He Who Listens* or *The Man from Beyond,* he used his gift to find a murderer from among ten catatonic inmates. In *He Who Listens* or *The Secret Service,* he improba-bly joined the title agency to ferret out a double agent counterfeiter. At Oliver's gleeful insistence, he filmed one comedic short, *He Who Listens* or *Duck!,* in which he shouted *I hear you!* and was promptly punched by the stuffed paw of a certain boxing kangaroo.

Before agreeing to do even a single one, he'd made demands. No sinking ships. No falling cannons.

"As contract demands go," Albin had said, "these are reasonable. Also, we don't have the budget to sink another ship."

"No water deaths," added Fleischl.

"Well, now we'll need to revise." And Oliver did. By the colorbursts of autumn 1910, Fleischl had found himself in thoroughly caked makeup, thrusting his fist toward Oliver's cinematographe in the glass-roofed studio outside the city.

"Say the line," Oliver had directed. "Then the first of many punches."

"I feel perfectly ludicrous," Fleischl had said. "I'm He Who Listens, not He Who Speaks."

"That's good," Albin had said approvingly. "We should use that."

His headache ebbed. The bones in his neck clicked in time to the galvanometer's newest modification, silvered wire. He paced the stage to get the blood flowing again, selected something to read from a heap of letters, periodicals and lecture notes, and bade goodbye to the ushers as he left. By seven o'clock he'd be back onstage, wiring up *altekachers*, giving a case study or two from among the many patients he'd treated over the years, and he would turn his back, always, on the *Elegy*. Every Sunday rain, shine or bombs; the Wintergarten served as a shelter. It also served as a haven, community center and unofficial *shul* for what seemed like half of Berlin's Jews. He supposed they had Alice Bliekroder to thank for that.

In the beginning, Alice came at least once a month. Sometimes she was in the company of other, similarly serious and refined women; other times she came alone. In either case, she never failed to provoke him and draw attention to herself. So thought Albin and Oliver, at least. Once, she'd appeared in the very balcony seat she'd occupied on the night he'd called her to the stage. She'd gesticulated wildly throughout the performance. It wasn't until the very end that he'd understood, she'd been making a show of the fact that there was no little light hanging above her.

At a show in 1913, she'd leapt suddenly from the wings to scare him, which she succeeded admirably at. She then ordered the startled audience to search among themselves for "anyone, possibly in disguise, who looks as if she heard something just now."

Stunts, Oliver called it. Narcissism, Albin offered. To Fleischl, though, her appearances indicated something else at work. A sadness that fed on itself, that needed something always out of her reach. He tried to tell his friends that when she startled him onstage and then called out the search for someone who heard, it didn't feel outrageous so much as pitiable.

"It reminded me of something she said once," he told Albin and Oliver, "about being impossible to love. There's a sad hope in what she does."

"She comes with the worst of intentions," Oliver reminded him, and he let the subject of Alice Bliekroder go. As did Alice herself; she'd ceased her visits to the Wintergarten by the end of 1913, when Albin gave up their Saturday night slots and began performing on Sundays. For Saturday was the Sabbath, and they'd begun to draw an inordinate number of Jews. Oliver suggested that they came, at first, because they'd heard about the argument with Alice; and then they kept coming because of Fleischl's growing reputation as a thinker (Talmudic, Oliver said), as a debater (rabbinical, Oliver said), and as one in communion with the fantastic.

"Which is Kabbalistic, of course," Albin declared. "Have you considered converting to Satanism? I think you have a gift for it."

Fleischl promised to give the idea serious thought.

The Sabbath was studiously avoided, and beginning on the first Sunday of 1914, *Under the Waves* took up once-weekly residence at seven sharp. Whether full, less full, or a *we did the show mainly for each other* level of empty, a celebratory dinner at the Adlon always followed.

Though the show's essential elements remained largely unchanged, the manner in which they were accomplished evolved with the times and the science. Wax cylinders gave way to discs. He added Einthoven strings to the machine and hoped the Bliekroders wouldn't sue him again. Along with the HWL series, Max began filming the volunteers as they underwent Fleischl's gentle stimulations. They set up an old phantasmascope in the Wintergarten lobby, where, for the price of a coffee, patron could watch previous audience members jump at the provocations of *He Who Listens*.

The majority of their audience was respectful and abided by the placard Albin placed in the lobby circa October 1914, following one interruption too many. *Herr Berger will entertain all questions, assertions, and entreaties, but there will be no more time given over to (1) accusations of fraud, or (2) questions about the one who heard.*

As he walked the three blocks westward from the Wintergarten to his favorite cafe three blocks west, he passed lines of people standing in the swelter, waiting for bread from the Backerei Merkle. Shoppes that were once full of life were now empty. The men who ran them had gone to war or had fallen into the deprivation and poverty brought on by the war. The ones who had returned from the front badly scarred or burned or with pieces of themselves missing altogether hid in their parlors for fear of scaring children. They couldn't sit at cafe tables and be seen. They couldn't save a chair for friends to come share a beer and a laugh. Those friends were among the dead.

At a window seat he ordered wine and some bitter cheese. He set his pen down next to a collection of photographs and letters from fellow psychiatrists with whom he corresponded. One photo was of a dog in the grip of a seizure, and the resulting alpha waves as they emanated from an Einthoven string, like the ones he used himself. There were photos of the newest in telegraph innovations and an industrial pamphlet extolling the virtues of silvered wire coiled in tight nautiloid fists. *Improved transmission!*

He paged absently through a scholarly article in a French periodical on the canals of Mars, and how best to deliver messages to the people up there. Some said a book in a specially constructed bottle, blasted past Earth's outer edges to float the rest of the way. Others called for light concentrated and cast skywards in a series of semaphores.

One collective cry, struck in coordination with all the peoples of the world, in hopes of being heard.

He lingered over that one.

Tidying the stack of loose papers, he rearranged his plate and stein so nothing touched. For the remainder of the afternoon, he wrote not a word. In the bread line across Potsdamer, the men looked down to avoid seeing each other's shabbiness, while the women looked skyward lest they miss the new century's miracles. Planes and shrieking air torpedoes punched holes in Turkey and Romania, so why not Berlin at this moment, out of a clear sky?

His call time was approaching. Oliver and Albin said they'd need him at the glass house at highest light.

By three that afternoon he was freshly dressed and seated among the crew, waiting for Oliver to start them on their latest HWL short opus, *He Who Listens* or *Mystery At The Asylum.* They would have seemed an odd assortment to anyone strolling by on their way to the city center. In what passed for the cruel Dr. Norcross' secret ice factory hideout beneath the titular asylum (the hastily decorated southern corner of the studio), pipes ran just below the steepled roof, suitable for swinging on. From Werner Krauss, the gruff actor portraying Norcross, they'd borrowed a dining table, which Oliver had disassembled, using parts to construct a conveyor belt. There was a simple piece of cardboard cut to the precise dimensions of a circular saw, as well as several wooden frames, each nearly the size of a woman's wardrobe, covered in blue cellophane—blocks of ice.

That day's damsel, played by Lili Feher, was a statuesque brunette. She served double duty as makeup artist. There were also four scoundrels who, as Fleischl understood the story, worked as factotums for the evil doctor. They seemed quite amiable, he thought. They kept to themselves and roughhoused when they weren't needed.

The way Oliver explained things probably made sense to someone, though not to him. It opened on He Who Listens lingering into the after-hours, studying the writings of all the psychiatric experts in the entire world, when distressed damsel Felice Le Grande runs from stage right with a sordid tale of kidnapping and lost memory. Her father, a kind and caring man, had refused suitor Dr. Alwin Norcross' bid for her hand. In a pique, Norcross snatches Felice and her father. Her father's calls to her are muffled. *I cannot remember the rest,* read Oliver's script, *only that it was dark and so terrifying as to provoke trembling.* Two intertitles, *He invokes her father's voice, and she remembers!* followed by *He Listens! As she describes a cold place he recognizes!* and *He arrives at the ice factory, ready to do battle.*

"For someone he's never met," said Fleischl, "wouldn't it be more believable if he just went to the police?"

"The line," Oliver sighed, "then the punch, and we can adjourn for some food."

Fleischl cleared his throat and waited for Oliver to signal him. *"I hear you!"* he cried.

"And… the punch."

He balled his hand into a chubby fist and threw a punch toward the camera box. A polite round of applause followed, from Le Grande junior, in the clutches of Ice Works scoundrels one through four, and Le Grande senior, who stood behind a blue cellophane curtain, the better to appear entombed in a block of ice.

"Ah, that's why his voice was muffled," Fleischl said as the scoundrels assembled for their turn.

"Frozen by Norcross," Oliver explained. "Moments away from an icy death."

"I suppose that will be on the placard."

"We have a better phrase for the advertisement," Oliver said. "Have some lunch. You kiss the girl next. Let me have my scoundrels."

Scoundrels one through four took their mark. Though they were men of differing heights and builds—one was slight and small, one quite portly, the others in between—they were dressed identically in dingy tan pants, red and white striped pullovers and obviously false black mustaches.

It must be a workplace rule, Fleischl thought as he watched them prepare themselves for the punch.

"And… punch," Oliver said. The scoundrels flung themselves to the floor, where they lay insensate until Max called the shot captured.

After, they all sat together in the yard sharing plates of small sandwiches. Lil applied more pancake to his face while he nibbled at his food. "You'll have to stand tiptoe if you want to kiss me," she said.

"We have a fruit box for him," Albin said.

Fleischl wasn't paying attention. All of the cast and crew were out enjoying a bit of sun and the pleasant breeze, but one of the scoundrels had taken up a position inside the studio by a window, and the way he stared at the world struck Fleischl as something worth watching. The man, bedecked like a little lord in striped top and the mustache, seemed at once content and a bit haunted. Then Albin tapped his shoulder and offered some schnapps for his tepid coffee, which he gladly accepted. When he glanced back, the scoundrel was gone.

Indeed, he was truly gone; in a while Oliver called places and only three scoundrels appeared at their marks.

"Where's the other one?" Oliver asked. "What was his name?"

The remaining scoundrels shrugged. After a few minutes' wait, Max reset the men so as to hide the loss of the fourth, slight little scoundrel.

"So," Fleischl said, "a new advertisement for this?"

Oliver wrote it out on a card, then showed Fleischl and Albin.

"Love and death holding hands," Fleischl read.

"It evokes," Oliver said, "without saying."

"Even I don't know what that means," said Albin.

"It means me," said Fleischl.

On the far street, a sleek, two-toned Horch sedan pulled up.

"Are you cross with me?" asked Oliver.

"No, my friend. It's a rather elegant way of thinking about it."

"About the day," said Albin.

"About the life to that moment," said Fleischl, before he was distracted by a man in chauffeur's attire making his way through the overgrown garden to the glass house door. He wasn't the driver Fleischl remembered from his days in Alice's apartment in the city. This one was young and slim, and he looked nervous.

"Herr Berger?" the driver asked.

"He's busy at the moment," said Oliver. "And you are?"

"Herr Bliekroder sent me. It's a matter of some importance." He held out an envelope.

"Not again," Albin said. "A writ, I presume?"

Fleischl opened it, then showed it to his friends.

I know something you don't, about her. Now Alice knows too. Please come. August

"I think I should go," he said.

Oliver shook his head. "You shouldn't be alone with that man. Or her, if she's any part of this."

"I'll be all right," said Fleischl. "I don't think they intend to kidnap me. Or, who knows? Maybe they employ scoundrels of their own."

"Speaking of which, let me get one more moment from you. And I'd still like to go with you. Having once patronized them, I don't trust them."

Fleischl told the chauffeur to wait at the car. Then he took his place among the toppled scoundrels, courtesy of the fists of HWL. It was all quite silly, and he would have laughed but for August's note. His stomach tightened terribly, and he felt flush with worry at the thought that there was something about her that had caused August Bliekroder to break a decade-long silence. But he had no choice. Greta could be hurt in some way—by their hands, even. *I don't forget,* Alice had said. *You don't get to keep this.*

He took his place with a fainted, soon to be revived Felice LeGrande in his arms. "I guess we're down a scoundrel," she said, arranging the pleats of her dress to expose a bit of thigh for Oliver's camera.

"It appears so."

"Just as well. I had the oddest feeling with that one's hand on my mouth. Quite odd."

"Oh?"

"I could have sworn it was a woman holding me."

Oliver's camera began rolling. It was a flywheel sound he'd grown fond of, clicks and whirs and subtle note that hinted at the alchemy taking place inside, one frame at a time. Warm notes of rising heat, chemicals, friction and the taking of light. But now it sounded like the strike of a match, the hiss and spark of a candle's wick. The last he'd seen of the odd scoundrel had been at the glass pane across from him, with its view of the garden where they'd all sat. The scoundrel had been watching, was all.

I should have been the one watching, he thought. Maybe it was her, watching from a window the way she used to. Or maybe I just need to believe that. Maybe I've learned nothing from a lost father.

Whether it was you or not, I won't let them hurt you.
I promise you, Greta.

★★★

He finally convinced Oliver to remain with the crew, that he could go it alone. August's chauffeur delivered Fleischl quickly through the city to the back door of the Bliekroder mansion. He recalled the canopy of boughs that lay beyond and was beset with the memory of all that had happened to him on Bliekroder soil.

From the lake's edge he saw a hunched figure in a wheelchair on the pontoon. A parasol, open against the afternoon sun, was fastened to the adjacent beam.

He walked down the planks to the midpoint above the brightly lit ballroom.

"Tell me what you see," said August.

Fleischl wasn't sure if he was referring to what was happening below the water or to the sight of August himself. Either way, there was much to take in. The outsized, intimidating industrialist was nowhere to be found. August's body was as twisted as a root. His bony hands rested atop the arms of his wheelchair like the curled paws of a dog. Deep hollows had opened in his face, under arches of cheekbone. He appeared to have shed a third of his body weight.

"You look well enough," August said, "and I don't. That must please you."

"I assure you it doesn't."

August gestured feebly with his hand for Fleischl to proceed toward the lake, and Fleischl obeyed. The ballroom was full of figures flitting back and forth among at least six tables full of boxy shapes and lengthy strands.

Equipment, Fleischl thought.

"I refused to pay for Alice's endeavor," August said, "but she found others to help her. Men of science down there with her, among others. She keeps company with whomever she pleases. Always has. Some are military, I believe. Others come from industry, the sciences. Anyone who shares her purpose. There might even be a psychiatrist or a Jew down there for all I know. It could have been you. Move me, would you? I find it interesting to watch them."

Fleischl took hold of the handles and turned August's chair to face the lake squarely.

"What's the wife of a wealthy man working on that would draw such prestigious assistants?" said Fleischl. "I was never good for much beyond helping magicians, but you already knew that."

"Alice is far more than the wife of a wealthy man," said August. "She's working on things that she encountered thanks to you. At this late hour in my life, it's finally becoming clear just how much of an influence you had on her. You and Greta."

Footfalls on the pontoon drew Fleischl's attention. The chauffeur approached carrying a small valise.

"A little something I wanted to show you," said August. "It's the reason I asked you to come."

The chauffeur stopped several feet away and set down the valise. He lit a cigarette and stared down at the water.

"Curt is one of the few remaining servants living here," said August. "Or perhaps he no longer does. I really don't know."

"Why am I here," Fleischl said flatly.

"You haven't asked why *they're* here. Alice is down there with all those thinkers because she's going to prove transmission."

"Transmission." He snorted. "And you're up here, a dying man watching his wife burn through the rest of his money chasing the impossible."

"There was a time when I would have agreed with your assessment. She might have agreed with you too, at least up to the moment she came across something of mine that she was never supposed to see. The missing piece, you might say. Now she's down there and they all want to be a part of it."

"What missing piece, August? You? Has she been waiting for you to die, to see if she hears you, because that's how much she loves you?"

An unmistakable flicker of pain registered on August's face. "You're not as civilized as you pretend to be."

"She's welcome to try proving transmission," Fleischl said. "It doesn't matter how many experts join her. It has no effect on me. The only reason I'm here is because of what you said about Greta. Tell me what it meant or tell your man to take me back where he found me."

"Bear with me, Fleischl. I won't get a second chance to speak to you. I don't speak to anyone, really. No one likes a dying man. It's too close. Curt, let me have one of those."

The chauffeur came over and put his cigarette in August's mouth. His parched lips puckered around it.

"It's to do with my liver," he said. "Weeks, a month. All the poison I've spread through myself has caught up to me at last. I've thought of making something poetic from that, but I'm no poet. Maybe Alice will. A eulogy about how I've always held the space she wanted someone else to fill. Someone she couldn't have. Don't look so shocked, Berger. Anything goes in today's Berlin. Alice is like you. Sentimental. Either one of you would pull down the entire world for love, or just to say you mattered. The only difference being that Alice has the courage to actually do something about it."

"I'm leaving." Fleischl walked past the chauffeur.

"You aren't the only one who loved Greta," August said.

"You're just the only one here on this pontoon."

You don't get to keep this. You sent away the love of a lifetime and in the process, made it clear how little I matter to anyone.

There above the ballroom, he remembered her in his apartment, attached to the electrodes they would one day fight over. Her attempt at being heard. *You aren't the one,* she'd said, *that I wanted to hear me.*

"Alice," he said. "All this time, in the midst of all of this, she loved Greta."

"Yes," August said bitterly. He wanted to laugh. A dying man who once brought home yet another plaything, only to see his wife fall in love with her. And then he saw himself, Fleischl, the one most blind to all of it, went and named himself He Who Listens.

He didn't laugh, nor did he leave. He walked back to August. Once again, a Bliekroder held him in his sway.

"That's what you wanted to tell me?" Fleischl said. "Your domestic troubles? Alice's unrequited love?"

"There's a little more to it than simple love. She wanted Greta to see her the way Greta saw you. Or should I say, the way Greta heard you that day in the ballroom."

"What?"

"She did hear you, Fleischl. It really happened. The proof is in there."

Curt opened the valise and withdrew a worn file. Turning it over, he showed Fleischl an aged, cracked wax seal.

"Look familiar?" August asked.

"Vaguely," said Fleischl.

"Alice had it once. Long ago. She would have told you it was my private file, not to be opened."

"August…"

"The color of someone's eye," August said. "How it just changed one day."

"Alright, yes. I do recall something about that. Someone's eye color changed for no apparent reason. What of it?"

"There was a reason, and it wasn't just someone. It was Greta."

Fleischl tore open the file. There was a medical report inside, along with a simple note describing a perfectly brown eye gone milky as a cloud one day. *29 October 1897*

"Ah, there he is. The man so gifted at listening. Is that the date of your misadventure at the army camp or isn't it? The day you were blinded?"

He didn't answer. He didn't have to.

"What happened to you that day happened to her. In one moment, your violence became hers. And now Alice knows."

His legs felt unsteady beneath him. It was no different than being aboard the *Elegy* or in Apia Bay, waiting again for water to bear him off.

"I remember seeing her eye," August said. "I thought it some freakish accident of the body owing to no cause or reason, until the day you revealed who Greta was to you and these ideas of yours. From that day I didn't know what to do with any of this. I only knew that Greta didn't deserve the persecution she would surely get if people found out. Well, they're going to find out now. She's proof that something impossible is possible."

"This can't be real," he said. "I've seen Greta since this. That first night here. With her father in the ballroom. I would have noticed."

"She's adept at hiding herself," said August, "or have you learned nothing about her?"

"I don't believe it. This file isn't proof of anything. It's a piece of paper. I want to see her for myself."

"So do we all, and no one more so than Alice. That's why she intends to publicize it. All of it. Including you."

All Fleischl could see was the work going on below, where once there was a winged dancer in fragile light, until a cliff fell and a scream struck from a world away. In his hands was proof of everything he'd chased after. A single sheet of paper. It was impossible.

"If this is real," he said, "if Alice cares for her as you say, this would destroy her. And after what I already did to her…"

Greta screaming at him while the window of her father's mind closed. *Is that what you'd have me hear, your dying.* Did she say that while looking at him through a cloud he'd put in her eye?

"I've now told the only person that matters," August said. "I won't be here to see how it all turns out."

"Need I even say it," Fleischl spat. "No one will hear you. No one will want to."

"That's fine. I'm not the sort to scream."

Below them, there was a figure in the ballroom standing amongst the men and machines. Alice. She stared up at the pontoon.

"It doesn't matter what you people do," Fleischl said. "This is what you fail to understand about Greta. You can't buy what happened and Alice can't will it. It happened to us. No one else. I hope it ruins what's left of all of you. Take this with you, wherever you're going. A girl who disappears and a Jew bested the Bliekroders whether it's true or not."

He stormed down the pontoon toward the house. Hearing hurried steps and the squealing turning of old wheels behind him, he told August to leave him alone.

"What will you do?" August asked as Curt pushed his chair across the grounds toward the house.

"Find her. After that, I don't know."

On the circular drive, August told Curt to take Fleischl back to the city. "I had her eye checked by the finest specialists in Berlin," said August. "They didn't have an answer. But I tried, Fleischl. And when I realized the connection to you, I kept silent. Part of me refused to believe it. Part of me still does, proof be damned. Part of me wanted to tell Alice just to punish her with the reality that she couldn't have what she wanted. But that just underscored the fact that nothing I did was ever going to be enough for her. So I resisted. It might be the only decent thing I've ever done."

"I don't care," said Fleischl. "I won't be seeing you again."

The chauffeur drove the car to where Fleischl stood and stopped. Fleischl opened the passenger door himself.

"Sometimes I wish I was a simpler man," said August. "You wouldn't understand."

"I understand very well," said Fleischl before disappearing into the car. "You wish you were Greta."

★★★

By eleven that night he was at Oliver's house, sitting near an ample fire with a brandy while Albin picked at the remains of a roasted chicken. The file lay on the table between them. Nothing but a yellowed old sheet with a few cursive words, and yet it brought down such unshakeable quiet.

Oliver broke the silence at last. "I did say Alice was pining for something. Little did we know."

"We'll ask around," said Albin. "Perhaps someone knows where Greta is. Where did you see her last?"

Fleischl mentioned the missing scoundrel.

Oliver shook his head in disbelief. "Right under our noses. I'll speak to the one who suggested him. Her. It's all rather stunning. But someone will know. She seems to pop up in these reels."

"You're my dear and trusted friend," said Fleischl. "But I need to ask about the day you filmed her in the ballroom."

"Of course you do. I swear to you, I didn't know. She ran away and wouldn't come out, as I've said. When she finally did, she was weeping and holding her head as if she'd been hurt."

"Or hiding what happened," suggested Albin.

"The next time I saw her was the night of the Bliekroders' dinner party where I met you, Fleischl. Then the play."

"And she was unscarred," Fleischl said. "I would have noticed it immediately."

He lay back and let the brandy numb him. "None of this

makes sense."

"Alice will do what she'll do," Oliver said. "Greta is strong and she's an expert at keeping herself away from everyone. It's you I'm worried about. Knowing Alice, she'll make this as large as she can and it will all land on you because you don't know how to disappear, not like Greta. It will be all anyone wants to talk about. They'll hound you."

"I don't care about myself."

"We suspend the show," said Albin. "It will blow over with time. For now, Fleischl, you need to come to peace with how this fits into your life. You know now. This happened to you."

"And her." He closed his eyes, but it felt too much like blindness.

"Listen to me," Albin said. "I've been writing something new. A film. Something strange, even by my own standards. I've found a director and am thinking about a crew. We'd go to the Carpathians. A gorgeous, faraway place. I don't know when we'll start, but when we do I want you and Oliver to come. We'll leave here and get lost for a while."

"An adventure might be just what we need," said Oliver. "A chance to think things through. What do you say?"

When they saw that Fleischl was crying, his friends went to him. They brought him from the dining table to a couch and held him while he sobbed.

"Did I hurt her?" he screamed.

His friends' embrace tightened, and everything within him crumbled and fell into the sea. It was much quieter this time.

CHAPTER Eighteen
Transmission

Though *Under the Waves* closed on the twenty second day of April, 1920, the Wintergarten remained open to serve as a haven for the war's injured and returned. It provided meager meals for a bit of belonging. But it wasn't the same without He Who Listens, and for those who came on the odd Sunday evening to gather in the shadow of the *Elegy's* faded bow, run aground at the bottom of the slide trap. Empty now of amity and argument, the place felt too quiet. The Kabarett Bretl troupe performed, but it wasn't enough to dispel the feeling that an era had ended.

Fleischl stayed away.

A few streets over, there was a newer, sleeker theatre, the Preussisches Staatstheater. During the spring months it was a hive of activity. Deliveries arrived throughout the day. The rumblings of construction from within its walls reverberated for blocks. One day in early June, a set of letters appeared on its marquee. *Will love and death hold hands at last?*

Fleischl stayed away from there as well.

Albin and Oliver made inquiries, true to their promises. As the date of departure for the Carpathians neared, they asked colleagues and acquaintances alike about Greta. No one, it seemed, had ever realized just who it was that moved through their dioramas as an old man, a beggar, a soldier returned from the front, a villager, and—in one instance that struck at Fleischl's heart, a blind woman.

How she looked, Oliver and Albin were told and in turn told him, was how everyone responsible for casting decisions met her. They didn't know her in any other form. They didn't know how to find her. She found them.

"Everyone seemed to like her," said one actor. "No one seemed to know her."

And when Alice Bliekroder's advertisement appeared in a mid-June edition of the Tageblatt as Fleischl knew it one day would, he did his best to stay away from newsstands.

Transmission of the Mind!

Sparing no expense, my experts have attuned the famed galvanic machine to the most minute of thoughts! I have contracted with no less than the Escape Artist himself, Harry Houdini, who will perform his death-defying water torture escape!

But more. Be it known that I call upon He Who Listens to come out of hiding and face the evidence that transmission is real, that he is involved with it despite his denials, and that he grievously wounded, by his mind, She Who Heard.

To that end, and by this advertisement, I call upon She Who Heard to come forth and tell us at last, yes or no. And if she will not, the authorities are prepared to arrest any and all parties perpetrating fraud and causing great physical injury.

It's now to you, Fleischl Berger. Enter the water. Hold death's hand.

When the following day's edition appeared, Fleischl couldn't resist. He bought a copy and read it.

She Who Heard has accepted! One empty chair filled. Does He Who Listens possess the courage?

Courtesy of the Kabarett's owner and his influence among the city's assorted ushers, cleaners and hostesses, Fleischl and Oliver soon found themselves in the Staatstheater's balcony, hidden from view and with a clear sightline to the stage. There was a glass water tank of monstrous size, with a padlock as big as the wheel of a truck on its outer door. Full to its brim, the tank shimmered under the bright aura of a candelabra.

Alice Bliekroder's version of a little light, Fleischl supposed.

Across from the tank, her galvanometer rested atop a long table. There were indeed two empty chairs. The machine didn't appear any different from the one he'd used, as far as he could tell. Silvered coil, electrodes sheathed in what looked like black rubber. Meant to be applied underwater, he surmised. Drowning and electrocution at once, beneath the surface. The only thing missing was a rope.

Oliver whispered in his ear. "I beg you, be with friends and away from this travesty. Don't give her the satisfaction."

The show began when Alice came onstage beneath the lights and placed one hand on the tank, which towered over her. She seemed so small next to it. A tiny figure, jeweled but incapable of wings.

"I need time to think," Fleischl said.

★★★

The following day he disembarked in Stralsund under a stark sun. Rapholtz greeted him in the library with a hug and a copy of the offending newspaper advertisement. "She's horrid to do this," Rapholtz said.

Fleischl was weary from the journey. They sat on the couch together and drank tea. "How is Dowid?"

Rapholtz gestured to the library window. "See for yourself."

Down at the docks, he spotted a figure sitting on the memorial bench, watching the sea.

"I presume he has his rope with him," said Fleischl.

"He takes it wherever he goes. Which is only ever these halls or, more recently, that bench."

"I hope he doesn't alarm anyone."

"All kinds here. He knows his way back."

"The tunnel?"

"Anton's parting gift. How long can you stay?"

"Just a day or so. I'm thinking of going away with Oliver and Albin. There's a film being done."

"One of yours, He Who Listens?"

Fleischl smiled. "No. I may be past all that."

"There's always a place for you here, my boy. No shortage of men with troubles."

He gave Fleischl a poorly wrapped box. Fleischl opened it and took out the old battery they'd built together so terribly long ago. Their life encapsulated.

"I don't care what this woman does," Rapholtz said, "or what anyone says. I believe you and I believe in you. I always have. And when my own time comes, there's no one I'd rather call to than you."

He took Fleischl's hand. "Listen for me, won't you? You're extraordinary, Fleischl, and you went in search of the even more extraordinary. Tell me you'll be all right when I go, that you'll be happy."

"You're stuck with me, and I with you, for a long time yet."

Their hands grew warm, but they didn't part. "Now," Rapholtz said, "tell me of your exciting life in the theatre. Did you eat yet?"

"Kippers, on the train."

"And how were they?"

"Hideous."

Rapholtz smiled, Fleischl took his smile and held it. He consecrated it.

"I'll try to improve upon that for dinner," said Rapholtz.

★★★

In the evening, Rapholtz dozed. Fleischl looked in on him and on Dowid perched the library window, then took a walk to the docks. There he discovered that the old shipyard had been leveled to make way for the Stralsund Universum.

He purchased a ticket and went in, if only to experience for himself what sitting in a cinema at the edge of the Baltic, at the scene of what was once his life, might feel like.

The lobby placard promised a comedy, The *Rosentopf* Case, and short reels. On a table by the curtained entry was a crate filled with bags of small pastries. *Just take one! Hermann*

The theatre itself was small, with sloping floors and no more than a dozen rows set before a rectangular screen. Fleischl took a seat near the front. He was still the only one there when the lights went down.

As he reached for a bit of streusel, an intertitle appeared in the same hand that had so politely offered pastry. *Stralsund's own He Who Listens*

Dowid's ghostly image appeared next, followed by the construction of the *Elegy*. Fleischl barely resisted the urge to bolt for the exit. The camera panned the docks before coming to rest on the finished ship. It took in the path, the far hill and Thalhammer. It swept past the sea tunnel and the buildings beyond.

He went to the projection booth and knocked.

The door opened and there appeared a younger man, not yet out of his twenties, with a cherubic face and a gap-toothed smile, and crumbs around his mouth.

"Are you Hermann?" said Fleischl.

"I am. I didn't know anyone came. This one's been showing for a while. It takes so long for new reels to get all the way here, you see."

"I understand. May I trouble you to show the reel you just played once more? The one with the ship?"

"Of course. Who are you? You look familiar."

"I'm in it, Hermann."

"Oh, is it you? He Who Listens?"

"It is, thank you."

"Aren't you sick of watching it by now?"

"In truth, I've never seen it before."

"I understand." By his tone, he didn't understand at all. Still, he replayed *Under the Waves*. Again there was the sea tunnel, just a glimpse before the camera's gaze slid by on its way to the hill and the *Elegy*. Through the tunnel, there was an apartment atop an old sausage shoppe, long since given over to something else. The apartment had a window. It could have been a reflection, a flaw of the camera, a grain on the frame. But it looked so perfect: a tiny glow, easily missed, though still stubbornly there to see in the windowpane for someone who knew to look.

★★★

He arrived back in the city just before dawn the following day. An unmarked envelope had been slid under his door. He opened it, read it, packed warm clothes, and went to Oliver's house.

Oliver looked at Fleischl's suitcase. "Going on a trip?" he asked.

"Yes."

He pointed at the envelopes Fleischl. "Are those…"

Fleischl handed him one. "Her," he said as Oliver read it.

Alice lied. I won't be at the Staatstheater. Where I'll be, she can't find me.

Don't go.

"What's the other one?"

"That one's for Alice," said Fleischl.

★★★

The Staatstheater's lights went down precisely at seven. It was sold out, much to Alice's delight. When the curtains parted to reveal the water tank, the table, two chairs, and Alice herself. There was a smattering of applause. She pulled out the two chairs with a flourish.

"The great Harry Houdini shall be with us momentarily. I now ask our other esteemed guests to come forward!"

A hush fell. A moment passed, then another. Alice fidgeted onstage as a restless murmur arose.

The sound of a slamming door broke the tension. The audience turned to see a figure emerge from the rear of the theatre. "Please, pardon my tardiness. A bit of weather."

"Who the hell are you?" Alice demanded of the young man in a telegram delivery boy's uniform.

The delivery boy opened a satchel and withdrew an envelope. "Telegram for an Alice Bliekroder."

Alice snatched it from his hand, tore it open and read it as the audience watched in utter confusion. She let it fall from her grasp. She stormed off, went out the side door, and was gone.

The audience began to shout. "At least let Houdini do something," cried one man. Several attendees clambered onto the stage to retrieve the telegram.

APOLOGIES STOP I WON'T BE THERE STOP NOR WILL SHE STOP I KNOW YOU TRIED TO REACH US STOP WE SIMPLY DIDN'T HEAR YOU STOP

HWL

CHAPTER Nineteen

Into the Carpathians

October 1920

"Regrets?" Oliver asked.

"None," Fleischl replied.

"Excellent. Now you enjoy the ride while I continue editing Albin's letter to the financiers."

It seems that our country caught fire in the war. Flu ravages city and town without regard to class. The empire is no more. Pride and identity, gone. What are we now but Spartakist rioters and disfigured cripples. We are the winter city.

There are echoes of this real world in the story. I suppose this is what art does. I don't know what anyone will make of this photoplay. I only know that whatever you may hear, it's not based on Bram Stoker's epistolary.

Please don't hesitate to contact us should you be served with papers.

The mountains they circumvented through Oravsky Poozamonva resembled the snaggle-teeth of Prussian giants, the eaters of men in old bedtime tales. Their caravan, some seven carts and carriages strong, sidled alongside the river Orava for what seemed like an eternity. The icy mountain flow became a kind of heart's beat.

Fleischl and Oliver shared their coach with a silent girl. She was in her late teens, Fleischl estimated, and pretty, though something in the way she leaned as if trying to flee her own body suggested the awkwardness of a younger age. Her eyes were brown and wide. She had a subtle spray of freckles across her nose which faded as they reached her prominent cheekbones.

"You're not paying attention," Oliver said to Fleischl. "Do tell us where you've been these last few moments."

"I was thinking of my father."

"This is how I'd know you were a Jew even if you never told me. Here I am, prepared to chastise you for not listening, and you make me feel guilty."

"I was thinking of him just this morning, and now I find myself on a cart, on a pitted road with no sense of where I'm going and no responsibility for the journey. There are the woods and the river and the sound of the wheels, and it's really just like the trips he took before he left for the sea, where I thought he'd be happiest."

Their cart hit a rock, throwing it sharply to the right and jostling the passengers severely. The driver recovered. They began to laugh, though the girl remained quiet. "That's what I deserve for being maudlin," said Fleischl.

"Another random rock in the course of Fleischl Berger's life," Oliver said. "You've a bit of the poet in you this morning. Consider writing, after you've made your triumphant return to the stage."

"If I ever do. But enough of me. Tell me when I'm to meet the stars?"

"I've actually never met them, though I understand our young traveling companion here is his assistant, is that right?"

The girl nodded.

"What's your name?" Fleischl asked.

"Adelita," she said in a disinterested voice.

"I'm Fleischl."

She shrugged.

"Tell us something about yourself, Adelita."

"Nothing to tell."

"You don't have any stories of yourself? What of your family?"

"I only have a mother."

"Where is she?"

"Somewhere."

"What do you do for the actor you assist?"

"I stay."

"So, companionship?"

"No more questions, please."

"Is he nice?"

"Can be."

"Is he mean?"

"No. Just… far."

"An interesting choice of words, Adelita."

"Must I do this?"

"He's a doctor of the mind," said Oliver. "Regrettably, he roots around as a dog through the trash."

"You say you want to hear my thoughts," she said, "but maybe it's your own you want to hear."

"My goodness," said Fleischl. He sat back. "I don't want to upset you or make the journey unpleasant."

"Then don't."

Their caravan emerged in a clearing below a great fist of high rock. The Orava flowed alongside them. Scatterings of children chased the slowest carts for a short distance, to the bounds of Oravsky.

To end the discomfort in the carriage, Oliver described the legal intricacies of the film. It was most assuredly not based upon Stoker's novel, which Fleischl had never heard of anyway. The producers were, respectively, a financier ready to bankrupt the newly created

Prana studio just to avoid paying the novelist's estate, and Albin, their occult master.

As his friend went on, Fleischl caught sight of a castle perched on a lime spur some three hundred meters in the air. Its spires were scarved in watery cloud. A magnificent structure, drenched in solitude and gray as the rock from which it pulled itself.

"Albin came across the story of a soldier," said Oliver. A cool ribbon of air passed them as their caravan began the gradual ascent to the castle on a path alongside a slim tributary of clear ice melt tumbling from the cliff top. "The man had been stationed in Serbia, in a village. He found himself billeted with a peasant whose father, he said, had been killed in a feud with a neighbor. A grudge that went back generations. The peasant's father, it seems, was on the wrong side of the matter as far as the village was concerned, so they buried him without the sacrament. The peasant said his father couldn't rest and came back to haunt the living as a vampire."

"A children's story," said Fleischl.

"The soldier said that the peasant provided him an official paper showing that his father's body was disinterred some sixteen months after his death. Astonishingly, it was perfectly preserved. Two sharp teeth protruded over his lower lip and he held a bouquet of flowers that bloomed as if they'd been picked that very day. The prefect ordered a stake driven through the heart of the nosferatu."

"The what?"

"Romanian, for undead."

"That's quite a tale."

"Isn't it? But think. A predator of good people, drinker of blood, bringer of vermin and infestation. Is it not us in everyone else's eyes? We come from the Pale, the Mitteleuropa, and we bring our ways; they hate to see our ships on their horizon."

"So this is to be a tale of the Jewish undead."

"Precisely!" Oliver laughed triumphantly.

At the base of the castle, everyone disembarked. The girl ran ahead and disappeared beneath an archway as Albin greeted them. The crew began the labor of unpacking cameras and tins. They erected a series of pedestals at varying heights, atop which the director, F. W. Murnau ordered large lamps be set. The scene, as Murnau blocked it out, was made of three features: the castle, in the foreground; the actor, Gustav von Wagenheim, as Thomas Hutter; and the central figure, Count Orlock.

While waiting for nightfall, they played games of figuerenspiel and schatkopf. They smoked and talked quietly, as men thrown together by circumstance invariably did. They grumbled about their wives, their labors and their pay, while Murnau peered through the keyhole lens of a small spyglass.

At a quarter past midnight, Murnau dropped the glass on the ground and cried, "we have a mist descending!"

Fleischl joined Oliver and Albin behind the first of two large cameras on tripods. The operators' hands rested on the cranks. The lenses were directed toward a long, pebble-strewn path leading to the deep-set archway he'd seen Adelita enter. Other crewmen lit lamps suspended high above, so the camera would pick up light but not the lamps themselves. Beneath the lamps, Murnau himself spread small bits of broken glass.

"Just for show," Oliver whispered. "It'll glint like little stars."

Murnau finished, inspected his handiwork, and called for Gustav. The actor stepped forward and hit his mark in the center of the path.

"We wait," Murnau said, and all eyes turned to the castle. The descending mist wrapped it over a ten-minute count. Soon the cloud came to curl at their feet. The air grew dank and cold. Fleischl felt the crisp burr of it in his throat. Something of it struck a note of panic in him. He recalled an odd bit of lore his father once told him on a night neither of them could sleep: that drowned men might be saved by clouds forced into their lungs.

Murnau nudged Gustav forward. "You've just arrived on a

coach of strange origin that left you at this lonely place to meet a host of whom you know nothing. There lies the archway and the tunnel beyond. There lies your future in the dark. Go to it in fear."

"That won't be hard," said Gustav.

"To the gate, Gustav. To the mouth of the Carpathians and lost times. See what comes for you."

Murnau and the cameraman turned the cranks of their machines as Gustav wandered to the archway.

"But I don't see…"

"Wait," said Murnau. And Gustav stopped abruptly.

He stood in the light thrown from the lamps. Something was emerging from the hazy darkness of the tunnel. It was a blade of a figure, tall and angular; as it came into view in the mouth of the archway, the crew gasped. Its face and head were vermin-like. Its tendriled fingers clasped together in an animalistic humility. It doffed the covering it wore, a rabbinical skullcap, and bid Gustav to follow.

"Go with him," said Murnau, still steadily turning the crank of his camera.

The figure receded into its tunnel, passing below the first arch, and then fading gradually back into the darkness.

"You don't want to go," said Murnau, "but look behind you. The gate has closed. The mist is so thick. The night is deep, where else is there for you? Go, until you can't be seen. And… end."

Gustav emerged swiftly back into the lamplight. "Please," he said. "Tell me I don't have to do that again."

"We have what we need," Murnau said. "Unsettling, isn't he?"

"He scarcely looked at me. Is this how it's to be for the rest of our time?"

"I expect so."

Adelita came to the mouth of the tunnel and lent the rodent called Orlock her slender arm. In the full light of the lamps, Orlock was a lonely figure.

"Quite an accomplishment," said Fleischl, almost to himself. "I wonder what this actor looks like without all that."

Murnau passed them. "So that we may foreclose discussion and endless questions, everyone please listen. This is how he will be. He wishes to remain as he looks, and I wish it as well, to provoke maximum reaction from all of you. Don't speak to him or approach him off-camera. Use his assistant if you must, but avoid him as you would a pestilent rat in the street. Consider this. Here, this is his world. In Wisborg, when he arrives aboard ship bearing coffins and vermin, he will be making your world his. This is how you react to him, until our work is done. Am I clear?"

"A question," Gustav said. "Have you conjured a real nosferatu?"

Murnau smiled. "That's the spirit. Come, to our lodging and a hearty breakfast."

Fleischl helped carry the equipment to the carts. He felt energized by the production, despite the long night. He and Oliver boarded their own carriage as the first shafts of sun broke from behind Castle Orava to paint the spires and trees. The murmur of the stream settled around him as they rode away, last in the line.

Near the tunnel, he saw Orlock and Adelita watching the caravan depart. The back of his neck went taut. He wasn't sure why, but he waved.

Orlock raised his taloned hand in return.

In town, Murnau treated everyone to a sumptuous breakfast in the wine cellar of an old inn. Fleischl and Oliver sat at the director's table with Albin.

"What did you think of that moment?" asked Albin.

"It was everything I could hope for," said Oliver. "Even the elements conspired to tell the story."

"And you, Fleischl?"

"It was an extraordinary moment. Despite knowing it to be stagecraft, I still felt such unease."

"What a weird thing we do, that your unease is a compliment of the highest order. But then, you're accustomed to strangeness, my friend."

"I've heard of you," Murnau said through a mouthful of dumpling. "Does everyone know who we have in our midst? He Who Listens. The lectures and the films. Oh, and the ship! Most intriguing. Quite a spectacle. I understand you've stopped doing them?"

"I have. Perhaps again one day."

"You used sights and sounds, yes?"

"Sound and vision," Albin corrected.

"Not that it's patented," Oliver said. "Let's not find out if there are courtrooms in the Carpathians."

"Weren't you moved to your profession by something rather extraordinary?" Murnau asked.

Adelita entered the inn's tavern and went to the buffet to pick at the remnants. She arranged a plate carefully, covered it with a napkin, and brought it to a far table where sat Orlock, in costume and in character.

"Wasn't there some sort of machine?" asked Murnau. "I apologize. I'm pestering you."

Despite his bemused protests, Fleischl soon found himself at the center of the inn's dining hall, encircled by tables of faces staring at him over steins. While one of the camera operators built a fresh fire in the cavernous hearth, he explained the show, starting with Professor Lischke and continuing through the *Elegy* and the galvanic machine. "I asked for volunteers," he said. "A soft stimulus. Nothing terrible."

Murnau rose from his seat, then picked it up and brought it to where Fleischl sat. He set it down and asked Fleischl to demonstrate on him.

"First," Fleischl said, "I'd attach electrodes to your head. You wouldn't feel a thing."

"And if you did," Albin said.

"It's not my machine!" Oliver finished with a grin.

"Then the stimulus," Fleischl said. He circled around Murnau, waited a moment, then clapped. Murnau jumped in his seat, to the obvious amusement of his crew.

Someone asked, "Have you ever done it to yourself?"

Fleischl looked up. It was Adelita, from the far corner where she sat with Orlock.

"Once," said Fleischl. "Long ago."

Orlock leaned over and whispered in Adelita's ear. "What did you use for stimulus?" asked Adelita.

"Interesting question," said Murnau.

"I do recall it," Fleischl said, "because I still have it."

He took a slim leather billfold out of his pocket. His hands trembled. That surprised him.

"What is that?" Murnau asked. "A letter?"

"A telegram."

He unfolded it and lay it gently across his lap. "It's funny; I haven't looked at this in years." It was jaundiced and creased to its fibrous heart in places, with an odd little dog ear at one of the bottom corners that he hadn't made on purpose. Yet there it was, never to be undone.

Fleischl did you die

"It's something you've seen before," Murnau observed. "Isn't its ability to stimulate diminished?"

"Not diminished. Different, in the same way I'm different." He smiled. "We've grown old together."

He looked at the faces of his dear friends in the fire's glow. Far beyond them, in the back, Orlock and Adelita huddled close together, their heads like black marble in the cast light.

One of them raised a hand. He thought it was Adelita. The other was at her ear again.

"What would we hear," she asked, "if this was your show?"

"You'd hear the strings. They vibrate according to the increasing electrical output from my brain, through the electrodes. If it was a better machine… if it was something different than it is, you could tell where in me it's coming from and what it might look like. I've imagined lightning, or a constellation, though really, I don't know. But perhaps that's not what you're asking."

The room grew quiet as he folded the telegram along its deep borders. "I believe if there was such a machine, you'd hear what runs between us, always. Once, it was so loud that someone heard it. For a time, I devoted my life to chasing it. I thought I'd prove it."

"One day," Oliver said. "If you feel you need to."

"Make a movie of it," Albin said. "No one reads anymore."

"So we would hear what that paper makes you feel," asked Adelita.

"You might have before, in the past, but no longer. You can't hear the impossible moment. No one can. Almost no one. I think you'd hear all the other moments I should have held more carefully."

He gazed at her and Orlock. "I"m a little drunk, I suppose."

Oliver raised his stein. "Here's to that."

As he returned the telegram to his pocket to rest against his father's old *Elegy* drawing, Murnau and the others closed in around him. They peppered him with questions and thought of nonsensical names for the movie they boasted they would make to mark HWL's triumphant return.

"So the thing they say happened to you," Adelita called from the corner of the inn. "You believe it really did happen."

"Perhaps we've asked Fleischl enough questions," said Oliver.

"There was something at another theatre," Adelita continued. "Someone was going to prove it. You were supposed to be there. You didn't go."

"No, I didn't."

"Why not?"

"I think that's enough," said Albin, but Fleischl held up a hand.

"I think I can answer one more," Fleischl said. He felt warmth from the fire and the drink, and from the sense that his father was sitting next to him, telling him something important, something worth carrying, like the telegram and the *Elegy*. He'd said a man should believe only what he can see. The soil if he is a farmer, if he is a ship-builder, the wood. *The sea if he was you, poppa. You spoke of belief in what can be seen, but you never told me what to do with what can be heard in this life.*

He felt old things stirring. The sensation of the world falling away, leaving only his need to know. To prove. The feeling had become entangled at some point with what it cost him.

"I didn't go," he said, "because the only thing it would have brought back is the man who once would have done anything to anyone, if it meant proving it. I don't want to be that man ever again. Instead, I hold the memory like any other, and I go on with life as it is for me now. I try to put as much right as I can for as many as I can."

Albin and Oliver came to him. Murnau told him the path he was on was where he ought to be. "Bravo," he said.

Soon it was afternoon, and everyone was asleep in their chairs. At some point, Adelita and her odd companion had left, though as he too roused himself from a drink-fueled lethargy to leave the tavern, he glanced at where they'd sat and it was as if some part of them remained in the configuration of chairs, the bread grown stale on the table, the spent and puddled candle.

In his room, he built a fire of his own, brewed some tea, fashioned a comfortable place for himself on the couch, and closed his eyes. Soon, he drifted off. He dreamed that as the embers ascended up the flume and went to ash, he went with them; and from his vantage point he saw that the Carpathians were gone. The castle was gone. The Orava, too, all gone. There was a strange landscape, and it took a moment for him to understand that it was all beneath the water. He continued to float until someone called to him from below; he woke with no sense of the time.

He rose stiffly and went to the window. It was deeply dark out. Then a fragile light ignited. He saw that it was small flame casting a dome of light over a silent scene. There, next to the the archway, the slender figure of Orlock cupped a candle, protecting it from the wind.

He left his room and went outside. The breeze stirred the leaves that carpeted the ground.

Orlock regarded him from the archway. Up close, Fleischl detected the seam of the latex headpiece, the falsity of the pointed ears.

"Did you call to me just now?" he asked, mildly unnerved. "I was sleeping."

"I know. I heard you."

Orlock removed a hand from his pocket to trace a path across Fleischl's cheek, through his tousled hair.

"Oh," said Fleischl, as he stared into her eyes.

"You always did dream loudly, Fleischl Berger," she said.

★★★

He watched Greta remove the last of her makeup while Adelita slept on his couch. She'd strewn his bed with components of her disguise. A latex headpiece, a dental bridge to create two rodent-like teeth, wadded towels caked with ashy makeup, wires she'd inserted painfully into her mouth at the gum line to force her jaw into a jutted grimace, lifts from her heavy boots, and all her clothes down to a slip. Inside her overcoat were thick pads she'd labored under to accentuate her shoulders and make a starved animal of her already thin frame.

"Who knows of you?" he asked her. "Oliver or Albin? Murnau? Did any of them know?"

"No one. Only you. I sent Murnau a photo of me as Orlock. I met him as Orlock. I wouldn't let myself be seen as anything other. The way you stare at me."

She sat down on the bed next to him. "I thought of coming to you before."

"Why didn't you? I would never have told anyone."

"I know you wouldn't. You, who knows how I disappear. I've stayed away a long time, no matter how badly I wanted to bridge the gap between us. I've come close a few times."

"The glass house."

"Yes. And the balcony at your first show."

When it occurred to him, it came as a physical sensation. Something long held back, loosed at last.

"Adelita," he said.

"She's ours, Fleischl."

"How old is she?"

"Nineteen. We made her that night at Stralsund, in my father's shoppe. She's so much me, but I watch her work things out, piece them together and fret over them. She's quiet and sometimes she's so sure of life, and sometimes she doesn't understand until she sees it through me. And in those times, I give what I can to her and then I hide away and cry because she's so much you."

"Where have you lived? How do you do all this?"

"My Fleischl. Puzzling me out even still."

She stroked his cheek. Her fingers slipped into his greying hair.

"I became old," he said, "while you weren't looking."

"I've always been looking. And I have a belly."

"Look at my hands. Spotted like an altekacher. Sometimes they tremble and I can't make them stop." His eyes filled. "I have a daughter. We missed years. Whole pieces of each other, gone."

He broke down.

"I've hidden and I've lied," she said. "I've kept her from you because the last I saw of you, you thought of my father as an animal to experiment on while telling yourself you did it for me. Are you still that man?"

"Your eye." His hand went to her face. "It looks brown, like it always has. I don't know what to believe. Did I blind you? My heart is tearing open. Did I hurt you that day?"

"No, you didn't blind me. You changed me."

She reached for her right eye. "I'm quite good at hiding. You know that."

Her hand lowered. "I know what they would have told you. August saw. I didn't want anyone to. I was terrified and yes, it hurt when it happened. At first I heard a rumbling from somewhere far, like a storm, only it didn't stop. It just stayed where it was. I thought, it's Oliver or one of his assistants rolling something down the steps. Or a ploy to scare me. But Oliver had told me, dance as though you're celebrating. It got louder. It wasn't thunder. It came through the ballroom dome. The way the water and the glass move light around and make it different, that's what it was with the sound. It came in crooked, cut up, and then it came together in me, and I thought the dome had burst open. Then I just *knew*. You were dead and I heard you die. It was all a matter of seconds. All I'd been doing was dancing. If you could see more than just a figurine the size of a pinhead, if you'd seen my face, you'd see the sound of you dying in there with me. And this is how my eye came back."

In her palm was a small disc, like a shallow little bowl the color of her eyes as they were.

"Do you see?" she asked.

"Your eye. It's blue."

"Like a spark," she said.

"It's impossible."

"It's you."

She put the colored lens in his hand.

"I don't know what to do," he said. "There's so much."

"I don't know either. But I've learned from my life to now, with Adelita and without you. We go on whether we know or not. We have to. So here we are, now, and we've time enough for sadness and love."

She kissed him. "If you remember what love looks like, show me. I can see just fine."

★★★

In two days, they left the castle and the Carpathians for the train. The film canisters were safely secreted in a storage car, the cameras and lighting fastened down, the kits of costumes and makeup packed in chests for the trip home.

The crew occupied the rear cars. There were parties in the more spacious and comfortable cars. Murnau held court in the evenings. Albin laid out plans for a series of Prana masterpieces, pre-suming Stoker's widow didn't sue it out of existence. Oliver wrote furiously and at each station, everyone disembarked to get word of the latest calamities in Berlin. Eventually, the mountain peaks fell away behind them. Flatlands went on into the distance for as far as anyone could see. The parties were over. They grew quieter, more introspective. They watched the landscape pass by outside the windows with the sense that they were heading into a country that was tearing itself apart.

In her car, in costume lest anyone come by, Greta read the note Fleischl gave her as they'd departed the Orava. She read it each day and again at night before bed.

I don't want to change you ever again. I want to find you in unex-pected places when I go to the cinema. I want to see you bring strange beings in, like Anton, like pageboys and witches. Like momma, like me. I want you to let no one but me see what you're holding. I want to be the reason you wander far, and I want to be the reason you return. We've been too long listening. Let's not be alone in the world anymore.

In his own car, Fleischl waited to hear her.

The night before they were to arrive at the Anhalter Bahnof, there was a knock at his compartment door. He opened it to Greta, her blue eyes full, his letter in her hand. Adelita stood next to her, staring at both of them in disbelief.

"Something happened to me," said Greta.

"Yes, it did. And to me."

"Can we make one life from all this?"

"Who in the world can stop us," he said, and brought them both in.

CHAPTER Twenty
Wilhelmplatz No. 8/9

1936
Thalhammer

"Patient files for today."

Fleischl waited his turn at the library window while Laszlo distributed assignments to the interns. Laszlo had at last relented and brought in a succession of thrice-yearly medical students willing to try their hand at psychiatry. Most couldn't leave fast enough once their four-month stints were finished, but occasionally one of them showed potential. Even Laszlo, who felt that he and Fleischl were managing just fine, came to appreciate the fresh perspectives that came with their youth.

There were two interns who'd managed to stay on, though Fleischl only liked one of them, Oskar. Oskar came to Stralsund from Freud's conservatory armed with psychoanalysis, gentleness, and a quiet relentlessness that Fleischl respected. He was soft spoken, well-mannered, and curious. He would do well, Fleischl felt. It was the other one that troubled him.

Where Oskar was keen to understand, Martin seemed to embody all of the more frightening things their country had become. He was harsh, rigid, cruel of temperament, and he believed in aversion as treatment. Once, no more than a week into his residency at Thalhammer, Fleischl came upon him in the library, paging through an issue of Revive Fleischl has assumed was long gone. *I should know better than to assume anything of the past goes missing,* he thought, as he surreptitiously took in Martin's fascination with hydrotherapy, Motrozal, insulin seizure articles, and photos of monkeys with their skulls removed. He saw the same glimmer in Martin's eyes when the intern deduced, from the number of Jews visiting Thalhammer to see Fleischl, that he was among them. Martin had requested a change in reporting relationship then, to Laszlo. When they passed one another in the corridors after that, Martin's rictus smile reminded Fleischl of the strapped monkey. A pathetic thing, grotesque and exposed.

Fleischl kept his distance. The country and the men it produced grew harder each day. It seemed to encourage men like Martin. It wanted the sort of unapologetic strength that valued shattered windows, checkpoints, and brown shirts.

He thought of asking Laszlo to send Martin away but didn't. He was certain Laszlo would do it if he understood the depth of the discomfort Martin aroused. But Fleischl feared retaliation and kept it to himself, as all Jews did. Martin nevertheless came to him in the late hours, to engage about a patient the Reich's Nuremburg laws forbade Fleischl from seeing lest a Jew minister to a German. Perhaps you could consult, Herr Doctor Berger. Perhaps you could just tell me what you think. Perhaps you could bring this one back but don't let anyone see you do it. Perhaps you could convert.

"I think this one's for you." Martin handed him a case file. "Older Jew given to bouts of melancholy," he said.

Fleischl saw the patient's name and said, "of course."

After Oskar and Martin left, Fleischl and Laszlo made their notes in the quiet of the library that they loved so well. Laszlo took

Anton's couch, and the thoroughly dented middle cushion that Fleischl delighted in reminding him had long since taken on the precise shape of his backside. Fleischl's spot was at the window, of course, where between scribbles he could gaze out at Stralsund's docks, the sea tunnel, the cemetery below, and the horizon beyond. He spotted Dowid walking along the water to the memorial bench. There he sat, close to the Baltic, to ponder… who knew what? Steps, perhaps, and whether counting them was necessary anymore.

"None of that native gloominess, Doctor Berger."

"Am I gloomy?" asked Fleischl. "I didn't realize."

"You are always gloomy," said Laszlo, "until Martin leaves." He joined Fleischl at the window.

"Is it that obvious?" asked Fleischl.

"Only to me, one who knows you longer than most. I do see what he is. It's best to manage these sorts of young men rather than antagonize them."

"Agreed."

"Is that our Dowid down there? You, me, him. We're all that remains of the Thalhammer that once was. I might give Dowid the position, should we ever rid ourselves of the little Fuhrer."

Fleischl laughed in spite of himself. "A bit of rope is preferable to a lecture on Aryan purity."

"Agreed."

Down at the sea tunnel entrance, there were three figures in matching brown shirts walking in. In a moment they would emerge on the other side, in the piazza. Stralsund had yet to grow accustomed to the sight of Hitler's zealous youth. In the minds of the peddlers, shopkeepers, and village constabulary, the brownshirts were aberrations. They were a pestilence of the city, not a harbinger of the country. They were treated as loud, boorish, overbearing novelties.

Fleischl, who traveled to the city regularly, saw them in a different light. They weren't visitors. They were here.

"When will you see them again?" Laszlo asked him. He knew

well enough what his friend was thinking, watching the youths make their way to Stralsund's heart.

"Tonight. I'll take the last train home."

"Mind yourself at the checkpoints. Don't draw attention."

"I will. And I never do."

"Maybe the burghemeister has some news for us on your papers, eh?"

"If he did, I would have heard from him."

"Have hope," Laszlo said. "See your patients, dine with me, and maybe we can take in a film before you have to leave. What's at the cinema?"

"Triumph of the Will."

"Propaganda garbage. You'll have to settle for my company, then."

"Agreed."

After his friend left for rounds, Fleischl asked for his first patient. "So," he said when the rebbe sat down on Anton's couch. "You're morose?"

"I'm a Jew," Rebbe Bernhard said. "What Jew do you know who isn't morose?"

The Rebbe had grown wobbly in his elder years. He leaned heavily on a cane, had trouble hearing, seeing, and digesting, but was still as stubbornly independent and quick-witted as any man Fleischl knew. He was also a warm and welcome reminder, much like the library. When they encountered one other on evening walks through Stralsund, they greeted one another with a quiet hug and a knowing smile.

"I remember you when you were just a boy," Rebbe Bernhard always said. One evening he said, "Your father…" and his voice trailed away. He shrugged. "Time. Such a thing. I know. I'll talk. You'll listen. A voice with a melody I hear in my own. What more do I need?"

"I'm still not much of a Jew, I'm afraid."

"You live and breathe in Germany. You're a Jew whether you like it or not."

He began to hum the Kaddish. Fleischl hummed along.

"For your father." He wagged a crooked finger. "Would you say it? It's been such a long time. Would you say it for an old man?"

"I hear you," Fleischl said.

Rebbe Bernhard nodded. "I miss those films. I never could afford the trip to see the stage show."

"It's always nice to be remembered."

★★★

The guild haus was still no better than a dark, wooden shanty, though now it was dressed up with curtains and a fashionably chunky table instead of the old desk. A woman's touch had informed the office. It even smelled of lilac soap. At least the ax remained on the wall where it belonged, behind the old burghemeister's son Willi, who proudly carried on the family tradition.

"Old ways," Willi said. "Some things should never change."

"Not like the world, at least," Laszlo said.

"Truer words." He patted the master roll. His pudgy face would always look young to Fleischl, even as it suggested his father's, in its moony roundness and high widow's peak.

"I've made the inquiry as I promised the doctor," said Willi. "He didn't mention that it was for you."

"I didn't want to cause you any trouble," Fleischl said.

"It's not my trouble that concerns me."

There was a list on the table. The roll from a recently departed ship.

"I remember the master roll well," Fleischl said. "It took on great meaning for me."

"A tradition carried on from my father. The best burghemeister Stralsund ever had."

"Your father was a good man. He was very kind to me when my own father died. May I ask, when did yours pass?"

"1928. His heart couldn't keep pace with his appetites."

"I'm very sorry. He will be missed. A great man, as I'm sure I see before me now."

Willi leaned over his desk. "Let me speak frankly," he said. "I worry about pressing the Ministry for travel papers for Jews. I fear that your somewhat open—shall we say—desire to leave the country would draw their attention and perhaps their ire. Something could happen."

"Something's already happened," said Fleischl. "Those I love live behind checkpoints. There are people on my street taken away for reasons I can't explain other than their being Jews. It will be me. It will be my family. There's no reason to it. Leaving is best for all."

Willi studied his face. "My friend, I'll do what I can. I promise. In the meantime, please stay safe."

Fleischl thanked him. With a last look at the roll, he walked to the guild door.

"My poppa used to tell me the story of you," Willi said.

"Thank you, Willi. For remembering me."

"It's not a story to forget. After so many years hearing about you, I can finally say I've come to know the Angel of Stralsund."

★★★

After a supper of sausage and potatoes at the bier haus, he and Rapholtz strolled past the theatre to the waterside path and back to Thalhammer, where he would pack his clothes and notes and make his way by hansom to the rail station at Rostock. With any luck, he would arrive before dawn, and as long as the checkpoints weren't manned by greener and therefore more zealous Schutzstaffel, he'd sneak into Oliver's apartment in time to see the sun rise. After that, and as long as the streets were clear, he'd make his way further down the street to Greta.

It was the way of things, and he hated it. There were laws, harsh realities, and Schutzstaffel to enforce it all. He hated what they had to become and what they had to live with, as if it was normal to fear being taken away.

He and Rapholtz passed a few brownshirt stragglers in the center of the piazza. Some of Stralsund's residents had gathered to listen to their speeches about gutter religions, mud people, the foulness of mixing races. As they walked by, he saw Martin among those lingering to listen.

"It's a sickness," Laszlo said as they gave wide berth. "Weak men trying to convince other weak men how strong they are, that they didn't lose, that it's someone else's fault. More and more Germans are believing this nonsense."

"The need to believe created these people," Fleischl said. "I should know. It created me."

★★★

By three the next morning he was waiting at a checkpoint on Handjerystrasse, waiting. He felt his pockets for his identification papers while, ahead of him in line, a woman and her son were taken to the side amid a cluster of Schutzstaffel. The woman rifled frantically through her purse, to no avail. In a moment, uniformed men walked her and her child down the block to an idling truck.

"No papers," a man behind Fleischl remarked. "What do you expect. Chilly day today."

"It is." He felt for the folds. They were newer, the paper smooth, not creased with age. Leaving the telegram and his father's drawing where they always were, he withdrew his identification papers and waited his turn. With any luck he'd pass through without incident, and then he could relax and enjoy the walk to Jenaer Strasse. Later he could find a patch of soft grass in the Volspark for a picnic, or a stroll past timbered homes to where the Comedian Harmonists might be found singing old Yiddish melodies. He would be happy. He would be with them, unless the evening to come brought another curfew.

He presented his papers to a uniformed boy who looked no more than eighteen. The boy examined them carefully under the watchful eye of an older officer who regarded Fleischl with a glimmer of recognition and no small amount of amusement. Such encounters were less frequent, but still there was always a chance that a man who sat in the audience weeping at Dowid or thrilling to the defeat of the malevolent Doctor Norcross, or who even volunteered his skull to the old electrodes, had since become a man with the power to pull him from line.

"It's fine," the older uniform said with a soft chuckle. "He can go."

The boy handed Fleischl his papers. "Go," he said with as much gruffness as he could muster. His demeanor reminded Fleischl of Martin, or whoever Martin might soon become.

As he passed, he saw the older man whisper to his pupil. The boy looked at Fleischl and shrugged, unimpressed.

He went to Oliver's apartment, locked the door, and had a bite of supper and some wine. He sat at the window to wait.

I shouldn't complain, he thought while the darkness began to lift with the dawn. There was some money saved from the old days, a job at Thalhammer, and an eroded yet persistent hope that he still could help people. He took to his tasks in the daylight hours, and at night he lay with his loves, whether they were with him or not. He listened for Greta and held the miracle that they'd found each other in his hands. The world outside their walls was on fire, but not always for them. Not if they were careful.

Dawn had only just broken when a tiny glow opened in a third-floor window down Jenaer Strasse from him. He grabbed his coat and left.

Greta greeted him at the door with a kiss that lingered until Oliver and Adelita could stand no more and came to break it up. Greta led him inside, took his coat, and sat in his lap while Adelita cooked a supper-like breakfast of pork tenderloin with apples. "Thank you," he told Oliver, "for watching over them."

"You're my family," Oliver said, and handed him a cup.

He sipped strong coffee and watched as Adelita stirred the drippings while reading a book. She was a voracious reader. Greta hated to read unless it was a script for a film she was to be in. There were fewer of those now. She didn't understand her daughter's need for a book in hand at all times. Where she yearned to bring others in,

Adelita wanted to be brought somewhere else.

"He promised to make inquiries," Fleischl told Greta and Oliver while Adelita hummed over her work. "I'll keep trying. At least for you and Adelita."

"We don't go unless we all go," Greta said.

"There may be an opportunity," Oliver said. "A film in the U.S. with Fritz is being discussed. There may be work visas. Albin is trying to arrange it, but he doesn't have the same influence."

"If it happens," asked Fleischl, "could you take them?"

"I won't leave you," Greta said, and Adelita cooked, and it was all a warm, quiet chat they'd had too many times, that didn't even raise voices anymore.

They cleared the table after breakfast, ate zimtschnecken from their favorite bakery on Sudwestkorso, then went up to the rooftop garden so Oliver could demonstrate his latest technological marvel.

"They're called cathode tubes," he said, gesturing to an array of exotic equipment. "Telefunken used them in the war for wireless. But they've been known for some time now. See here, the electrode? Plucker and Hittorf found some sort of ray coming from the cathode, and Schuster discovered the ability to deflect those rays with an electrical field..."

Fleischl smiled. This was what a good and quiet life looked like, he thought, when brought in by people like us. Each of his loves and what they most cared about. There was always the unease, of course, the pit in the stomach, the rumor of some harder thing coming. As Fleischl watched Oliver stretch a canvas sheet along a clothesline, he decided that there would always be some disquiet in the world. He was nothing special. Men existed between what they loved and what they couldn't bear. Men lived with such things all the time.

"Adelita," said Oliver, "I need a volunteer. You as well, Greta."

He positioned them before the canvas, then shone a bright light on their faces through a spinning disk fitted with lenses he'd installed on an adapted phonograph. "Is it not extraordinary? The light sweeps across them. Over there, the cathodes take the light and convert it to a signal of electricity. Each hole in the disk produces one line of image. Look there, at the screen."

It took time, and it was as dissolute as a dream, but the new contraption produced an image. Two faces pressed together, suggested with barely a hint of detail. But Oliver felt in his glory and Adelita was entirely content to be pressed cheek to cheek with her mother.

"Implications for your work," Oliver was saying to him as the image faded into a chaos of black dots across the screen. The clothesline sagged, dropping the canvas sheet, and beyond lay the city lights, glowing through low clouds. In the morning, they would return to the world. But there, then, it was easy to look at Berlin in the misty dark and call it home.

That night, he and Greta sat with Adelita in her bed. She liked company until she fell asleep, adulthood be damned, and he liked to be the last thing she saw, so she had something to hold onto for the nights he couldn't be with her.

"Tell me something," she said, as she always did. She loved stories before saying goodnight.

When they'd arrived back from the Carpathians and began the slow process of building a life together, she scarcely spoke to him. She was surly and refused to laugh at his jokes even if any sane person would think them funny. She watched him constantly. She didn't trust anything about him. His presence, whether it would last, her mother's deep and stunning love for him, all were suspect.

The first time Greta left them alone together, Adelita moved through the apartment they shared as if no one else was there, until the night she called to him from her bed. "Tell me something," she said in such a small voice that he wanted to cry.

"What do you want me to tell?" he asked her that night. Tonight he asked her the very same thing again as they lay back together in a different apartment they no longer shared, their bellies full of pork and apple, because it had become ritual, even though they all lived apart. That had become ritual too. The fear that what could befall him at any moment could befall them if they were together.

"You," said Adelita.

That first night, he'd humiliated himself in hopes of gaining her sympathy, or at least a chuckle at his own expense. So he told her of the old paper's retitling, The Electric Love Song, and how he'd used that title for a magic trick. Then he performed the static sleight with a blank page from one of her many journals. He didn't recall her smiling, exactly. But she'd rolled over and fallen into a contented sleep. That was before the laws and the danger he posed to her simply by being with pure German women, one of whom carried his blood.

This time he told her of flax carts, of lying beneath tub water and holding his breath for an impossibly long time, until her grand-poppa Jurgen, whom she would have adored, said get out. He told her of the Angel and the shipyard, and then he brought her to Kiel and the crumbling cliffs before performing the waxed pfennig trick. He omitted details. Men fell in the spaces between what he told her. He could see in her eyes she knew they were dead. She heard well enough.

He held all the threads within himself. All the random moments. Sometimes it struck him so sharply, the life he'd led to now.

"I don't like you not being here," she said. "You should just always be here."

"Agreed. Remember the first carriage ride?"

"I didn't like you."

"I didn't think you'd ever like me."

"I still don't."

"No. You love me."

She smiled. She loved it well, the story of how he worked for her affection again and again until, finally, she heard him. I guess we can call the part of me that's you, She Who Listens. It was her favorite joke. It was also his.

"Soon," he said. "These laws will end and the men who made them will be gone, and we'll be together so much you'll get sick of me.

I'll bore you to tears, sitting around getting fat on your cooking and writing dull papers."

"Let me know when you've finished your paper on the energy," she said. "I want to read it."

"You'll be the first," he said, because it had become part of the ritual. That he would never write it didn't matter.

"I'll keep an eye on her," said Oliver when they returned to the living room. "Just be careful. I've heard a couple of vehicles. Maybe they're patrolling."

"You leave first," Greta said. "I'll meet you at the Kino."

"I'll save the seat in front of me," said Fleischl.

"It's late. No one will be there."

"There are always others."

After thirty minutes of navigating back streets, he arrived at the doors of the Mozartsaal Kino, in Schoneberg's Nollendorfplatz. He knocked, and waited until a heavy-lidded man opened the door, took his money, and allowed him to pass.

He adored the old theatre. The sumptuous interiors betrayed its concert hall heritage. Safe within its Noveau walls, he didn't have to think about shattered storefronts or torchlit marches. All the toxic resentments the Nazis fanned daily. He could just lose himself in the dreams onscreen. The stories never mattered to him quite as much as the balletic movement of images. A boyhood spent peering into a phantasmascope had left him with a childlike wonder at what so many frames-per-second could conjure: the world. That's what she told him.

There were others in the dark. Men and women seated a few chairs apart. Some passed notes while others stared at the lighted screen, searching out one anothers' silhouettes.

Only when Greta sat in front of him did his heart quiet.

"Nothing bad will happen," she said. "I promise."

"I promise too," he said softly, and put his hand on her shoulder.

"Find me," she said.

It was a picturesque enough film. There were the Alps and a

vague superstition about blue gleaming crystals and essential goodness. Outside the theatre were leaflets railing against Jews and Communists and Roma. Daily there were rallies. Thugs beat men because of the way they dressed or the shape of their accent. Shops owned by the wrong types were burned down. There was inflation again, and illness again, and lines, and lost work. But not in the light onscreen. In there, he searched every scene because she could be around the next corner, or the next, or the next.

Onscreen, the heroine scrambled up a mountainside while below her, townspeople celebrated the looting of crystals from a sacred grotto in the crags of the Dolomites, or witchery, or whatnot. He studied the villagers dancing in the streets over their trove of blue lights.

"There you are."

He pointed to the corner. It was always a corner. An old woman holding a crystal aloft to dazzle in the Alpen light. He couldn't see her face, but it was her. The way her shadow cast something like wings against the wall it could be no one else.

Greta lay her head back so he could reach her. "You always find me," she said.

They walked back to Jenaer Strasse. The streets were theirs and just for the time it took to turn the corner, he felt as if the empty quiet world was theirs as well. Her hand was warm in his. They leaned in to one other like two people listening closely. Under the lengths of telephone wire at Oliver's end of the block, he kissed her in the dark. "I love you," he said, just before they were swept by a beam of light.

Down at the opposite end, near her apartment, a car had turned a corner.

"Go," he told her, and he let her hand slip free. She crossed the street into an alley. There were back ways where she could reach home without being seen.

The car continued down Jenaer. Just a car, he thought. Just people.

He crossed toward the alley, intending to catch up with her—if his creaky knees could tolerate a light jog. Then he'd cradle her while she slept, just to add one more memory of her to all those he already held.

He grinned at his own sentimentality. She would tease him mercilessly if she knew.

The sound of a motor caught his attention and he turned to it without thinking. The car had reversed direction and was now driving toward him.

He froze. If it was a patrol, he had papers. If it was a pack of brownshirts looking for a victim to beat up and spit on, he would let them satisfy themselves with him. He wouldn't let them roam the streets until they found the woman with one blue eye who hadn't yet made it home.

Reaching into his pocket, he withdrew the key to Oliver's building and inserted it into the lock, careful not to appear in a hurry, or suspicious, or as terrified as he was. Just a man on a walk, returning home to one of the myriad flats inside.

Oliver appeared at the top of the steps above the mail slots in the lobby. They stared at one another through the entryway glass. The alarm on Oliver's face told the story: he'd seen the car too.

Fleischl opened the entryway door just a crack and told Oliver to stay out of sight.

"Come inside," said Oliver. There was a tremor in his voice. "Come hide."

"If they search, who knows who they'll take. Tell Greta and Adelita. I'll come as soon as I can."

"No, Fleischl."

"I've no intention of disappearing. Not after all we've come through."

Behind him, the car came to a stop. "Papers," said a man.

Oliver's lips moved soundlessly. *Schutzstaffel.* Then he slipped around the corner, where another short flight of stairs led to the second floor.

When he heard the car door open, and the unmistakable

concussive report of boots against pavement, Fleischl turned to face them, papers in hand.

"Do you live here?"

Three uniformed men formed a circle around him. Another remained behind the wheel. The one who'd spoken was young, clean of face, with the sort of zeal he saw more and more frequently in newsreels, at rallies, and on street corners. A tranquil confidence shone in the eyes of these blonde boys. As days wore on under the Reich, it became clear that rules applied differently to boys like the ones before him. And even those rules would fall away, leaving plain license. Consequences were for others.

To be the ones who demanded papers, he thought.

"I don't live here," said Fleischl.

"And yet you have a key."

"I live a good ways away from here, near the university. I'm just visiting a friend."

"Late at night, with a key."

"She's married." He tried to smile. It was a lazy lie and he was terrible at lying anyway. He hoped it would be enough. Perhaps they'd settle for a few punches.

The officer examined his papers. "We were told you'd been seen in this area before, Herr Berger. I suppose that's the reason why."

His stomach turned.

"May I go?" he asked.

"Mustn't keep her waiting, eh? Regrettably, no. We've been tasked with locating you. You're being summoned for a meeting at the Ministry."

"Can I ask what this is about?"

One of the other uniformed men opened the car door while the driver spoke into his radio. Fleischl heard his name go out across the waves.

"Of course you can ask," said the one holding his papers, and then he smiled.

★★★

In thirty minutes, their car idled on Wilhelmplatz No. 8/9, on the northern corner of Wilhelmplatz with Wilhelmstrasse. The Ordenspalais was an assemblage of monolithic, windowed slabs abutting an immense plaza, a cement city unto itself. Cars and pedestrians passed through by the hundreds.

His Schutzstaffel escorts walked him up a marble staircase to the Reich Ministry of Enlightenment and Propaganda. They waited with him in the reception area until a young woman in a pencil skirt brought him down a corridor to a wood-paneled office that smelled of cigars and cologne.

"Herr Berger. Come in."

The man seated behind a grand desk lit a cigarette, then offered one to the woman seated beside him.

"My name is Werner Naumann," he said. "I am State Secretary for the Reich Ministry. I believe you know my companion here."

Alice lit her cigarette. "Yes," she said. "We know each other."

"We used to," said Fleischl.

Naumann was a watchful, cautious man with a bitter air and a tightness around his mouth, as if nothing suited him. He wore a dress uniform with the Reich insignias prominent on both lapels, and a swastika band on his right arm. He was chilly, elegant, and affectedly aristocratic.

Were it not for his expertly tailored clothes, he might be taken for an accountant.

Alice wore a swastika pin that stood out in stark relief against the blue fabric of her blouse. She wore no other jewelry.

She caught his gaze and looked away. He couldn't remember ever seeing Alice Bliekroder being careful.

"It's a pleasure," Naumann said, "to make the acquaintance of the famous He Who Listens. I saw one of your shows. The Wintergarten, correct? Very entertaining. Those old silents. And that other one, with the man and the ship. I was a boy of course. Quite thrilling. Later, I came to understand that you did it to help him. Tell me, is he still alive?"

"He is."

"How is he now?"

"Better," Fleischl said.

"Well. I suppose that's something, isn't it. Does he know you when he sees you?"

"He thinks he does."

"Frau Bliekroder, perhaps you can let He Who Listens know why I am taking the time to see him."

Alice sat next to Fleischl. "Of course," she said, before turning to address Fleischl: "You've expressed a desire to leave. There was an inquiry opened in your name by a burghemeister in Stralsund. Travel papers. It leaves the impression that you want nothing more than to abandon the country that's given you everything you've enjoyed. You and your family."

This was the Alice he remembered. Erudite. A reasonable woman asking questions and stating facts, a woman who didn't need to demand a reply.

"The burghemeister made the inquiry at my request," said Fleischl. "Please don't involve him."

"What if we told you," said Alice, "that all necessary papers could be expedited for your family, and perhaps you, as an ambassador of German science and thought? Why flee the only home you've ever known when you could represent it proudly around the world?"

"I don't understand," Fleischl said carefully, "how such a thing might be possible."

"By you doing what you do best. Talking. This time on film."

"We want you to make a film for the Ministry," Naumann said. "The return of He Who Listens in the name of German greatness, marking the tremendous advances Germany's made in the sciences. We take you on a tour of one of the facilities. You visit with doctors and experts. You watch them work. You comment on their achievements.

And you let the community at large know that Germany leads the world. Germany is to be respected. She's to be trusted. The community doesn't seem to receive these facts very well from us. There's no reason for this, but perhaps they'll receive it from you and others like you."

"What community are you concerned about," he said.

"The community that either understands its place in the new Germany or loses its place in the new Germany."

"Shall we tell you more?" Alice asked. "Or shall we return you to where we found you?"

Beneath the prim clothes and practiced authority, there she was. The bruised woman expecting the return of what was taken.

"I'm listening," he said.

★★★

In the car, Alice removed the pin from her blouse.

"There are benefits to working with them," she said.

"That's why you're doing this."

Their car passed the plaza on its way back to Berlin's bustling heart. "That's why they're doing this too," she said. "Put aside the speeches and the smart uniforms. Ideology is for the underclass. At the top, it's only power that matters."

"And me?" he asked. "What power do I lend them?"

"You're not the only one they're reaching out to. The Ministry understands perfectly well that the transition has been heated for certain parts of the country. The Reich isn't trusted. They've given good reason, not that they want to hear that. But nothing about this is nefarious. Germany is entitled to recreate herself. Everyone can have a place. Maybe not an equal place. They aren't communists, after all."

"Transition. Ideology. You sound well-rehearsed. But I don't think you see what I see. People are being taken away. Transition is too sterile a word for what they're doing."

"Maybe those people wouldn't have trouble if they acted more like Germans. That they act like their allegiance is elsewhere first, Germany last, is why the war was lost and the peace worse still."

"If you truly believed that," Fleischl said, "you'd have left the pin on."

The car turned onto Jenaer Strasse and came to a halt in front of Oliver's building.

At least they don't know, he thought.

"You're a forgotten actor," she said. "A psychiatrist known only by other psychiatrists. There are other, far more important people who will help the Reich turn a positive light onto Germany. But your people remember you. They may even trust you. And so your name came to their mind. And your name led to my name. It seems we're linked even now."

"If I do this, you'll grant us passage?"

"If you don't, they won't grant passage to any of you. That much is clear."

A car pulled to the curb behind theirs. Its engine rattled between its steel walls. He turned to see more Schutzstaffel in the front and rear seats.

"They'll be here through the night," she said, "and they'll bring you tomorrow morning. A bit of advice. Don't be open in your desire to leave. It's counter to the image you need to portray to get you through this. With luck, it's tomorrow and no further, and you all leave."

She lifted a fresh cigarette to her lips. Her hands trembled ever so lightly. That was all it took for what was left of the old Bliekroder façade to crumble. He took her lighter, ignited it and held it near the face of a woman living in fear. It was only the second time he'd seen her cry.

"Do it for her," she said. "She needs to leave. Now. I don't know if they'll let you leave. I'll help if I can. Do this for Greta before it's too late to do anything."

"Please tell me what's happening."

"I don't know. I just do as I'm told." She inhaled deeply and held it inside. "August is dead. That occurred long ago. It's customary to offer condolences."

"Let me know who's mourning him and I'll do so."

"Fair." She lay her head back against the seat. For a moment he wondered if she would try to lay it on his shoulder. But she knew better.

"There's never been a place for me," she said. "I've looked for it everywhere. The world of men, the company of… special people, shall we say. Whether they wanted me or not. I just wanted someone who would let me belong. They never have. I suppose you're all that's left. How odd, that you know me best."

"It sounds as if they know you too," he said. She turned away as a tear fell. "I understand why you're afraid. Checkpoints aren't just for Jews."

"No, they aren't." She gathered herself. "Until tomorrow. Wear a decent suit."

He stepped out onto the sidewalk. Two Schutzstaffel emerged from their car and waited.

Alice rolled down her window. "The last time I saw her, she was a witch holding a jewel. You aren't the only one looking for her in dark theaters."

"At least tell me what it is I'm supposed to see tomorrow."

"Isn't it obvious? Sound and vision."

In Oliver's apartment, he brought a chair to the window and waited. All through the day he saw at least one uniform stationed at the entrance to the building.

He thought of using the telephone but was too afraid. Could they listen to the lines coming from anywhere? Could they know which apartment he was in? No, he decided. She and I have our own ways. Oliver was with them. They know what's happened. She'll be watching.

He fought sleep.

Just before nine that night, a tiny light flickered to life at the far end of Jenaer Strasse. He lit his own candle and placed it in the window. He sat in its glow and spoke as if to her. Don't come out. Don't.

When he saw a lone figure dart across the street into an alley, his heart gave way. He waited at the window, feeling as if the room was filling with water. How long had it been since a young man in a false ship had to hold his breath like this?

She never came back onto the street, or to the entrance where the Schutzstaffel were. He didn't see her anywhere.

Leaving the apartment, he went to the roof to look for her. He opened the stairwell door and walked through pitch black to the edge. A whisper came to him across the gap between Oliver's building and the next.

"Here."

His eyes adjusted. The shape of a figure stood against the netting of stars above the roof of the building across the alley. He couldn't see her face and didn't need to. She was home for him, dark or light.

"Those men down there," she said softly.

He told her what happened.

"Don't trust her," she said. "Go somewhere. Don't let them find you."

"If there's a chance for you and Adelita to leave, I have to try."

"You'll go tomorrow and never come back."

"I'll light a candle in the window when I get back home. But don't come out if those men are still here. And until I'm back, don't stay in one place. Stay on the move. I don't want them to come looking for you because of me."

"Like the old days. Living out of a suitcase." She grew quiet. "What if there's no candle," she said.

"Then take Adelita and do what you do best. Disappear, my love."

He heard a soft gust of air. She cried.

"I don't want to test it anymore," she said. "How we find each other. It's been enough and now we're finally here. We should be here."

"All our years," he said, "we've only had this a little while."

"They've been my happiest days. For a dull, unimaginative boy, you've surprised me. Just when I think I have your voice in me, it changes."

"I hope to surprise you a little each day. Each week, maybe."

"I like seeing you with Adelita best. She needs her father."

"Yes."

"But we don't need to tell each other these things. These are things for distances."

"We have plenty of time to tell each other," he said.

"Nothing can happen to you. Do you understand?"

"Or to you."

"I don't want to hear you. Never again."

"Never," he said.

CHAPTER Twenty One
Vera

They took him the following morning, as promised.

Over the course of the night he'd experienced an unsettling, ambient sense that the world was accelerating, that by dawn he would step out and find something unrecognizable. A strange city standing where Jenaer and Berlin had been. That he would be no different than Alice. The two of them, in a place with no place for the likes of them. It felt entirely plausible, as all dislodging fears did, before the light opened down the street where his loves were.

As the sun began to climb and the knock came at his door, it still felt real. But it wasn't until he walked out to the street flanked by Schutzstaffel that he accepted it. The world hadn't been replaced by some sleight of hand. There were the tenements and the wires and poles, the waiting car. The sky beneath which they'd drive him away was the same sky, and one less man wouldn't matter to all but a few. That was the real world.

Neighbors came to their doors and windows to see who had brought the Reich out. The majority of them were poor, Jewish, and not at all used to such pomp surrounding the mere taking of one of their own. It was always done quietly. A snatching from a queue, or a knock late at night. Some knew who he'd once been, and to them there was a grim pride to be found in the treatment the Reich afforded. So many men. Such a clean car.

Fleischl climbed into the backseat between two officers. A sidearm poked him in the ribs.

The car rolled smoothly away from the curb onto Jenaer Strasse, bound for the end of the block. There were more people along the streetsides and more faces at windows. In one there was a candle, pale and fading into the rising light, and three faces gathered at the glass. Oliver was there. Of course he was. He would have rushed to be with them, and he would stay until it was clearer, whatever it was. A different world, perhaps, or the unimaginable future.

He didn't want to turn and gaze at them as the car idled by. A turn of his head told things those men shouldn't know. Perhaps it would say too much to Greta. *I need to see you because my eyes may close too soon.*

So he left them where they were, in the window, and he took what he could of them. He took the image of them sitting all together, of the houseplant next to Adelita as she sat in her favorite corner of the couch, and of the painting above them, an impressionist landscape of a barn at sunset.

It didn't have to last all his life, he thought, though it could. It was strong enough.

A question occurred to him, there in the rear of the sedan. Oliver, the perpetual bachelor. Had he ever been in love? With whom? Surely he dreamt of more than making the world into moving pictures. In his secret heart, he must make the world up and then put someone in it who was meant for him alone. Or maybe he too feared checkpoints.

He wanted to tell Oliver how sorry he was for never asking. Whoever they are, he would say when he returned, they'll have a home with us.

He didn't ask the men with him where they were going. What difference would it make?

The Havel River shone beautifully along the way, beneath a high, bright sun. He did what he could to let it overrun him, so there would be nothing else to consider. He held on to Greta, Adelita, Oliver, the painting, the plant. Of course there would be a next time that he saw them.

In the late morning, they arrived at an unmarked gate of iron and stone. The buildings beyond were in various stages of construction. Between the silhouettes of cranes and geometrically stacked rail ties ran a paved road that split the center of a great triangle. There was a broad white building with a tower rising from it. The entire perimeter was walled in with a barricade some ten feet high. The flat buildings he saw across the grounds reminded him of Kiel's barracks, the cramped cot-filled quarters. In the distance, an appelplatz anchored the triangle's base. It vaguely resembled the piazza.

Everywhere there were echoes.

A stern, humorless man in uniform opened his car door. He was thick and pugnacious, with a slit for a mouth and a rodent's sour expression. His closely set, callow eyes scanned Fleischl and found him lacking. "I am Sturmbannfuhrer Lippert. Welcome to Sachsenhausen."

There was a platform at the curved edge of the field. It was covered in ribbons and fronted with rows of chairs. A string quartet played Schubert for guests milling about while children moved in tight formations among them under the watchful eyes of uniformed matrons, passing out yellow carnations while the cameras captured guests patting their heads. Crowds lined either side of the appelplatz. Another cluster of cameras had been assembled against the lip of the stage, where a considerable gathering of gray-clothed figures left the barrack buildings. Like starlings, they came in streams to the seating area. There they waited.

As he took it all in, a camera appeared alongside the car that brought him. A mannish woman with a spray of curly, unkempt hair

tucked beneath a hat told one of the cameramen to capture him as
he exited the car. Next to her, a man holding a microphone said in a
jaunty voice, "now comes a Jew star of yesteryear, He Who Listens, to
witness Germany's scientific excellence."

"Herr Berger," the woman said, "walk to the stage. I'll tell you
when to stop or turn. Look as if you're seeing something wondrous.
No talking to the others unless I instruct you. Walk, please."

While walking, he mustered what he hoped might pass for
wonderment. The grey-clothed crowds gathered across the field were
quiet until a guard gestured to them. Then they cheered for whoever
passed them by. Some of them were permitted to step forward and
greet the men and women exiting their own vehicles, wearing finery
and picking up uniformed escorts who led them to their seats. He
saw an actress he recognized from films he'd sat through in search of
Greta, and an athlete of some sort, though he couldn't recall what he
did. Faces from newsreels, filmed rallies, stage and screen; he counted a
dozen that he knew from somewhere.

The camera followed him closely, so he maintained a wide-
eyed wonder as he entered the crowd emerging from barracks. There
were odd badges sewn to their chests. Many wore Stars of David the
color of the fading carnations gripped by the children among them.
They held those flowers closely, as if they were all that mattered.

A little girl with hair the color of straw gave him one.

"Thank you, Fraulein," he said. The child's face sank when the
carnation left her hand.

Another guard selected six men and women and told them
to step forward. The men extended hands for Fleischl to shake. The
women came closer and waited. Neither they nor he knew what to do.

A frail looking man in a tweed coat shook his hand. "I saw all
your films," he said as the guard glanced at the woman directing her
cameramen. She nodded.

"You can answer," the guard told Fleischl.

"Thank you. I'm grateful. I hope they brought you comfort."

"And your lectures. They were wonderful days." His eyes filled. "I will remember this." The guard told him to move back.

The director instructed Fleischl to move on. He climbed the stage and sat where she told him, at the end of a row of chairs. The other guests sat together drinking champagne, as a contingent of soldiers marched, high-kicking in lockstep for their benefit. A line of rigorously smiling children marched alongside, their little legs churning furiously. The guests applauded as the man with the microphone moved among them, collecting their comments.

There were speeches extolling the installation's design and its purpose, to inspire hard work and freedom, or some such. Fleischl gazed at what could be seen beyond the stage, beneath the tower. Groups of people in the same drab clothing strung thick spools of wire along the top of the perimeter wall. Others dug trenches and painted railings near the southern end of the appelplatz. Here and there, the symbol of the Reich adorned buildings. The interlocked, twisted Zs. There was a building on the far side of the field marked with a sign over its door. Brausebad Baracke X. Beyond it was a brick structure with a chimney, like a small factory. Flowers grew alongside it. They didn't seem to belong, nor did the knot of dour women huddled together in its shadow, picking over a pile of clothes. Occasionally they drew something out and ripped it to pieces before tossing it into a new pile of odds and ends for the others to go through. Some of the pants and dresses looked no bigger than the marching children.

He spotted Alice in the audience, among other dignified, well-dressed invitees. She glared at him as if to warn him. Perhaps I don't look suitably wonderstruck, he thought.

Sometime in the early afternoon, the last speech, a terse discussion of order from Sturmbahnfuhrer Lippert, reached its orderly conclusion. Then he heard the distant whistle of a train. The guests left the stage for the appelplatz, and he followed. As he passed through the crowd, a woman asked him why he was there. She wore a yellow star.

He told her he'd been invited to see scientists work.

"Are you staying?" She smiled as she spoke because the cameras could find them at any moment. It was a terrible thing, he thought. A smile such as that.

"No," he said.

"Are they making you stay?"

"Sha," a man next to her said.

"It's alright," she said. "Meshpucha."

"It's not alright. The trains. There are more coming."

"Who's coming?" Fleischl asked.

"Us," the woman said and smiled as a camera swung around to face them.

A beefy arm landed heavily on Fleischl's shoulders. The man before him had the face of a wrestler. "An old colleague from the silent days!" Paul Wegener said. "Not everyone can make the move to sound. Tell me, what are you doing with yourself these days?"

They shook hands. "I'm a psychiatrist."

"Oh, have I troubles to tell you!" He laughed for the camera.

"We've met before," Fleischl said. "I don't know if you'll recall."

"You do look familiar," Wegener said without conviction. "Do I know you from somewhere other than your films?"

"I attended a performance of Nathan Der Wiese in Berlin. I was acquainted with one of the members of your troupe."

He saw recognition alight in Wegener's eyes. "I remember. You knew Greta." The cameras felt so close.

"Are you still acquainted with her?"

Behind the bank of men with their lenses and microphones, Alice lingered.

"No," said Fleischl.

"Separate ways and all that. Do give her my best, should you ever see her. Her ability with makeup and prosthesis was an astonishment."

"I've seen for myself."

Alice glanced at an impatient Lippert. "They want us at the train platform," she said. "Take some flowers to hand out."

"Flowers?" asked Fleischl.

"Just do what they say," said Alice. Fleischl wondered at the beads on her brow and the carnations in her hand.

Lippert took them to the platform as the first train came to a slow rolling halt. Through a cloud of steam, people clambered out of crowded cars. There were no seats. They'd been standing body to body for who knew how long.

Guards separated them into two long, silent lines, then questioned each of them. They didn't look like prisoners. They didn't look dangerous or deserving of any of it. They were just people, just old and young and married and families, and they didn't meet the eyes of the guards or of Fleischl, Alice or the guests as they obeyed the director's instruction to hand out flowers.

"We welcome you," Fleischl said, following the words written on a whiteboard held up by one of the cameramen.

Then the newly arrived were separated. Parents were taken from weeping children; they told their babies not to cry, that they would see one other soon, that this was just formality, as if the word had the power to cure.

There was a system of some sort at work, Fleischl thought, but he couldn't guess what it was. The guards must specialize in this sort of thing. The unstitching of ties, like the work of seamstresses.

Lippert prowled the aisles of refugees until he found what he was looking for. Then he walked past Fleischl and Alice with two girls. Twins.

"Come," Lippert told him, and he followed with Alice. The cameras came after them.

Lippert took the girls to an array of barracks near the little factory. Curls of grey smoke rose from its chimney to fade against the clear sky.

"What is that building?" Fleischl asked.

"New showers," Lippert said. "Better hygiene."

"And the other? The one with a fireplace?"

"For the doctors. No more questions."

He brought the girls to one of the barracks, where a matron waited in the open doorway. The faces of women filled the space behind her. When the director pointed cameras toward them, the women all smiled and curtsied. One stepped forward to tell the girls to come in and make themselves comfortable. "Your momma and poppa will be here soon," she said. In her smile and her star, Fleischl heard, *Are you staying? Are they making you stay?*

At the matron's command, the girls turned to the cameras and waved. Just beyond the doorway, another child stood waiting. She held two yellow stars and some thread.

The cameras were well placed. They only captured the girls as they disappeared inside.

"Ten minutes," the director told Lippert, and went on ahead to the little factory.

"You'll see the scientists next," said Lippert. "There will be things for you to say."

As they left the barracks behind, Fleischl saw the girls in a window, standing patiently as their stars were sewn.

Lippert brought him and Alice to an industrial yard ringed with construction. For the cameras, Lippert named the structures to come. A brickworks, a canal bridge, a path for testing shoes, a line to assemble components for nearby factories. Useful things, he said. Honest labor for Germany's uplift.

They entered a well–lit building adjacent to the shower facility. It was sleek in design, with an outer lobby and corridors gleaming from a recent cleaning. They came to a large conference room where the other guests were already seated. At the front of the room were several tables with posters and a film projector. White coated men stood beside each segmented presentation, awaiting their turn.

The lights dimmed as Fleischl and Alice took their seats. For two hours they watched films and listened to lectures on scientific achievements for the benefit of all Germans. There was a clear military bent to it. Dogs, monkeys and pigs were opened and cauterized. Their ability to withstand altitude was measured in pressure chambers. Their limbs' ability to heal, their bodies' ability to fight plague, assaulted by the contents of tubes. Horrifyingly, their eye color was altered by injections to improve night vision.

He had to look away from it. A furtive glance told him Alice did too.

When each experiment was complete, the films continued. They showed the animals' bodies being borne off in bags, across the industrial yard to somewhere near Baracke X, to the building Lippert had identified as being for the men on stage. Each time a film ended, after each experiment, but before the scientist responsible for what appeared onscreen came forward to applause and questions on cards, a bit more film of the animals' bodies gently borne off in bags, across the industrial yard to somewhere near Baracke X and the building Lippert said was for the men onstage, with its hearth fire and its slender fingers of smoke.

At the conclusion of the day's presentations, the guests gathered before the cameras to recite whatever appeared on raised cards. The director—Fleischl heard Lippert refer to her as Leni—darted among them to check lighting and angles.

"Perhaps we can go," Fleischl said. "No one seems concerned with my saying anything."

"All I know," Alice told him, "is that there's an experiment for you to observe. Sound and vision, that's all they said. Someone will tell us more if we need to know more."

"So you don't know what it is."

"I don't know what else there is to this. I'm just trying to do what they want me to do. Please, Fleischl."

Lippert came for them. "You're somewhere else," he said.

They followed him out of the building, toward Baracke X.

"Showers?" Fleischl asked.

"Something with water, maybe," Alice said, nodding in agreement with herself. "They saw that film of yours with the fake ship.

There was a time when you couldn't get away from it."

A Schutzstaffel let them in to an anteroom with blank concrete walls the color of snow, benches, and empty shelves. At the far end was a formidable steel door. The last of several camera operators was positioned there, alongside a guard. All the other cameras aimed at Fleischl as he walked toward the table in the middle of the room. Leni waited there with another white-coated scientist, a gleaming machine, and a viper's nest of electrodes trailing along the floor and leading to the head of one of the twin girls Lippert took from the train. She couldn't have been older than ten.

There was something about the camera at the far end that dried his throat. The way it pointed at the door, not the room.

He didn't see the girl's twin anywhere.

"I am Dr. von Bolschwing," said the man in the white coat. He enunciated each word for the benefit of the microphone in his face. "Herr Berger, He Who Listens. Do you recognize this array?"

A card rose behind the doctor. "That is a galvanometer," he read. "Only it's far more advanced than any I ever worked with. What are those?"

He pointed where instructed, at the cathodes bunched next to the machine. It looked like a bouquet of flowers. Dr. von Bolschwing explained cathodes to him. Oliver's version was better.

"Do you recognize the experiment?" the doctor asked him.

"Yes," Fleischl read.

von Bolschwing turned the galvanometer on. The cathodes ignited. The girl trembled in her chair.

"Come and see," von Bolschwing pronounced, "the real version of what you used to talk about in your act."

Fleischl came closer. Something gaseous and alight rose to the underside of the cathodes' glass heads. They were like emergent clouds, each to a region of the girl's brain, each its own little nebula of candlelight.

God help him that for a brief moment, he felt the stirrings of the man to whom only one thing mattered.

"Stimulus one," von Bolschwing said.

But no one came to the girl to snap their fingers or tickle her neck. No one did anything.

von Bolschwing pointed to one of the tube heads. "Cocoa," he said, then prodded the child's arm. "Did you taste it?"

"Yes," the girl said dully, reading the card held up for her just off camera.

Fleischl exchanged looks with Alice. She wore the same sinking expression, which only sunk further as the true nature of the experiment began to emerge.

"Stimulus two," said von Bolschwing. A loud shattering came from beyond the steel door. "See the areas of the brain," he told Fleischl.

No one held a whiteboard up. There was nothing for him to say. Every tube head flared.

Now they held starry skies. The lights were firing.

This is what it looks like, Fleischl thought, when the mind wants to be heard.

"This is transmission," he whispered to Alice. She stared straight ahead, frozen.

"No talking," Lippert warned.

The girl whimpered. Her eyes were locked on the far door. "I'm a twin," she said softly. "Make them stop."

Now Fleischl watched the far door too.

"Stimulus three," von Bolschwing said.

They waited. All was silence in that closed room where the camera operator hung his head after peering through the lens.

"Maybe they stopped," Alice said under her breath. "Maybe we're done."

In the cathodes, the child's mind was violence. She was terrified and it welled up in her like a storm. She was a baby, this twin they took from a train, walked to a barrack, sewed to a star. He never saw Adelita at that age. He had missed all of that.

"German science and ingenuity," declared von Bolschwing. "For the benefit of the world that will see this, tell us, He Who Listens. Have we established transmission for the first time?"

Whiteboards went up just off camera. Yes, his whiteboard read. *This is what I always dreamt of seeing but never did.*

I hear you, the girl's read.

That's my line (smile) but you say it much better than I ever did.

"I hear you," the girl read. She was breaking.

Lippert came to the side of the man holding Fleischl's whiteboard, glaring.

"Say it," Alice muttered, "so we can be done with this."

It was there before him. The words to say and the words the child said, out loud and in a place where only tubes and the clouds of her could hear. He was at last seeing what it really looked like, in a concrete bunker with a metal door and men with arms bands like blood, and a twin with her own star sewn to her, and people just off cattle cars. The Reich's map of steps led to women rending children's clothes because the children were gone somewhere into Sachsenhausen. It happened thanks to a baby lying about hearing anything because her twin was gone somewhere into a room behind a door. For all he knew, he was gone as well.

"That's my line," he began, then knelt to the girl. The way her body shook brought back the crumbling cliffs at Kiel.

"What's your name?" he asked her.

"Vera Kugelmann." Her soft voice was inflected with an accent from the interior of the continent.

"Did you know that kugel is a food?" he said. "It's noodles made in a casserole. Quite delicious. And my name, Fleischl, is meat in German. So we're both named after food. Don't be afraid."

"I had to walk across dead bodies," she said. "On the train."

"Where's your momma and poppa?"

"I walked across poppa."

"I promise not to hurt you, Vera."

"They don't promise."

She began to cry. She called for her mother and her sister, but not her papa. She was still so young but she knew, there was no point. Her twin was named Eva; she cried for her. She cried for her home. He managed to gather that the Kugels came from Hungary on the train.

"I lost my poppa too," he said, and felt himself sinking.

Somewhere in the time it took, while the lights in the glass cathode heads dwindled, the cameras stopped. Everyone stared at him.

"Either you say what you're supposed to say," Lippert told him, "or I'll place you under arrest."

"What stimulus did you use?" he asked von Bolschwing, who glanced at Lippert.

"That's not what you're supposed to say," Leni noted. "It's on the whiteboard."

Lippert patted his sidearm. Alice mouthed his name, and please. There were more words to say. That's what they wanted from him. After that, he knew he was dispensable. So was Vera. Eva.

"The only thing the cathodes show," he said, "is that you terrified this girl. That's all there is."

What must it have been, he thought, for a man in the sea up to his lips, who would never come home, and all that mattered was the last few words that needed to be said, and needed to be carried away by the first of one thousand seven hundred and two steps.

He thought of his loves. How many steps away are you.

"Show Eva to me," he said and felt himself fall.

Lippert told the director to clear the room of the cameras. "At this moment," he said to Fleischl, "you are placed under arrest for violation of the Law for the Protection of German Blood and Honor. And all those who aid and abet you will be arrested."

A Schutzstaffel officer came from his post at the metal door. He pulled Fleischl's arms behind his back.

"Leave the child alone," Fleischl said to von Bolschwing, to Lippert, to Leni, to the lifeless lenses of the cameras. "She gave you what you want. She said she heard. Let her sister go."

"You want to see the sister," Lippert said. "Go see her."

He pointed to the metal door.

The Schutzstaffel released his arms. Ahead, the camera operator cleared away his equipment and left. There was a small, rectangular window in the door where the lens had been. Like a porthole.

He wanted to stay where he was. He didn't want to walk as he did, past Lippert and Alice to the doors and that little window. He wasn't a brave or special man. His days had been alike as two drops of rain in a storm. A dull, unimaginative boy, dreaming of no particular thing. Never dreaming of this.

But he pressed his face to the glass and saw the last of the girl as she left.

She was a mirror's image of the child behind him. She lay on the floor beneath shower heads, only there was no water. This was not a roundhouse under the sea. The room held only her and a few desiccated pellets. It held air.

The pellets were blue. He wanted to vomit.

Minutes had passed since von Bolschwing called for the third stimulus. It took minutes more for Vera's twin, Eva, to stop breathing.

"You filmed this," Fleischl said to no one.

Men in gas masks came into the showers from another door when it was over. They carried a large bag, which they lay alongside Eva's still form. When they stretched it between them and unzipped it, he left the glass.

Alice didn't meet his gaze.

"Don't look," Fleischl told her. "On the other side of the door, just a little ways past the glass, you'd see where you've gone to, looking for a place to belong. Don't see it for yourself. Just stay where you are."

He went to Vera as Lippert closed in on him. Somewhere behind them all, a door to the showers opened, then closed. In a moment the masked men passed by the window of the room.

They carried the bag, each to his end. The bag bowed at the

center. It held weight.

They were heading for the little factory where all the animals went. Soon, the ash of Eva would leave this place.

"Did you see her?" Vera asked.

"I saw her," he said.

Lippert took him away from the building and the showers. They went past what he now knew was a crematorium, toward the barracks. The sky above him was different from afternoons in the city, the way he and his loves saw it from home's window, with the dusting of coppery rust on the balcony railing. How small a balcony it was. Room for the birds at most. Shall we luncheon on our spacious balcony? Adelita would say in a terrible accent that mocked the rich. It always made him think of the Bliekroders.

He thought of them, and the couch, the plant, the painting, and all he knew and didn't know, and he remembered them as they watched him leave from their window in the pale circle of a candle.

He knew now, it was the last time he'd see them. He would die in this terrible place, and it didn't feel real. He wanted to wake up. But he could only think of how to reach Greta. They all had to get out.

At the door to one of the barracks, Lippert called out the elder. "You have an honored guest. He Who Listens, from your old days. This man just spent time with your daughters, Kugelmann."

Across the appelplatz, a man shoveled something into a hole outside the little factory while thin fingers of smoke unwound from its chimney stack into the sky.

He listened for any sounds but heard only a faraway whistle. Another train.

"Find a place for him," Lippert said, and left him there.

Kugelmann motioned to Fleischl. "Inside," he said.

He entered behind the elder man. Hundreds of men were crammed into berths atop splitting sacks of straw. The walls were crude and flimsy against the elements. There was an adjoining room just like this one, with more faces protruding from its rack–like berths to stare, and beyond it was yet another doorway with more berths and more gaunt men; on and on it went like mirrors at a carnival.

The barrack elder pointed to an empty bunk. "This one," he said. "Next to me."

The door to the barrack closed, and Kugelmann came close. "You saw my children? You spoke to them?"

"A little while ago," Fleischl said, and hoped nothing showed.

"Are they safe?"

Kugelmann held out his hands. In them was a needle and thread, and a yellow star. In them, too, was the need to be held up.

"They're well," said Fleischl.

All the men watched him.

"I… I will make inquiries about them."

"Yes," said Kugelmann. "You can bring them back to me. They brought you here. He Who Listens. An important man. They'll listen to you. Or why else?"

He put the star and thread into Fleischl's hands. Fleischl smiled even as a tear rolled down his stubbly cheek.

"I sold flax," he said, "and isn't it a ridiculous thing, but I never learned how to sew."

★★★

After Lippert left him in the barrack, Fleischl passed the hours by studying the metal joist brackets above him, the teardrop contour of some mildewy condensation on the wall, and the faint whorl in the center of the stain. It could have been a fingerprint; a thumb, he decided.

He studied the flakes of flakes of ash dusting the ground around the crematorium across the way. He knew those ashes were Eva. They were small and delicate. The slightest stirring of air set them dancing beneath the lights. He wondered if Eva had been a dancer before.

All was silent since Lippert walked away. The crematorium, the barrack, but for the quiet service murmured by a minyan with the

twins' father presiding. It was a silent world. He thought of Vera somewhere. Of Poppa before Dowid. Of Momma before Greta behind the
sheet. Of Greta in the little globe of light at the bottom of a lake. That
was before he knew who it was down there. The love of his life.

All the things, he thought in the bunk, *that over time have come to
me to break their silence and ask, bring me back.*

He used the time to make mental notes. How to end the paper
he would never finish.

We are all stories, it would say, *and mine was electric.*

*It began in the sea and along telegraph wires, and it will end behind a
door. In between, a life.*

*Something happened to me, but only once, and only because love and
death held hands and screamed. I was a storm in the one who loved me and no
one can change that.*

Deep in the night, a guard brought him across the appelplatz to
the arch of Sachsenhausen's gate, where Alice waited.

"Five minutes," the guard said.

Fleischl waited for the guard to step back. "Did you know?"
he asked.

"No." She lit a cigarette and drew deeply. "They're going to
put you on trial. Race defilement."

"That means Greta," Fleischl said.

"I know."

"Lippert said they would arrest anyone who aided and abetted.
Do you understand what that means? Greta, Adelita, Oliver…"

"Me," said Alice. "That's why I can't do anything. I can't."

"Help me."

"If I even try, I'll be in there with you. You know that."

"You're a coward."

"I always have been."

"Look at the train tracks. Did you see how many came yesterday? More will come. This is what they're doing. Did you look through
the window? Did you see it for yourself?"

"I didn't. They didn't tell me. I won't ask."

"Finish," said the guard.

"Help her. Get her whatever papers she needs. I don't care how you do it. Get her out."

"Don't you understand what's next? They're going to sweep all of Berlin. They're rounding up whole neighborhoods. Naumann told me last night. She's there somewhere and he doesn't believe me when I say I don't know where. They'll find her with or without you. I can't stop it. I'm not who I was. None of us are since they took power. If I was, would I be here with them? With you?"

"Do you want to know what I saw behind the door? A child gassed to death to see if her sister heard. Where did they learn about that? From you? Your advertisements and your show? Love and death, holding hands at last? Remember that, Alice? You told me to do this for Greta. You wept for her. You love her. You put me here and now you tell me you can't do anything? I'll do whatever they want. I'll sign a confession. I'll admit any crime. Just don't let this happen, I'm begging you."

"Don't ask it of me. I just needed to tell you. I needed you to know that whatever else is true, I didn't want this for you or for her. I'm sorry for all of it. I should never have brought you to them. They're going to try you and execute you for everyone to see, Fleischl."

She turned and walked away.

There were guards coming toward him and for all he knew, he would be shot there and then. In an hour or a day or a week, other men would storm down Jenaer Strasse and eventually they would come to the apartment with a candle in the window. He couldn't crumple, not now.

I never want to hear you again, she'd said.

And it came to him. The only thing left to do. The impossible thing.

"They don't need a trial, Alice."

The light caught the damp surface of her eyes.

"They need a show," he said as the guards took hold of him. "The one you wanted, for the world to see."

The last thing he saw before the butt of a rifle came down on him was Alice, still standing beneath Sachsenhausen's arch.

★★★

The following morning, guards jarred him from a shallow, troubled sleep. They pulled him from his bunk and took him out of the barracks.

When he saw they were walking toward the showers, he wept. The guards were amused by the terrified old Jew with trembling legs and a liturgy of mumbled names pouring out of him. They didn't understand how the man they half-carried across the appelplatz had lain awake all night, thinking of the words to say, nor did they appreciate that he was, with each step, reaching the end of a most unusual and decidedly non-Talmudic prayer.

They veered away from the grey metal door of the showers and brought him around to the other side. There, in the anteroom, men waited to see the famous He Who Used To Listen.

It didn't occur to the guards to ask why the old Jew's incantations had stopped.

Alice and Lippert sat at a table in the anteroom. There was a third man with them. He stood and turned at the sound of Fleischl's steps.

"Herr Berger," Naumann said. "Good of you to join us. I was just indulging a rather peculiar proposal from the Fraulein, and I thought it sensible to include the cornerstone of this odd little venture. Come, sit."

There was no chair for him. He knelt to the floor.

"By all means," Naumann told Alice, "continue."

"The footage of the girl, hearing," she said. "Followed by He Who Listens and his stimulus, that no one will hear. German science triumphant. It would make for great theatre, and it would be highly useful for the Ministry's needs. I can see it playing in cinemas across

Germany. Maybe elsewhere."

"But how will we know Berger failed? I mean, of course he will. This is all nonsense, let's just say that here and now. To prove this stunt of yours."

"His," Alice said. "I merely supply the venue."

"His stunt," Naumann continued, "would we not need to produce the one who supposedly heard him, so she can say she didn't hear anything? Where is this woman?"

"I don't know, as I've said. Neither does Berger. Disappearing is one of her specialties, it seems."

"We can remedy that," Naumann said.

"I'll tell you both how you'll know if I fail."

Fleischl pulled himself to his feet. "You'll know I failed if you find her. Because if I succeed, you never will."

Lippert came to him and slapped him hard enough to split his lip. Blood flowed down over his chin.

"For your arrogance," said Lippert.

"Deserved," Naumann added. "His arrogance aside, these are meaningless words. As I've stated quite clearly, none of this is real. I will disavow all knowledge of this meeting and the comments made, as will each of you, but this Jew didn't do anything, and the girl didn't do anything. The wires and the machine are the stuff of cheap charlatans in alleyways. There are days when I wonder what Goebbels was thinking, peddling nonsense to the masses. This is swill, and beneath me to even entertain. To what end is all this, Bliekroder? I ask you, not him. He's going to be placed on trial. That is inevitable. The charge is as serious as the rest of this is trivial. A show? It buys him time, nothing more. And what would he do with that time, I ask? Plot against us? No. It's out of the question."

"If I fail," Fleischl said, "I'll do so in front of as wide a world as you can gather up to watch. And I'll say I failed. I'll say you're right about all of us. Jews, Roma, Communists, homosexuals."

Alice reached for a cigarette, her eyes fixed on her purse.

"Every low form of German society you despise, I'll speak for all of them. I'll say I've lied all my life. We're treacherous, deviant misers and hook-nosed drinkers of pure Aryan children's blood. I'll say that if we don't accept Germany's role for us, then we deserve whatever comes next. I'll say whatever you want."

He turned to Alice. "And you tell her, if you find her, that you were right about me and she was wrong. Maybe she'll see at last who you really are, after all the time you spent trying to convince her."

Alice's eyes narrowed. He saw the pinch of her lips, the beads sprouting across her forehead.

You're here too, he thought. And you know it.

"The mere fact that you beg for this so openly and pathetically," Naumann said, "makes me suspect you all the more. And it must occur in a... what did you say this place is?"

"My ballroom," said Alice with some hesitation. "Built underwater."

"Of course it will make you money, I've no doubt of that."

"It's the only place where it happened," Fleischl said. "Including here, as you admit, Herr Naumann. As far as you are concerned, I failed to prove anything. Well, so did you. There is one place. There are two people. That's it, in all the world no matter the money, the might, or the fine German minds. It happened to me, to her, while we were far from each other. That's how it has to be."

"And you ask nothing for yourself," Naumann said. "I find that very hard to believe."

"There's no point to it. I'm begging enough as it is. You won't give me what I ask for."

"No, I won't. No papers for your family and no reprieve for you. You are to be an example."

"I've no power," Fleischl said. "I've nothing left but begging, and so I beg you with everything I have. If you ask, what do I want, I want you never to find them. But if you do find them, leave them where they are. Don't bring them here, or anywhere like here. Let them be. They've done nothing. I will take all the blame and all the consequences."

"Anything else?" Naumann was enjoying the exchange.

"A piece of the old days to have with me," Fleischl said. "During the show."

"There will be no show. To even participate further in this is an insult to the Ministry and the Reich. My answer is no."

"Are you afraid, Herr Naumann?" He saw Lippert stand. "Me, a charlatan Jew, against the might of the Reich. How can I do anything but fail? And yet, I'm a good listener, and I don't hear the insult that you describe. I hear doubt. Do you doubt what you can do? Or perhaps you doubt that I'll fail?"

Naumann ended the meeting with a call for Lippert to slap Fleischl again, followed by pitying shake of his head and one word for Fleischl as he left the anteroom in the grasp of two guards.

"Buffoon," Naumann said.

The guards escorted him out. Alice followed them to the barrack, where she asked for a moment to speak to Fleischl.

The twins' father waited at the barrack window. The sight of him sank Fleischl's stomach.

He thinks this was a meeting about his girls. Look at the important man out there.

"Are you insane?" Alice spat. "What is it that you think you're doing, antagonizing them like that? Do you want to die so badly?"

"I'm doing the only thing I can," said Fleischl.

"Tell me. I won't say anything. I truly need to understand what just happened. Are you thinking there will be some chance to escape? I promise you there won't be. No? Are you hoping to impress them with your act, and they'll anoint you ambassador and send you around the world to convert Jews to the cause of German greatness? You truly are a buffoon if you believe any of this. For that little speech of yours, they'll most likely shoot you today in the yard, and me right after you, for ever darkening their door with the likes of you. Jesus Christ, what's wrong with you?"

"Let me tell you precisely what's wrong with me, though I'm certain you can guess, intelligent and accomplished woman of German society that you are. What's wrong is I can't get to my family and I can't escape. I can't help them and I know it. You can't help them because you're too afraid of ending up in here, and I know that as well. You're not in the least troubled to step over gassed children if it means you'll live. So what else would you have me do? Do you really think I'll do nothing and simply die? I have to try."

"Try what? If you think I'm the coward here, let's see you do something. Overpower a guard. Shoot your way out. I'd like to see that."

"It wouldn't help them."

"Nothing will help them, can't you get that through your thick skull? You'll be put on trial and they'll go looking for your family if they haven't already started."

"Berlin's big," Fleischl said.

"So are they."

She checked her timepiece. "You asked for my ballroom. Fine. But they won't do it. They don't need to. They'll try you and execute you. Or maybe just execute you outright."

"Need is a funny thing," said Fleischl. "You didn't need to keep showing up at the Wintergarten, but you did. You didn't need to take out all those advertisements or sue me over and over or try to stop her from showing up onscreen. But you did because you couldn't help yourself. There's a quaint notion in psychiatric circles. Out of awareness, but not out of operation. Meaning, even when you think you're done with me or with her, you aren't whether you know it or not. You can't stop yourself. I'm always there in your every thought. So is she. You've never been able to get us out. And now, neither will Naumann. He'll do it because he thinks he has to in order to cleanse himself of me. An arrogant old Jew who thinks he's better than he is. Just like you. You watch. And I'll do it because I did it before and you know it."

"You'll fail," said Alice.

"Say it enough times. Maybe you'll start believing it."

She nodded to the guard and said, "we're concluded."

The guard pushed Fleischl inside the barrack and closed the door.

Kugelmann came to him with his daughters glistening in his eyes. "They're safe. You did it. Tell me you did it."

Fleischl could do nothing but meet the gaze of a father with only one child left, and he thought, should Kugelmann have come to the empty chair onstage and ask the same of him—*tell me you brought them back*—Einthoven strings would have traced the lines of a mourner's kaddish. But maybe they would have traced hope as well. They would have sent it over the same wires. The chance that it was true.

All the clouds in Vera's firing mind, he thought, and who's to say that among the lights, one didn't burn for the belief that Eva lived. Our lights must burn as brightly for hope as horror, or else we're already dead. Love and death hold hands. No one ever said death had to be the one in charge.

My loves aren't dead, he thought as he returned Kugelmann's gaze. Neither am I. But for them, I soon will be.

"Have hope," he told the father before him.

CHAPTER Twenty Two
Get Out

Over the following week, while a crew was assembled and preparations were made to the ballroom, Vera and her father saw each other from across the appelplatz every day at role. Kugelmann, whose first name Fleischl learned was Josef, wept on each of those days at who wasn't there next to his remaining daughter.

The night before they came to take Fleischl to Alice's ballroom, he joined Josef and the other men of the barrack in a recitation of kaddish. After, they shared a bit of stale, stolen bread in the name of those not with them.

All that evening, as the Sachsenhausen sky grew purple, he recited his own kaddishim for every empty chair in his life—and for himself, so the words would come readily when he needed them. So they would come with no hesitation. So they would be loud.

Lippert and his men entered the barrack at dawn. They found him weeping and terrified. Morning, so soon. But he knew what needed to be done this day.

Lippert patted his holster. "Get up."

The promise of rain informed the air. Nothing imminent,

Fleischl thought, as they walked him to a car waiting at the gate. Just an outpost of thunderheads on the horizon and the odd, fizzy, grey beneath them that spoke of sweeping storms falling on whatever lay below.

Rain from a distance looked like ash, he thought.

Along the journey he watched the Oranienburg give way to Berlin's outskirts. The lands turned over and a skyline emerged from the fog. The drive was over before he was ready and they entered the crescent drive and parked near the main house. Men in the black uniforms of the Schutzstaffel formed perimeters on either side of the walk, rifles slung cavalierly across their chests.

Lippert brought him through the house and out to the path. He almost buckled as they walked. His mouth was dry. Sweat crept down his back. Cramps cascaded through his gut, and the old ache in his leg returned from nowhere. From the past.

They emerged from the bough canopy into the clearing near the steps down to the aqueous green glow of the ballroom. There were guards on the dock, watching the water.

They all had guns.

One of the guards opened the entrance. "Lock it after us," Lippert told him.

Fleischl heard a padlock click behind them as they descended.

The ballroom seemed small with so many in it. There were three cameras and men to operate them. Alice sat behind Naumann, near the center of the room. A wall of sheets hung tautly from a line of thin wire, spanning the width of the ballroom.

Lippert pushed Fleischl toward a table set up behind the chairs. A projector rested on it, and a film canister with its top off. A spool was attached and a fresh, brown strip had already been threaded.

All the cameras were filming. He heard the movement of the parts. The dome still tinged everything below it in lights of different seasons, and far from all of it he heard the water turn. That much hadn't changed.

"Alice," he said as the camera at the corridor entry turned to capture them.

"This is impossible for me," she said quietly. "To see what's to become of you. I could never have imagined this, Fleischl."

"Nothing's impossible, Alice. Not even for you. You always know more than the men around you."

He went to the table as Lippert instructed. The sheets filled with spatters of dust, then went to a brilliant white. The ballroom dimmed.

Alongside the projector, Fleischl watched Vera float across the screen at the end of a nest of electrodes. Behind her, light bloomed in the cathode tube heads to indicate the fear inside her. The cameramen in the ballroom captured it all. The screen, Naumann watching, and him.

I hear you, Vera said onscreen as the cameras converged on him. Vera faded to black.

"Now it's your turn," said Naumann.

"Yes," said Lippert. "By all means, show us a miracle."

Baruch hashem. The ballroom glowed and iris light opened on the sheet. It speckled the glass of the dome with tiny flecks. He saw one among the constellation. Blue.

Beneath the strikes of the projector's gears and the moving lake above them, there was an audible and steady pulse in his ears. It was the reel, or his heart falling. The screen filled with the old view from the dock, looking down at the water. The camera's eye beheld the glow at the bottom and a tiny figure inside it, spinning slow circles.

He felt her turnings in his chest. She hummed in the wires of him, a small and insistent thing surrounded by water. A faint, far light he refused to lose.

He heard Greta's voice, young and out of reach, telling him of his electric birth. Greta, older, telling him of their daughter. And he understood, it had to be now. It couldn't wait.

The lake pressed against the glass. It was quiet, the way it was when he lay beneath the surface of the tub, reaching for rings of rain and his father above them.

On the sheet, Greta was just a moment away from running with her hands at her eyes as the sound of him came through the glass all those years ago to find her here. Right here.

He grabbed hold of the table because the room felt as if it was shivering in a storm and he couldn't stay upright. He was sobbing. He saw himself in the camera lens.

"Is he actually doing anything besides crying?" Naumann asked.

"Are we finished?" demanded Lippert.

"Do it here," Fleischl said. He couldn't hear the sound of his words, only the pounding in his ears. "Now."

Naumann stood. "You mean kill you?" He went to the corridor entrance. "Have my car brought round," he called. "Enough of this. Fraulein, you will answer for this monumental waste of the Ministry's time, I promise you. I want this woman found by the end of the day. Lippert, take this idiot out of my sight."

Lippert's shadow fell across the sheet, wiping Greta away.

"Find this Greta," Naumann was saying. "I want her in Sachsenhausen. And the daughter. Both of them."

Fleischl's hand brushed the film canister and closed around it. Greta was lost inside the great fanning that was Lippert. She was gone and he couldn't bear it.

Spinning, he held the canister out like a book. A sheet of pain coursed through his shoulder as the canister hit something hard and unyielding. He thought he'd hit the projector, but it still flickered the last of Greta onscreen as she ran away.

Go, he thought. Go as far away as you can. Disappear, my love.

Lippert glared at Fleischl as a thin ribbon of blood descended from below his hairline, between his eyes. More followed. Swooning drunkenly, he crumpled.

Onscreen, Greta was gone. Somewhere in the projector light,

her eye made its way to blue.

He picked the projector up and dropped it hard on Lippert's head. Lippert twitched, then was still.

He crouched down and came back up with Lippert's sidearm in his hand. He pointed it at Naumann.

A muffled, percussive rumble came from somewhere high. Running. The Schutzstaffel saw it all from the pontoon. It wouldn't take long.

"You should go," he told Alice. "But you…" He trained the gun at Naumann's head. "You stay." He pushed Naumann to the floor and held him under his foot.

"They're coming to kill you," said Alice.

"I know."

"And then we'll find your family," said Naumann.

"I'll find them first."

Footfalls in the corridor. They'd broken through the lock.

Alice froze at the entrance to the corridor as he placed the muzzle against his own temple. The first of the names and the words came, burning bright.

"Go now," he told her. "Save yourself from them if you can."

He moved the gun away from himself and aimed it high. "But in Greta's name, you don't get to keep this."

Alice turned and ran as the words rolled over him and took him down.

You hear me wherever I am. You always have. Hear me this last time. Momma, poppa, Kiel, Anton, Gert, Sachsenhausen, Eva, all of you can have me, just take me to them. Take this to my love, hear me one last time, Greta. Listen, my love. It's not a storm. It's me.

As Naumann screamed, he fired at the dome.

GET OUT

It shattered. The lake came in a jet. The rest of the dome buckled drunkenly, then exploded, and it was the entire sky falling on him.

He closed his eyes and as the water pummeled him into the collapsing wall, he went home.

CHAPTER Twenty Three
Balsa Wings

The lake swept everything under. It filled the ballroom corridor to the top of the staircase and spilled from the entrance onto the grounds, carrying the first bits of destruction with it. Old sheets, a Sturmbahnfuhrer's hat, a gun.

For the Schutzstaffel who'd stayed behind when one of the tiny figures in the room below was seen hitting the other, the lake's surface was calm at first. Then there was a flash of bright light followed closely by total darkness and sudden waves.

It would be a good while longer before anyone noticed the odd way the water peeled gradually back from shore.

All was silence below, where the upheaval churned the water violently, and Fleischl with it. It spun him dizzyingly and he saw only clouds. He heard voices, but he didn't know if it they were real or if it was simply the lake, filling him with all that it had heard over the years.

He opened his mouth and called for his loves to get out, and everything slowed. After the initial pounding of the flood, nothing hurt.

He thought he saw light crossing the water above him and reached for it. In a moment, he understood; he wasn't in the water anymore, turning and turning. He was on shore, buried face first in mud.

The screams of men reached him there. They were far away. Dazed, he glanced around for anyone coming as beams of light split the distance. He'd floated the length of the lake to a small embankment just below a road.

I held my breath a long time, he thought.

Men shouted for Lippert and Naumann. Their flashlight beams interlaced. They searched the surface of the water.

The soft rumble of a motor car came from the road. He waited for it to pass, then stumbled to a line of trees on the other side, careful to remain in the wild, untended thicket. There he hid himself and tried to stop shaking. Do something, he thought. Make a plan. A map of steps. Remain in the shadows. Look for a way to get somewhere, and from there somewhere else, until home. Go home. See if they're home.

With luck, it would be a while before they knew he wasn't down where he ought to be. They would come looking for him, but he would be far away by then, with his loves. He had to be.

He tore the star from his shirt, balled it up and pressed it into the pocket of his trousers. Then he began to walk.

The lights of Alice's estate soon fell away behind him, but the city was still so far.

★★★

Officials of the Reich Ministry and the Schutzstaffel questioned each of the men who'd been assigned to guard the grounds, from the ballroom to the house and the garden to the lake. They reported what they saw, and to a man they provided the same account. The ballroom was a jewel beneath the water with tiny figures in it. Movement, like a fight. Some ran to see and the rest stayed on the dock, where they witnessed a disturbance in the water—in the very air, said a few—followed by a massive thud and the churning of the surface.

An engineer summoned to the telephone from his bed at nearly midnight estimated several days at least before the lake settled atop a new bottom composed of shattered glass, layered mud, the remains of the ballroom foundation, and the bodies of Lippert, Naumann, and some unlucky cameramen who weren't fast enough and fell to the flood. And, of course, the Jew responsible for all of it.

"Certainly, he's down there," Alice told a Ministry official on the dock, where he'd found her and asked for her own account of the incident. "I don't know where else he could be. Down there in death, with good Germans taken by his treachery. How many lost?"

"Secretary Naumann," the official told her. "Lippert. At least three others, likely swept away. The rest are accounted for. They ran back up your staircase ahead of the flood."

"You'll forgive me," she said, pulling her wrap tighter. "It's been a long and terrible night. I'd like to rest."

"Why did you let him do this here," the official asked. " Of all places?"

"Herr Naumann agreed to it."

"My question."

She reached into her pocket for a cigarette. None.

"Wouldn't it have been something," she said, "if the impossible actually happened."

"There are rumors," the official said. "About why you would do this."

"I didn't love him, if that's what you're suggesting."

"Not him. Her."

Her wrap was thin and offered little resistance to the chill. In the house was a better one she'd stored away. An ermine. Old. She would put that on instead.

"I'm not nearly daring enough to be that sort of German," she said, and walked past him.

"Do you think anyone ever heard anything?" the official asked.

She paused on the dock. The ballroom had once been directly below her.

"I can't imagine," he added.

"Neither can I," said Alice.

★★★

Keeping to side streets and alleys, Fleischl made his way along the rows of walk-ups lining Danzigerstrasse. He didn't know the hour, only that it was late. The gritty area was a sure bet for after-hours festivities of a drunken, prurient nature even in the hardest times. He expected to see the usual revelries on the stoops of the apartments and through windows thrown open so the whole of Prenzlauer Berg could hear the rowdy sounds of sex and argument. But nothing was lit and nothing moved. Only a stench in the air, of something burnt.

He managed to reach Niedstrasse and Stubenrauchstrasse. It was the same desolation there. As he neared home, the acrid smell became heavy and pungent. It stank of rubber and left a coppery tang. In the distance he saw flashes of lightning burst erratically above Wilmersdorf and home.

Down the mouth of an alley he went, emerging on Jenaer Strasse. There he froze.

Dozens of military men prowled the street to the end of the block. The bursts he'd seen were the arcing fireworks spitting from a downed line quivering on Jenaer Strasse's hard pavement in front of her burning building. The power was out and beneath the intermittent canopies of sparks, he could see figures moving past the darkened windows of the apartments.

One soldier came to his tiny balcony, the very balcony that he and Adelita used to joke was the most capacious in all the world, capable of holding precisely two potted plants and a chair.

"Clear," the Schutzstaffel called down to the street.

Uniformed men came to open windows and said the same, down the street. Then they were gone from sight, into the bowels of the buildings.

He turned away with nightmares in his eyes. The ash and smoke of Greta and Adelita rising into the sky. They were shot dead and left to burn like cordwood in the hall. They'd already been taken away, and what he witnessed was a sweep for stragglers. They were cowering in the dark somewhere, waiting for him to find them as the smoke swept into their lungs in search of the sea to push out.

When some soldiers left her building and crossed the street toward Oliver's and his alley, he ran.

In the park where they'd liked to picnic, he washed himself as best he could in a pond, dressed, and turned back to the city in a sort of dream state. The sky was bruised with color and the occasional bleat of a car horn invaded the silence. He aimed himself at the lights and told himself to walk, until a train, or until the sea, or until they find you. How will I ever find you? Are you alive? Greta, did you die?

He withdrew the star from his pocket. It was stained with blood. Lippert's, he supposed.

He patted the pocket, feeling for the telegram and his father's drawing. They were gone. Of course they were. Maybe destroyed in the lake. They had been through so much. In the end, they weren't meant to last forever.

★★★

In two days, the Reich Ministry's engineers assembled an army of men and equipment at the estate. They ran long lengths of tubing down the ballroom stairs and from the dock. Engines roared in locations around the property. On the morning of the third day the lake began to pour out in muddy torrents down the curved drive, into the surrounding forest, and eventually onto the road at the far end. Schutzstaffel guarded every downspout with orders to keep careful watch for any bodies that emerged. They were ordered first to determine if the body wore a uniform or a star.

Draining the lake proved a more logistically challenging undertaking than first thought. More engineers were brought in. Debates were held. New hydraulics were ordered on an expedited basis from America, a fact kept as quiet as possible. Blueprints were commissioned, dividing the lake into quadrants, each to be isolated behind metal retaining walls. The engineer who suggested, without understanding or irony, that they make use of a quaint method known in medical circles as "ten-twenty" was whisked off to parts unknown.

The same day the lake began to leave, Fleischl Berger's name and likeness appeared on movie screens across Germany. Between newsreels reporting the failing health of the President and tributes to the Reich Chancellor, dire warnings of a "lake incident" and a malevolent, quite-possibly-dead-but-just-maybe-alive Jew rumbled through the theaters, with the admonition to report him, should he be spotted.

On the fourth evening of pumps and water torrents, a grimy, bent film reel rose to the dwindling surface. Stirred loose by the suction, it floated atop the lake's remains but didn't quite reach shore.

Alice watched it pirouette across the laketop. If anyone wanted it, she decided, they could fish it out for themselves. She'd do no favors. Certainly, no one would do any for her. Her social circle of Party wives took unholy delight in telling her about the newsreel they'd seen at cinema. The renegade Jew was no doubt among the dead, but what if he wasn't? Didn't she know him? Would she describe him as a friend? Would he reach out to her? Would she harbor him? What would she do?

She took a final drag from her cigarette, threw the butt to the water to float with the spool, and returned to the house to pack her things.

"If he lived," the Ministry official had asked her on the night of it all, "where would such a man go?"

"Fleischl Berger was a man whose days were as alike as two raindrops," she'd said. "Had he lived, he would go where he always went."

On the next night in Berlin, the Reich Office of Communications sent three communiqués. One legalized plans to merge the roles of Reich Chancellor and president as soon as Hindenburg died at last. One voided any and all contracts, whether written or oral, between the Party and all industries, whatever the sector, in which August Bliekroder held even a negligible interest.

The last ordered all forces national and local to scour Pasewalk, Berlin, and Stralsund especially. As many men as it took for as long as it took to locate He Who Listens.

The following night, Alice left folders of paperwork detailing her eroded holdings, separated into orderly piles. Then, thinking better of it, she tossed the folders into the dank air of the mansion and let the crumbs of the grand Bliekroder empire fall where they may.

She jotted a brief note and left it atop the mess.

I have nothing left but this house and a lake full of wreckage. You're welcome to all of it.

A.B.

She left late that night without a word to anyone. There was no one to tell.

On that same night, the storage car door of a train bound north was finally pried open after much effort. After a moment considering what it would be like to climb over the bodies, a weak and hungry man pulled himself up and closed himself inside.

★★★

Ahead, the Baltic rolled below the moon. It was nearly three in the morning. He didn't know what day it was or how long he'd been traveling.

He stumbled through the piazza tunnel with tears in his eyes. There were few vehicles on the road. When he saw headlights break open the darkness, he lay flat in a ditch until they disappeared, and his heart stopped thumping.

Who knew if cart sellers even came anymore? Somewhere in the time that had gone by, they'd paved and widened the roads for cars and trucks. The tunnels remained, but two of them—the one he entered and the one adjacent to it—were lined with electric lights that looked like bright shower heads.

He arrived at the docks and fell against a pole. Some trucks were already parked. A crane split the sky above a freighter. Its wire works were in place to lift cargo. Gone was the forest of masts, the lantern lights. New days had come to replace the old.

It dawned on him what pole he leaned against. Its wood was ancient and pitted. The hands of lovers had once memorialized their union on its base. Initials inside hearts, as high as the tallest of the two could reach.

Had he time, he could listen for the hum of the wires. Instead, he left the docks, went to the switchback and made his way up to Thalhammer.

The man who answered the door was gray. His once youthful cheeks were puffy and grizzled with stubble. His orderly coat was buttoned to the very top.

"I still have it," said the man, smiling. "It's in my room. I've kept it all these years."

"I knew you would, Dowid. It's so good to see you, but I've very little time. I need help."

"I can help. I work here now. Why are you like that?"

"I got hurt. Don't worry."

"Fleischl, my boy!"

Rapholtz rolled up behind Dowid. He brought his wheelchair to a stop and held out a violently trembling hand. "You're home."

Fleischl took it and fought tears. There would be time enough.

"The SS has already come here asking questions," Rapholtz told him.

"I know. They're looking for me."

"You're hurt. You need medical attention."

"I need to use your telephone."

They went to the library through empty corridors and locked the door behind them. There was a telephone on the table next to Anton's couch. He picked up the receiver and called Greta's home. He hung up after several minutes, but the sound followed him. The incessant ring, echoing in the air.

"There was a fire," he began. "Power outage, I don't know. A line was down. Something happened. I need to get to the telegraph office and get Greta and Adelita out, get Oliver…"

"First, you rest," said Rapholtz. He asked Dowid to find blankets and lamps before turning back to Fleischl. "Who knows who's looking for you? We'll get word through somehow, but not now. You'll tell us what happened when you've had some food and sleep."

He told his friend about the camp, as best he could. Someone else had to know.

"God above," said Rapholtz. "We'll go tonight, after everyone is gone. I'll send word to Willi."

"I don't want to get you in any trouble."

"You're the only family I have in this world," said Rapholtz.

The moon poked through the low clouds on its descent to the sea. Its light crept across the library window and left pale patches on the floor.

He went to the window in spite of himself, to see the manner of ship announcing itself from the dock.

"You shouldn't be at the window," said Rapholtz. "You can't be seen by anyone."

"Only us," said Dowid.

"Only you," said Fleischl.

"How many steps?"

"One thousand, seven hundred and two," Rapholtz replied.

"It hasn't changed," said Fleischl.

"Not for me," said Dowid.

The library window offered its clear view of the dock, and Fleischl took it for a few more moments. A man emerged from the guild haus carrying an old crate to the foot of a gangplank of the ship anchored there. Soon, other figures approached the dock. Some shuffled along wearily, their steps informed by the early hour and by lives spent toiling at sea. Others, the uniformed ones bearing weapons, came to see who it was trying to board the ship. They all approached the slip and formed a queue extending back from the man on the crate. Even at the distance, Fleischl made out the master roll in Willi's hands.

"The old ways," he muttered.

The first man in line rolled his thumb across the ink pad, then the list. He wrote his initials and walked to the gangplank. The smallest gestures, the thumbprint and the initials, were obscured by the distance. But Fleischl knew them.

"The sun will be up soon," said Rapholtz. "It will be too easy to see you here at the window."

"Yes." He stepped back but kept watch over the ship.

"They'll come here again, looking for you," said Rapholtz. "But they won't find you. No one will know you're here. As long as you need. Go now. I'll bring you some food. Tonight we'll see the burghemeister about a telegram."

Fleischl went to open the old library door.

"You know," said Rapholtz, "I always suspected I'd find some use for that one day."

The tunnel was dank, mossy, and cold, but there were things that could make it better. Some light, a surface to sleep on, books and blankets and a chair. He'd make sure the far end was covered and couldn't be opened save by his own hand.

Dowid came just as he was closing the tunnel. "I still have your things." He handed Fleischl the rope. "See?"

"This has always been yours, Dowid. Would you continue keeping it for me?"

"And these?"

Dowid held out a crumple of balsa and paper, and some poorly glued feathers. "Maybe they can be fixed?"

"Maybe they can." He pressed the wings gently to his heart.

"I hope they don't make you sad," said Dowid.

"They don't, Dowid. If you like, close the door and listen. I shouldn't be seen. But I can tell you their story."

"I'd like that. Read it to me like you did on board."

Dowid pushed the door closed. In the murk of the tunnel, Fleischl heard him slide to the floor. He heard the rope drop into his lap.

In the faint light, he studied the wings. Some glue, yes, and perhaps another rod of balsa or two. Anyone else would give them up as beyond saving.

"This," he began, "is the story of the first time I almost died."

★★★

In the pale glow of a single candle, he saw the ax on the wall.

"I received Rapholtz' message," Willi said sleepily.

"I've been trying to place a call," said Fleischl, "but no one is answering. I saw lines down."

"You must be speaking of Berlin. I've heard things. Some sort of trouble in one of the neighborhoods. Sabotage, according to the Ministry. The power went out. There was a fire of some sort. They haven't released any other information."

"Do you know when it might be restored?"

"No idea, my friend."

"Do you know if anyone is there?" he asked. And Willi saw all he needed to see in Fleischl's eyes.

"I'll keep trying for you. You shouldn't make calls from Thalhammer if anyone is listening. And they may be."

"I'm grateful."

"How long do you think they'll look for you?"

"When they don't find me in the lake," he said, "they'll take all the time in the world."

★★★

For six months, men of the Schutzstaffel searched every building on Jenaer Strasse, repeatedly, until the neighborhood became as familiar to them as their childhood homes. They perused the rows of every movie theater in Berlin, looking for the old Jew who was enamored of the cinema. They sought out past colleagues, only to discover that Fleischl Berger really didn't have any. His friends Oliver Galeen and Albin Grau had gone to America to make a film with director Fritz Lang and never returned. His old peers at a university he never actually attended claimed scant recollection, until they were reminded of a vague incident involving a skulless monkey staring at a piece of paper, and the near electrocution of the deceased Chancellor's wife. That led to laughter and unkind words like *hubris* and *quitter* from those few who remembered, along with the sentiment that Fleischl Berger was almost certainly dead. He was not a man built to persevere.

They came to Stralsund as an occupying force. They organized Nazi rallies in the piazza to celebrate Hitler's ascension, at which they and a few stalwarts, including a long unemployed Martin, were the only attendees. Between marches and speeches given primarily for one other, they ransacked homes in search of the Jew who may or may not have been buried deep in the bottom of the lake, never to be found. They boarded docked ships and combed through the master rolls. They questioned every citizen and on more than one occasion posed for pictures outside the guild hall, with the mighty axe in the background. They looked in closets and crawlspaces, and on the evening of each day they made their pilgrimage to Thalhammer. There they interrogated the staff, including an exhausted old doctor in a wheelchair, searched each room, including the wash area and the library, and marched through the cemetery, where they never failed to trample the graves of Fleischl's parents.

They intercepted every telegram and listened in on phone lines. Before bed, they contacted commanding officers and advised that another day had passed with no trace. Then they slept in the hotel that was once a cheap pension for travelers hoping to meet their futures at the Baltic's edge. Over time, the men of the Schutzstaffel took to waving good night to the odd figure in Thalhammer's window who held a rope as a mother might hold her baby, and who told them each time they searched the library how many steps to the sea.

Still, Stralsund maintained a certain normality. Shoppes opened and closed, wares were sold in the piazza, and the dock hosted ships new and, occasionally, old.

Every other night, Willi sent word from the guild to the asylum. *No one answers on Jenaer Strasse.*

At Thalhammer, Rapholtz found an orderly to push him to his daily destination, the bier haus, for bags of sausage, fried potatoes and good crusty bread that he took back with him. His orderly would push him into the library, receive a generous tip, and lock the doors while the doctor set the food out on a table that had been in place since a time before most of the asylum staff were born.

"Dowid," Rapholtz said after returning with food on the evening of the Schutzstaffel's umpteenth departure, accompanied as it always was with a warning that they'd be back, "would you let him know? I'm going to lie down a while."

Dowid helped the old man out of his chair onto Anton's couch, covered him with a soft blanket and went to rap gently on the bookcase. In a moment, an answering knock sounded.

Dowid went to the window so he could keep watch over Fleischl as he ate, Rapholtz as he slept, the Schutzstaffel as they departed, and the sea.

"Do they think you're dead now?" he asked Fleischl, as he always did.

"They might," said Fleischl through a bite of bread. "But they all know me. My name and my face."

"So you can stay with us longer?"

"I can."

"I'm so glad."

Fleischl kissed the sleeping Rapholtz' forehead and joined Dowid at the window.

"One thousand, seven hundred and two steps," Dowid said.

"It's good to know some things remain."

He glanced at the cemetery grounds. Deep in the night, he might hazard going out to tend to his parents. Down a little ways from their graves was an undistinguished plot where Rapholtz hoped to rest. "Will you see to me," he'd asked Fleischl, "when my eyes close?"

"As to my own," said Fleischl, "for you are and have been."

They'd wept together, but only a while.

Dawn always came swiftly and with it, his return to the tunnel.

Dowid held the rope out to him, as he always did. "Do you want to keep this now?

"It belongs to you, my friend. I have all I need." Fleischl held up the restored wings.

Dowid smiled. "So you'll be here?"

"I will, until it's safe."

"Stay here until you're older. Then they won't know you."

"A good idea."

"Do you miss your friends? The ones you ask the burghemeister to call?"

"I miss them terribly."

"Where did they go?"

"I don't know."

"But they got there?"

Dowid turned to watch the black night sea. His lips moved soundlessly. The numbers, each its own prayer.

"I believe they did." Fleischl looked onto the Baltic, at the ships he could vaguely make out, and the piazza wall and the dimly lit tunnels to the water and back again. "Or else I would have heard something."

CHAPTER Twenty Four
Stories

November 1940

He wrote one last entry into a medical chart, then stood up from the cozy trap of Rapholtz' favorite couch. The orderlies had moved it to the window that spring, near the end, when Laszlo was no longer able to make rounds. At that time, Fleischl assumed responsibility for notating all the charts of Thalhammer's young doctors with observations, dosages, and suggestions on topics to try in session. *Behind the fear,* he wrote often, *lies the territory you want to reach. Find the first day of their fear and you've found the last day of their joy. There lies the work.*

Then, listen.

The young psychiatrists had made peace with the odd routine of rounds at Thalhammer. Each evening they left their folders neatly stacked by the locked library door. In the morning, they picked up robust feedback that they presumed to be Dr. Rapholtz', which was remarkable because their grandfatherly mentor had essentially dropped from sight, until the day in September when at last his heart gave out.

More remarkable still was the fact the charts continued to be filled.

They rarely caught sight of the mystery doctor rumored to be living in the library. They never learned Fleischl's name nor heard a word from him aloud. They knew only two things: Dr. Rapholtz had trusted him with their careers and his own health, and they received his undivided (if silent) attention to their files, rendered in a pedestrian cursive each day without fail. Alike as two raindrops.

★★★

Laying the charts outside the door, he closed the library up once again and went to the window to finish his coffee. It was almost midnight. If he hurried, he would be in his seat by a quarter past.

He opened the tunnel. Before leaving, he straightened the shawl draped over Anton's couch, so its patterned weave lay symmetrically. He'd kissed Rapholtz' forehead a last time on that couch, and in a certain light he could almost see the outline of his old friend's backside indented in the worn brown leather.

Bundling himself against the cold sweeping in from the sea, he hurried through Stralsund's empty piazza to the movie house that sat atop the bones of the the former shipyard.

Its doors were locked, as always. The last showing was long over. It was another slickly produced piece of Nazi propaganda, but no one went to see it. Rot and claptrap, something to do with the head of a munitions factory leaving the business to the Fatherland, instead of his children. It was hardly worth the risk to skulk over and watch it. Fleischl preferred the sort of showing he came for now. It was just him, occasionally Willi if his wife was in good spirits, some treats and a grand old silent.

Hermann greeted him at the door. He'd aged into a ruddy and generally stoic man with a hoarse voice, goiter and a spray of liver spots across his bald head that always put Fleischl in mind of days past. The ten-twenty days.

"Ah, herr Berger. I feared you were running late."

"Good evening, Hermann, and thank you as always."

He presented Hermann with some coins. "Not tonight,

herr Berger. This is a special night. I'll be watching myself."

"Oh? What's on the menu?"

"Something we are decidedly not supposed to watch."

"Dear God, not another one of those. What was the last one, 'Getting His Goat?'"

"Nothing of that sort. Come, we've been waiting for you."

He followed Hermann through the lobby and into the theater. Willi sat in a middle row. When he saw Fleischl, he held up a basket of fruit tarts. Fleischl took the seat next to him and selected a mohnstuck-chen. He bit into it, savoring the sweet poppy seeds.

"What are we seeing? Hermann wouldn't tell me."

Willi shook his head. "No idea. I just hope we skip the news-reel. Nothing but depression and malaise."

"Yes, please." He took another bite. He was developing a gut, though not like Willi's, whose girth rivaled his father's barrel of a body. "It was all I could do not to be shattered for days by the last one."

"The burning shoppes, the murders. If this is the new era, God help us all. They say thousands are being put in the camps now."

"I heard." He fell quiet.

"I'm so sorry, my friend. May you never go back."

"May no one."

"Remain hidden. We have you safe."

Hermann came down the aisle and sat down. "I'll start it soon," he said as the beam made its bright path above them. "Straight from America. It's a film from Fritz, and then an extra reel. "I haven't seen any of it.

"His work is banned," said Fleischl. "How did you get this? You'd have trouble if the Ministry knew."

"Fleischl, sha," Willi said. "There's a black market for every-thing, even if it takes years."

"Maybe your friend Oliver wrote it," Hermann said.

"Oh, my dear friends. This is more than I could ask for."

"You can ask for another tart," Willi said. "You look too thin, old man."

They ate and talked a while. Hermann went to make sure all the doors were locked and the heavy velvet blackout curtains drawn. Patrols were uncommon, but not unheard of. When he was satisfied, he ascended the stairs to the projection booth, closed the door and threaded the film spool.

By then, Fleischl had grown quiet. His friends were used to his subdued demeanor. He'd grown reticent in his old age; he preferred to listen. Sometimes, in the theater, they observed him with his eyes closed. The first time, during their screening of a worn print of Metropolis that Hermann kept well hidden, they'd nudged him, thinking he'd fallen asleep.

"I'm awake," he said, and it was true. "I'm listening."

"But it's silent," Willi had teased. "Nothing but music."

"No. I hear it," he said as, onscreen, Rotwang resurrected his lost love in the soul of a machine. He'd listened because the robot gestured in such a way as to suggest holding something like a book, and he heard Greta in the metal skin. Clever, clever Greta. For the rest of the movie, he told himself, *Yes, it's her. She's always disappearing. Somewhere out there is a new movie, and she's hiding, and she's safe.*

Telling himself he'd found her in each old movie he watched helped ease the nights in Thalhammer's tunnel, when the quiet was not knowing and the smell of the hearth fire left ashes in his mouth. In the tunnel's grainy dark he kept company with old wings and faces peering at him from row upon row of decrepit bunks. He would tell them *all my loves got out. They are not with you. They are not ash clouds above Germany.*

It had been years since the last time he called their apartment only to hear the ringing that wouldn't stop. Over those years, Willi and Hermann had learned, He Who Listened still heard things whether he wanted to or not.

Hermann knocked on the projection booth window. The film began right after. For ninety-two minutes they watched the story of a falsely accused man take his revenge.

Everywhere, Fleischl saw all that Fritz had come to know and all that Oliver believed. The words. The play of shadow and light around corners and from rooftops as a mob descended on a jail to lynch a man for something he didn't do. The sweeping away of innocents.

He closed his eyes and listened.

The credits rolled. "Spencer Tracy," said Willi. "Such an actor."

"There's one more reel," Hermann called from the top of the stairs. "Let me thread it."

After a few moments, the empty space onscreen filled with the jail house from the movie.

The crowd was gone. In one of the building's windows, a candle flickered.

Fleischl sat forward as a man's voice began to speak.

"Rumors of atrocities continue to make their way through the embargo in Nazi Germany."

Images of Hitler came quickly in succession: speaking at one of his rallies, saluting soldiers as they marched in lockstep past his viewing platform, shaking hands with blonde, blue-eyed youth as they smiled at him beatifically.

"But instances of uprisings are increasing. Recent arrivals from Germany describe acts of persecution and defiance. One such occurrence, from the spring of 1936, is still talked about in refugee circles, when a night of suspected sabotage roused a neighborhood in Berlin. That night, an old telegraph line came down, cutting power to several city blocks. There were reports of at least two women racing through the streets, telling terrified residents who'd come to their windows to get out. The military swept through, looking for the saboteurs, but by that time only a few hundred remained in an area where thousands once lived."

Oliver appeared onscreen, seated at a table behind a glossy typewriter. His glasses perched on his head, he pecked diligently away as his name scrawled across the bottom. He was grayer, fuller in his face, and when he looked up at the camera and smiled in that way he had, Fleischl wanted to reach out and touch his friend's cheek.

"We think of the ones who didn't get out," Oliver said, now on a city street. The breeze ruffled his thinning hair. "The ones we can't reach, and who can't reach us."

The camera shifted left, making a dream of the buildings behind. It came to rest on her.

"We hope against hope that they're alive and somewhere safe, where they can hear us as we hear them," she said. Next to her, Adelita held her mother's freckled hand.

"The night," said the narrator, "became known in German immigrant circles as 'Nacht der Leerenstuhle.' The night of empty chairs."

"Is it them?" asked Willi. "How old is this?"

"Four years almost," said Hermann.

"We can call the studio," said Willi.

"MGM," Hermann told him. "Fleischl, is it them?"

Fleischl smiled stupidly. Tears bathed his face. How many nights had he looked out to a future he couldn't name, a life without ever knowing.

I thought I lost you.

"It's them," he said, and stared at the snowy space where the film's last held image had been. Their faces, broadcast to the world in hopes of finding him alive beneath the death's head soldiers and the concentration camps. The years it took to finally find him.

My love, he thought, *it was so much faster the way we did it.*

★★★

By the early spring of 1941, the grass around his parents' graves had grown lush and verdant. It had something to do with the prevailing winds from the Baltic's current, or so said Willi, burghemeister and self-styled expert on all things Stralsund. It had been Willi's idea to plant cornflower near the resting places of his parents, Rapholtz and Anton, and his friend had been right. The rains brought out clusters of a deep and lasting blue in that corner of the grounds.

He visited them all for the last time on a clear April day. "Poppa," he said, "you'll appreciate this. I believe you told Momma once, 'flax will be our future.'"

He unfolded the telegram Fritz sent Willi in reply to the carefully crafted message left for MGM's legal counsel the winter before.

WILL ENJOY RECEIVING YOUR GOODS STOP WILL LEAVE NECESSARY PAPERWORK FOR FLAX IMPORT WITH SPANISH CONSULATE STOP

Fleischl sifted the vivid blue petals adorning the ground.

CIRCUITOUS ROUTES ARE WHAT WE HAVE IN UNCERTAIN TIMES STOP PLEASE SEND FLAX SWIFTLY STOP EAGERLY AWAITING STOP

"My passport." He held it up to all the stones. "Papers, whatever it is I need to be admitted to the United States. Willi forged an identification card for me. He told me, 'I've no plans to go anywhere. This is my home, and it's yours for whenever this is all over and you can come back for a drink and an old movie. But home for you is where they are.' A good man. A good friend."

He tucked his papers safely into in his pocket. It will always feel empty, he thought, without something old and tattered in there.

"I suppose I could fly or take a train from place to place, but I'm not a brave man. There are so many ways, Poppa. So many chances for me to be taken. Who knows if they still look for me. So I'll be on a ship. Can you imagine the strange line my life follows. I'll be Willi in the master roll. But I am your Fleischl, and I'll come back to this spot one day to see you. No one should lie where they can't be found. Until then, I take you all with me. When I come home to you, it will be with them."

Plucking a blue flower, he placed it in his pocket, next to the wadded piece of yellow cloth. Then he stood, touched each stone, and said Kaddish.

That night he had dinner in the library. It was just him and Dowid, seated at the window with their plates in their laps and their glasses on the sill.

"I guess I'll see more of the new doctors now," Dowid said.

"They're quite good."

"I've become so used to seeing you and Dr. Rapholtz. Things take forever to change, and then they change, and you say, 'that happened so quickly.'"

"Have you ever considered leaving, Dowid?"

Dowid smiled. He nibbled on a pastry. "I like it here. When Anton died, I remember thinking, I shall be him one day. None of us are so crazy that we can't find our way out there. It's only one thousand seven hundred and two steps. But none of us are so crazy that we think a world like that is a place to go to."

"You're one of the sanest men I've come across in all my experiences."

"I'll be right here tomorrow. Will you wave?"

"I will. I promise."

"You never broke your promises to me. Not once."

"It's been so many years we've shared. Have I made you promises before?"

Dowid patted his rope. "Yes. You have."

★★★

The ship *Scharnhorst* was scheduled to depart at four in the morning, with various ports of call before reaching Spain in the early summer, smooth seas allowing. Fleischl roused himself two hours early, having slept only a little. He made sure he'd packed his meager belongings, and he left Thalhammer through the front door. He had with him some clean clothes, some writing implements, some money, his original thesis paper, now yellowed, and a few tins containing splicings of silent films, courtesy of Hermann. There was the nosferatu, a bit of the boxing kangaroo, and his dancer, twirling at the bottom of a vanished lake.

He'd followed the news from a distance, through glimpses of Stralsund's local paper, the Tageblatt and the Der Sturmer when it was available (and he could stomach it), newsreels, and word from local businessmen in the piazza, passed from Willi. It had taken months, in the end, to drain the lake. During the process, bodies floated up and were identified. None wore a star.

He'd heard of Alice, but only once. She was teaching at university again. A class on statistics.

Belongings in hand, he walked to the bottom of the hill. There, he waved in the direction of the asylum, toward the cemetery and the library window. It was too dark to see, but he knew Dowid was there.

The dock was empty but for sellers waiting to board, a few officers, and Willi with the roll. "An old seafaring custom," Willi explained to a curious uniformed man. "We see them off."

"I've been here for other ships," said the officer. "I don't recall seeing this."

"It's an old ship. So, an old custom."

"Ah."

Those few in line pressed their thumbs and left their initials in the roll, then displayed their identification beneath the officer's flashlight beam. Some of them smiled. They were old, and remembered well the old ways of Stralsund's docks.

Fleischl stepped forward. He left Willi's initials and pressed his thumb as if such a thing was meaningless and didn't conjure the dead at the water's edge. He showed the officer his card. "Safe travels," the officer told him.

Fleischl walked along the gangplank and onto the deck. He wondered if he was ever so young to have beheld his father standing at a ship's rail, with the sea and the future and the horizon line always just ahead.

The sky was beginning to blister at the margins. There were clouds above Stralsund, mountainous and threaded with pale color. It was still too dark to see if they carried rain.

Willi's figure emerged from the early gloom. Some others wandered to the dock from the direction of the piazza. He took them for latecomers, and he felt for them, that the gangplank and anchor were already up. But they went to Willi's side and remained.

He felt the unmooring and the drift. It was happening. He was leaving.

In the pale light that crept over the seam where the Baltic touched land, he saw dozens of figures, and more still coming from the tunnels to the port. He saw Willi and Hermann standing together. Willi raised a hand. Fleischl waved.

Willi's hand glowed blue. One by one, all of them raised their hands. The lights they held ignited blue.

In Thalhammer's window, a blue light rose.

More came with their lights raised high. By the time the *Scharnhorst* began its turn in the water to face its direction, the port of Stralsund was a sky of blue lights reflecting atop the shallows, below the old wires.

"I hear you," he whispered.

He remained at the rail despite the deep cold, listening to the sea washing against the hull, and to the steps of those on board retreating to their quarters while the working men did what was needed to run the ship through the Baltic to the next sea. The wings had been too fragile to pack, so he kept them in his coat. When he needed to hear the wind pass through them, he could take them out and listen.

He waited, shivering, until the last of the blue lights disappeared. By then the clouds he'd seen over Stralsund had drifted off. Reaching into his pocket, he took out the yellow star and held it over the rail, and incanted the names of the ones he loved, the ones he knew enough to say, and the places where the loves of others crumpled among little pellets of poison to become ash and cloud. Momma. Poppa. The men of Kiel. Anton. The Burghemeister. Rapholtz. Eva.

Vera. Sachsenhausen. Dachau. Buchenwald. Auschwitz. Bergen Belsen. Berlin. Germany. You are all my Kaddish. *Yitgadal v'yitkadash sh'mei raba* stop.

The names rose. It was nothing he could see. But even this far out, even if he didn't want to, he could hear.

He let the star go. It fell into the Baltic. When it soaked up all the water it could hold, it descended.

He went to his cabin. For eleven days, he listened.

★★★

They docked at Algeciras, and in a small office belonging to a mayoral attaché, he picked up a new passport and boarded a different freighter for the long voyage to California. He ate with the crew and occasionally with the captain, a Dutchman of good humor who was content to tell salty jokes and never asked questions. No one did, which made Fleischl wonder if everyone aboard left something behind.

Once, in a port of call in Genoa, he saw a family gathered at the dock. The patriarch was dressed in black, with a wide-brimmed hat and a thick forelock lying against his cheek. Their eyes met. Fleischl's filled. So did the man's. They nodded to one other and went their ways.

On a late May afternoon, the freighter docked in a city the crew called Long Beach. He took his belongings, safeguarded the wings beneath his rumpled coat, and disembarked beneath the warm sun. At the bottom of the gangplank, Oliver and Albin pulled him into their embrace.

"For such a drab old man, you make quite the entrance," Oliver said. "Everyone's waiting for you."

They clung to each other and sobbed. He heard every tear fall from somewhere deep within, like rain on water, bringing all the stories down with them. There was so much more than he could ever hope to tell.

Albin drove them to Santa Monica. They pulled up in front of a modest, well-kept house on a street lined with trees and cars the likes of which he could never have imagined. The trees bore wide-winged plumage at their pinnacles. But the trunks. So straight and slim. Like telegraph poles.

The home belonged to a woman from Galicia, said Albin. The Mother of All Émigrés, he called her. "Everyone who's far from home knows her. You'll be meeting some remarkable people. They're most gracious to include an old Satanist."

"I don't fit," said Fleischl. They smiled, because no one believed that anymore.

A small, attractive woman emerged from the house. "You must be Fleischl," she said. "I'm Salka. I'm so pleased to meet you."

They went inside. Fleischl looked around as Salka took his case from him. "Where…"

He peered into the next room. There was a wide table filled with food, and an immense chocolate cake in the center, adorned with a single flickering candle. There were people seated, and an older woman standing unsteadily with assistance from the woman next to her.

He went to them. Greta felt so frail. She was thin, slightly bent at the shoulders, and in her hair were the first threads of snow woven among the curls. There were a few faint lines around Adelita's eyes, and when she whispered that she loved him, her voice had a warm burr that he welled up at the sound of. It had been so long since he'd heard it.

They held each other while everyone clapped and wept. Oliver introduced him to a younger, watchful man named José. That evening Fleischl learned the man was an actor who performed under a different, more exotic name. He'd met Oliver in the very home of The Mother of All Émigrés, and émigrés came not just from different countries but from different secret hearts.

He learned as well how happy his dearest friend was.

"Wherever it is that we make our home," he told Oliver that evening, "it will always be your home too."

They ate cake and sipped tea, and no one asked anything of him but to rest and feel safe.

He held his loves' hands. He craved the feel of them in his.

"Poppa," said Adelita, and behind her there was a man with a small, nervous girl in his arms.

"Hello," Fleischl said, and he knew they were now his family. Their faces were new ports for him. For the story of him. "I'm your grandpa," he said to the child. "What's your name?" She glanced at her father, because his accent was impenetrable.

"Ask him, Ava," said Adelita's husband. Fleischl would, that evening, learn that his name was Jerrold, that not very many people spelled it that way, that he worked with his father and brother in a small office selling advertising for car dealers, and after some wine, that he respected his father but wondered if he was loved.

"She's only four," Adelita said. "It's not you."

Fleischl smiled, went to fetch his coat, and came back with wings. "You're an angel now," he said.

He put the wings on her tiny back. They were loose and would need some tending or else they'd fall off. Ava walked away, her little body twisting this way and that so she could catch a glimpse of the feathers.

Greta's arms slipped around his waist. When he met her blue eye, it was filled. "There was a moment," she said. "I thought you'd finally come home. I turned on the light, but the lines. Then there were flames outside the window."

"And you told who you could," he said, and it was just the two of them in the room and the world.

"Did I dream you?" she asked.

"Get out," he said. "And you heard it and told others." He began to cry. "Did I hurt you?"

She looked at him as if he was new. "You changed me, and you saved us."

"I broke my promise," he said. "That you never hear me again."

"Make me another one. We are never apart again."

"I promise you."

"I promise you."

Oliver came bearing more drinks. "The night of empty chairs?" Fleischl asked him. "I'm pretty sure that was your idea. It sounds like you."

"Who would he be," Albin said with a grin, "if he didn't apply a flourish."

That evening, they all drove in a caravan to a pier. On the way, Salka told him that soon, when he was rested and ready to talk, there were people who wanted to hear the story of what happened. They wanted to help those in the camps get out.

"I want nothing more," he said.

At the edge of the land, they followed the planked path and watched the sun sink into the Pacific. The wind from the ocean felt bracing, but with a ribbon of warmth at its center that he savored deep in his skin. Greta took his hand. They held each other up as they walked through the sand. Jerrold and Adelita told Ava not to stare, but she couldn't take her young eyes off of him, not for a moment, and there was such disquiet in them that he asked if she wanted to hold his hand too. She said nothing, then ran past him to the edge of the water. The wings flapped in the air.

He walked ahead to reach her before she went too far into the shallows. He felt tired, and the rest of the world felt new.

The last of the light slipped away. Greta was at his side, and Adelita and Oliver were just a little ways behind. His granddaughter watched the tide roll over her feet. She looked afraid. The wings had fallen off, and she held them tightly to her chest. He wanted to say, be careful, Ava. You'll break them. They're fragile. They've been through too much. But he didn't want to chastise her. She didn't know him. So he told her, you have such a beautiful name. I once knew of a girl with a name quite like yours. One letter off, is all. She was older. She was.

Ava was quiet and still. Her eyes were full of fear and something like wonder. They were the color of the sea. The deep blue of it. Like Greta's, now.

"Are you okay?" he asked her. "Are you afraid?"

"I'm listening." She had a small, wise voice, with a hint of a lisp.

"Listening to what? Are you listening to the sea?" She held the wings to her soft cheek and shrugged.

Greta touched his shoulder. Her hand remained.

Adelita told her daughter, "Grandpoppa's nice, and he's all better now." It was remarkable to see the mother in her.

Ava stepped carefully into the shallows. When she heard him grunting as he removed his shoes and socks, she pointed to the spot where she wanted him to be. Standing next to her, in the wide and fading rings she'd made.

"Cold," he said as the frigid sea lapped at his ankles. "Should we get out?"

"No."

She dipped her hand below the surface. Her little body bent at the waist. She leaned over until her hair brushed the top of the sea. But she was careful; the wings remained safely in the air.

"Come," she said.

He waded over, and at first he wasn't sure what she was doing. Scooping water up in her palm, he thought. Playing. Making ready to splash.

He saw her hand under the water. She'd curled it so that her finger pointed up. Its tip hovered just below the underside of the surface. Breaking it, she felt the cool air tingle her fingertip. She held it just at the meridian between water and world and waited for him to touch her back.

He brought his finger to hers. Maybe it surprised her, he thought. Or maybe the last of the sun was right behind him, making of him something else. The way she gazed up at him, it was as if he was hard to see.

"One day," he said, "I'll tell you stories. The sea carries so many stories. Did you know? Ships and ballrooms and people and love. Always, love. Do you like stories, Ava?"

"Something happened," Ava said.

"It did?"

"To you," she said. She held the wings out for him. Open, like a book.

"Yes," Fleischl said. "Something happened. That's a story too. Did you hear something of that one?"

"Yes. I don't know who told me."

For a moment, he saw a glimmer in her eyes, and he wondered if it belonged to her. It came and went, and he couldn't be sure what color it was, or whether it was ever really there at all.

"Do you want to know a secret I learned, Ava? All stories are woven with love. Maybe when all the stories come to have their silences broken, when they come to be heard, they come to those who love them. Who listen just for them."

"Don't get out," she said, "and don't get lost."

"I won't," said Fleischl.